YOTAM OTTOLENGHI

JERUSALEM

A COOKBOOK

SAMI TAMIMI

Ten Speed Press

BERKELEY

Additional text by Nomi Abeliovich and Noam Bar

Food photography by Jonathan Lovekin

Location photography by Adam Hinton

Contents

Introduction 8

    Jerusalem food 10

    The passion in the air 12

    The recipes 15

    A comment about ownership 16

    History 18

Vegetables 24

Beans & Grains 94

Soups 130

Stuffed 150

Meat 172

Fish 214

Savory Pastries 240

Sweets & Desserts 256

Condiments 296

Index 310

Acknowledgments 318

Introduction

One of our favorite recipes in this collection, a simple couscous with tomato and onion, is based on a dish Sami's mum, Na'ama, used to cook for him when he was a child in Muslim east Jerusalem. At around the same time, in the Jewish west of the city, Yotam's dad, Michael, was making a very similar dish. Being Italian, Michael's dish was made with small pasta balls called *ptitim*. Both versions were beautifully comforting and delicious.

A dish just like Michael's is part of the Jewish Tripolitan (Libyan) cuisine. It is called *shorba* and is a result of the Italian influence on Libyan food during the years of Italian rule of the country, in the early twentieth century. So Michael's *ptitim* was possibly inspired by Tripolitan cooking in Jerusalem, which in turn was influenced by Michael's original Italian culture. The anecdotal icing on this cross-cultural cake is that Michael's great uncle, Aldo Ascoli, was an admiral in the colonial Italian navy that raided Tripoli and occupied Libya in 1911.

Confusing? This is Jerusalem in a nutshell: very personal, private stories immersed in great culinary traditions that often overlap and interact in unpredictable ways, creating food mixes and culinary

combinations that belong to specific groups but also belong to everybody else. Many of the city's best-loved foods have just as complicated a pedigree as this one.

This book and this journey into the food of Jerusalem form part of a private odyssey. We both grew up in the city, Sami in the Muslim east and Yotam in the Jewish west, but never knew each other. We lived there as children in the 1970s and 1980s and then left in the 1990s, first to Tel Aviv and then to London. Only there did we meet and discover our parallel histories; we became close friends and then business partners, alongside others in Ottolenghi.

Although we often spoke about Jerusalem, our hometown, we never focused much on the city's food. Recently, however—is it age?—we have begun to reminisce over old food haunts and forgotten treats. Hummus—which we hardly ever talked about before—has become an obsession.

It is more than twenty years since we both left the city. This is a serious chunk of time, longer than the years we spent living there. Yet we still think of Jerusalem as our home. Not home in the sense of the place you conduct your daily life or constantly return to. In fact, Jerusalem is our home almost against our wills. It is our home because it defines us, whether we like it or not.

The flavors and smells of this city are our mother tongue. We imagine them and dream in them, even though we've adopted some new, perhaps more sophisticated languages. They define comfort for us, excitement, joy, serene bliss. Everything we taste and everything we cook is filtered through the prism of our childhood experiences: foods our mothers fed us, wild herbs picked on school trips, days spent in markets, the smell of the dry soil on a summer's day, goat and sheep roaming the hills, fresh pitas with ground lamb, chopped parsley, chopped liver, black figs, smoky chops, syrupy cakes, crumbly cookies. The list is endless—too long to recall and too complex to describe. Most of our food images lie well beyond our consciousness: we just cook and eat, relying on our impulses for what feels right, looks beautiful, and tastes delicious to us.

And this is what we set out to explore in this book. We want to offer our readers a glimpse into a hidden treasure, and at the same time explore our own culinary DNA, unravel the sensations and the alphabet of the city that made us the food creatures we are.

In all honesty, this is also a self-indulgent, nostalgic trip into our pasts. We go back, first and foremost, to experience again those magnificent flavors of our childhood, to satisfy the need most grown-ups have to relive those first food experiences to which nothing holds a candle in later life. We want to eat, cook, and be inspired by the richness of a city with four thousand years of history, that has changed hands endlessly and that now stands as the center of three massive faiths and is occupied by residents of such utter diversity it puts the old tower of Babylon to shame.

Jerusalem food

Is there even such a thing as Jerusalem food, though? Consider this: there are Greek Orthodox monks in this city; Russian Orthodox priests; Hasidic Jews originating from Poland; non-Orthodox Jews from Tunisia, from Libya, from France, or from Britain; there are Sephardic Jews that have been here for generations; there are Palestinian Muslims from the West Bank and many others from the city and well beyond; there are secular Ashkenazic Jews from Romania, Germany, and Lithuania and more recently arrived Sephardim from Morocco, Iraq, Iran, or Turkey; there are Christian Arabs and Armenian Orthodox; there are Yemeni Jews and Ethiopian Jews but there are also Ethiopian Copts; there are Jews from Argentina and others from southern India; there are Russian nuns looking after monasteries and a whole neighborhood of Jews from Bukhara (Uzbekistan).

All of these, and many, many more, create an immense tapestry of cuisines. It is impossible to count the number of cultures and subcultures residing in this city. Jerusalem is an intricate, convoluted mosaic of peoples. It is therefore very tempting to say there isn't such a thing as a local cuisine. And indeed, if you go to the ultra-Orthodox neighborhood of Me'ah She'arim and compare the prepared food sold in grocery shops there to the selection laid out by a Palestinian mother for her children in the neighborhood of A-tur in the east of the city, you couldn't be blamed for assuming these two live on two different culinary planets.

However, if you take a step back and look at the greater picture, there are some typical elements that are easily identifiable in most local cuisines and crop up throughout the city. Everybody, absolutely everybody, uses chopped cucumber and tomatoes to create an Arab salad or an Israeli salad, depending on point of view. Stuffed vegetables with rice or rice and meat also appear on almost every dinner table, as does an array of pickled vegetables. Extensive use of olive oil, lemon juice, and olives is also commonplace. Baked pastries stuffed with cheese in all sorts of guises are found in most cultures.

EVERYBODY, ABSOLUTELY EVERYBODY, USES CHOPPED CUCUMBER AND TOMATOES TO CREATE AN ARAB SALAD OR AN ISRAELI SALAD, DEPENDING ON POINT OF VIEW.

Then there are looser affinities, those shared by a few cuisines but not all of them: bulgur or semolina cases stuffed with meat (*kubbeh*), burnt eggplant salads, white bean soups, the combination of meat with dried fruits. Eventually, these separate links among the different groups join all of the groups together into one clear and identifiable local cuisine.

Aside from that, there are the local ingredients. Jerusalemites tend to eat seasonally and cook with what grows in the area. The list is endless. It is made up of dozens of vegetables—tomatoes, okra, string beans, cauliflower, artichokes, beets, carrots, peppers, cucumbers, celery root, kohlrabi, zucchini, eggplants—fruits—figs, lemons, peaches, pears, strawberries, pomegranates, plums, apricots—herbs, nuts, dairy products, grains and beans, lamb, and chicken.

The passion in the air

The diversity and richness of Jerusalem, both in terms of the cooks and their disparate backgrounds and the ingredients they use, make it fascinating to any outsider. But what makes this city doubly exciting is the emotional and spiritual energy that pervades it. When it comes to people's emotions, it is hard to overstate how unique the city is.

Four thousand years of intense political and religious wrangling (SEE PAGE 18) are impossible to hide. Wherever you go—in Jewish parts in the city center or within the walls of the ancient Old City—people are zealously fighting to protect and maintain what they see as their piece of land, their endangered culture, or their right to a certain way of life. More often than not, this is pretty ugly. Intolerance and trampling over other people's basic rights are routine in this city. Currently, the Palestinian minority bears the brunt with no sign of it regaining control over its destiny, while the secular Jews are seeing their way of life being gradually marginalized by a growing Orthodox population.

The other, more positive side of this coin is that the inherent passion and energy that Jerusalemites have in abundance results in some fantastic food and culinary creativity. The best hummus joints, where methods have been perfected over generations, are in the city (and locals are happy to go into some seriously heated debates about the best one), as are some of the country's most creative modern restaurants. There is something about the heated, highly animated spirit of the city's residents that creates unparalleled delicious food. It also has a very obvious effect on the flavors, which are strong and bold, with lots of sour and sweet. The Jerusalem Palestinian hummus is patently sharp, as are the Friday night Sephardi soups.

On top of that, there is a spirit of warmth and generosity that is sometimes almost overbearing. Guests are always served mountains of food. Nothing is done sparingly. Eat More is a local motto. It is unthinkable not to eat what you are served. Going into a friend's restaurant, or a friend of a friend, you are never expected to pay. It is a combination of the famous Middle Eastern hospitality that goes back to the days of Abraham and the typical way in which Jews and Arabs shower guests and relatives with delights, lest they "go home hungry." Heaven forbid.

Alas, although Jerusalemites have so much in common, food, at the moment, seems to be the only unifying force in this highly fractured place. The dialogue between Jews and Arabs, and often among Jews themselves, is almost nonexistent. It is sad to note how little daily interaction there is between communities, with people sticking together in closed, homogenous groups. Food, however,

IT TAKES A GIANT LEAP
OF FAITH, BUT WE ARE
HAPPY TO TAKE IT . . . TO
IMAGINE THAT HUMMUS
WILL EVENTUALLY
BRING JERUSALEMITES
TOGETHER, IF NOTHING
ELSE WILL.

seems to break down those boundaries on occasion. You can
see people shop together in food markets, or eat in one another's
restaurants. On rare occasions, they work together in partnership in
food establishments. It takes a giant leap of faith, but we are happy
to take it—what have we got to lose?—to imagine that hummus will
eventually bring Jerusalemites together, if nothing else will.

The recipes

Our selection of recipes here includes traditional, age-old dishes, cooked just as they should be, with no change or modern touch. Others are fairly traditional, but we allowed ourselves poetic license and updated them to suit the times or our sensibilities. And then there are recipes that are loosely inspired by the flavors of Jerusalem—delicious concoctions that could have easily fitted on many Jerusalem dinner tables but have yet to become local classics.

We don't mean to cover all of the city's foods, or even substantial numbers of them, nor all of its communities. This is impossible. Smarter people have delved deep into Jewish and Arab cuisines and have documented both extensively. Other communities in the city have also had their foods written about. So a lot is omitted. Some typical local dishes like kugel (slow-cooked noodle cake), bagel (Arab or Jewish), *pashtida* (savory flan), *pastelikos* (little Sephardic meat pies), *tchulent* or *hamin* (everything cooked in one pot overnight for Shabbat), strudel, challah (sweet Shabbat bread)—all are left neglected. Ashkenazic foods in particular are underrepresented. This has to do with our personal backgrounds and the types of flavors we tend to cook and eat.

As we draw deep inspiration from Jerusalem and its food but are in no way trying to represent its realities, the justification for this collection of recipes is our preferences and cooking habits and those of our readers. The cooks who like our style and flavor combinations lead a (usually) Western, modern lifestyle. They have a certain set of ingredients available to them and a twenty-first-century mind-set (use less oil in the food, spend less time in the kitchen . . .). We can only hope that through our haphazard, often eccentric selective process and through our modifications we have succeeded in distilling the spirit of the place that made us and shaped us.

———

WE DRAW DEEP INSPIRATION FROM JERUSALEM AND ITS FOOD BUT ARE IN NO WAY TRYING TO REPRESENT ITS REALITIES.

———

A comment about ownership

In the part of the world we are dealing with everybody wants to own everything. Existence feels so uncertain and so fragile that people fight fiercely and with great passion to hold onto things: land, culture, religious symbols, food—everything is in danger of being snatched away or of disappearing. The result is fiery arguments about ownership, about provenance, about who and what came first.

As we have seen through our investigations, and will become blatantly apparent to anyone reading and cooking from this book, these arguments are futile.

Firstly, they are futile because it doesn't really matter. Looking back in time or far afield into distant lands is simply distracting. The beauty of food and of eating is that they are rooted in the now. Food is a basic, hedonistic pleasure, a sensual instinct we all share and revel in. It is a shame to spoil it.

Secondly, you can always search further back in time. Hummus for example, a highly explosive subject, is undeniably a staple of the local Palestinian population, but it was also a permanent feature on dinner tables of Aleppine Jews who have lived in Syria for millennia and then arrived in Jerusalem in the 1950s and 1960s. Who is more deserving of calling hummus their own? Neither. Nobody "owns" a dish because it is very likely that someone else cooked it before them and another person before that.

Thirdly, and this is the most crucial point, in this soup of a city it is completely impossible to find out who invented this delicacy and who brought that one with them. The food cultures are mashed and fused together in a way that is impossible to unravel. They interact all the time and influence one another constantly, so nothing is pure any more. In fact, nothing ever was. Jerusalem was never an isolated bastion. Over millennia it has seen countless immigrants, occupiers, visitors, and merchants—all bringing foods and recipes from the four corners of the earth.

As a result, as much as we try to attribute foods to nations, to ascertain the origin of a dish, we often end up discovering a dozen other dishes that are extremely similar, that work with the same ingredients and the same principles to make a final result that is just ever so slightly different, a variation on a theme.

—

FOOD IS A BASIC, HEDONISTIC PLEASURE, A SENSUAL INSTINCT WE ALL SHARE AND REVEL IN. IT IS A SHAME TO SPOIL IT.

—

History

The complexity and vibrancy of the food in Jerusalem stems from its location as a meeting point between Europe, Asia, and Africa and the incredible richness of its history. Jerusalem was traditionally depicted, as in this medieval map (below), as the center of the universe, surrounded by three continents. Indeed, there are few places in the world to match its importance. Yet Jerusalem has never been a great metropolis. It has never had temples as big as those of Luxor, art as refined as that of Greece, or public buildings as magnificent as those of Rome. It didn't possess large imperial courts like those of China or India, or busy commerce hubs as in central Asia. It has always been a rather small and crowded city, built of the stone of its surrounding hills.

The energy of Jerusalem is introspective. It is born out of an interplay between the peoples that have been coming and going for millennia, and the spirit that seems to hover among the olive trees, over the hills, and in the valleys. It is not through anything material but through faith, learning, devotion, and, sadly, fanaticism that Jerusalem gained its importance.

When King David founded it as his capital, in around 1000 BC, it was, as it is now, a collection of rugged hills with little vegetation or water. David was a warrior and chose his capital for strategic reasons—it was at the center of his kingdom. His son Solomon, the most glorious Jewish king, built the first temple in Jerusalem and sanctified its place as Temple Mount. Following Solomon's death, the young Jewish kingdom was broken up by squabbling relatives and often attacked from the north. This culminated in 587 BC, when Babylon attacked Jerusalem, burnt the city and the temple, and dispersed its inhabitants.

It is then that we first see one of the greatest emotions attached to Jerusalem: yearning. We are told of two Jewish leaders, Ezra and Nehemiah, who successfully made it their life mission to restore the temple in Jerusalem and the Jewish nation in its homeland. This yearning will play out again and again, in Jews, Muslims, and Christians, from all parts of the world. Indeed, it is so strong that psychiatrists have identified the Jerusalem Syndrome—pilgrims who break down when their life goal, the long-anticipated journey to the holy city, is accomplished.

In 332 BC, the Persian empire fell to Alexander the Great and a few centuries of Hellenistic influence followed. A protracted war of cultures took place between the modern, frivolous, and inter-marrying Hellenistic Jews and the more traditional Jews. For a while, a rebellion of Jewish traditionalists—Maccabees—gained the upper hand and managed to control the religious life. This revolt gave us Hanukkah, the festival of lights, based on the story that, upon restoring the temple to its Jewish traditions, a little jug of oil could miraculously feed the sacred light of the temple for eight days.

While for many the Maccabean revolt is a story of liberation and inspiration, some scholars see it as another episode in a centuries-long struggle between traditionalists and cosmopolitan Jews. This is another pattern that is played out in Jerusalem again and again, nowadays manifested as the struggle between the Orthodox and the secular Jews in the city.

The Romans—following hot on the heels of the Hellenistic influence—first appeared in Jerusalem in 63 BC, and then gradually asserted their authority against Jewish resistance, which culminated in a failed revolt in AD 70, when the second, and last, temple was destroyed. This event is painfully etched in Jewish history as the onset of a slow process of decline that would not end until the advent of Zionism.

Jesus Christ lived some decades before this momentous event, at a time of great political, military, cultural, and spiritual upheaval. His presence is, of course, still evident in many monuments in the city, first and foremost in the Church of the Holy Sepulchre, the site of the Resurrection. This is a collection of dimly lit caves, buildings, and churches, encompassing seventeen centuries, each attributed to a different creed of Christianity but all connected. As usual in

IN 587 BC . . .
BABYLON ATTACKED
JERUSALEM, BURNT
THE CITY AND
THE TEMPLE, AND
DISPERSED ITS
INHABITANTS. IT
IS THEN THAT WE FIRST
SEE ONE OF
THE GREATEST
EMOTIONS ATTACHED
TO JERUSALEM:
YEARNING.

Jerusalem, there is no splendor there, but there is in the crowds of the pilgrims, the secluded little corners where people kneel and pray to the light of a candle, the glimpses of exquisite art, and the meaning loaded onto every stone—a truly moving experience, perhaps even a transcendental one.

Alongside the slow development of the nascent religion, the Roman Jewish conflict continued to simmer, and came to a head in another revolt, in AD 132, after which Jews were banned from the city—bar one day a year—for many centuries. The city was renamed Aelia Capitolina, and with the Christianization of the Byzantine Empire it was adorned with Christian churches, and became a veritable Christian city, devoid of any Jewish presence.

This, and similar periods, are considered by Palestinian historians as proof that not only the Jews, but also the Palestinians (many of whom are Christian), have a long-lasting historical claim on the city. In fact, some Palestinians claim that they are descendants of the Jebusites, the original inhabitants of Jerusalem, who were deposed by King David.

Islam was born in the seventh century, and with it came another claim on the city. Jerusalem, or Al-Quds in Arabic, meaning "The Holy," is the third holiest site for Sunni Muslims. It is from here, believe Muslims, that the prophet Mohammad ascended to heaven. After the death of the prophet the Muslims went on a conquering spree of a huge scale, Jerusalem included. Temple Mount, the site of the long-demolished Jewish temple, was consecrated by Islam with the building of two large mosques, one of them the golden dome of the rock, which still dominates the skyline of the Old City. Temple Mount remains exclusively Muslim, with Jews only using the Western Wall, also called the Wailing Wall—remnant of the ancient wall that surrounded the Jewish temple's courtyard and a place where some still weep over the temple lost two thousand years ago.

——

DURING THE CRUSADERS' RULE, A NETWORK OF MARKETS WAS BUILT ALONG ANCIENT ROMAN PATHS. . . . AT THE HERB MARKET YOU COULD FIND FRESH PRODUCE, MALQUISINAT WAS THE FAST-FOOD MARKET . . . AND "THE COVERED MARKET" WAS USED BY CLOTH VENDORS.

——

Over a millennium of Muslim control followed, with different Muslim powers vying for power. Christians staked a new claim for the city in the Middle Ages, when the Catholic Church managed to bring together forces from all around Europe to recapture the Holy Land. It was an ambitious project, with knights coming from as far away as Norway. The crusaders controlled the city from 1099 to 1187, but then lost it again. During the crusaders' rule, a network of markets was built along ancient Roman paths in the Old City that survives to this day. In each of the three alleys, specific produce was sold: at the herb market you could find fresh produce, *malquisinat* was the fast-food market, offering meals to the many pilgrims that flocked to the city, and "the covered market" was used by cloth vendors.

Jerusalem then became a rather neglected place, changing hands as the (mostly) Muslim rulers came and went. The Muslim authorities were, by and large, quite tolerant, certainly more tolerant than the Christians. Jews were allowed to stay in the city and Christians allowed to worship there. In the nineteenth century, under Ottoman control, Jerusalem still enjoyed some glory due to the wide, if sparse, international presence. However, most visitors described it as a miserable, congested, and squalid provincial town.

The British conquered Jerusalem in 1917, during the First World War, and the city became anything but sleepy. The Brits brought a definite push for modernization, and this was intertwined with the growth of the Palestinian national identity and the Zionist reclaim of Israel. Jerusalem has since been at the heart of the struggle between these two fierce nationalistic movements, and when the UN decided in 1947 to divide Palestine between them, Jerusalem was given to international administration. But a war, rather than peaceful division, is what followed. Interestingly, this war has different names: for the Jews it is the War of Independence, an assertive act of bravery after the trauma of the holocaust; for Arabs, however, it is called a nakba, "the catastrophe." The young Israeli state managed to hold onto the western part of the city while losing its eastern, ancient part, which has been densely populated by Arabs. Eastern Jerusalem was controlled by Jordan until the 1967 war, when Israel took over the whole of Jerusalem, along with the surrounding areas.

The population grew quickly throughout the twentieth century. Arabs settled in the city as part of a general urbanization trend, and Jews arrived from around the world to the refounded national home. Entire communities immigrated and usually settled in particular areas, maintaining their traditions. This insularity, combined with the fact that most families—both Jewish and Arab— have many mouths to feed and not a lot to live on, creates a real microcosm of tradition.

Jerusalem is claimed by Israel as the "eternal capital of the Jewish people" and by the Palestinians as the capital of their state. The question of this city is at the heart of the Israeli-Palestinian conflict, and its resolution is essential for achieving that elusive dream of peace in the Middle East. Perhaps naively, we hope that the city can be acknowledged by all as part of the world heritage— undoubtedly a true reflection of reality— and provide the key for sharing, acceptance, and coexistence.

VEGETABLES

Roasted sweet potatoes & fresh figs

Figs are abundant in Jerusalem and many trees, bearing the most delectable fruit, actually belong to no one, so anybody can help themselves. Summer months are always tinted with the smell of wild herbs and ripe figs. The mother of Sami's childhood neighbor and friend, Jabbar, used her roof to dry the glut of figs (and tomatoes) in the hot summer sun, spending hours cleaning and sorting them meticulously. Poor Um Jabbar—Sami and her son never wasted time and used to sneak up to her roof regularly, stealing her figs at their peak and causing havoc. This wasn't enough for Jabbar, though. The boy had such a sweet tooth that he always carried around with him an old match box full of sugar cubes, just in case. Unfortunately, this habit had clear ramifications, evident in his "charming" smile.

---

4 small sweet potatoes (2¼ lb / 1 kg in total)
5 tbsp olive oil
scant 3 tbsp / 40 ml balsamic vinegar (you can use a commercial rather than a premium aged grade)
1½ tbsp / 20 g superfine sugar
12 green onions, halved lengthwise and cut into 1½-in / 4cm segments
1 red chile, thinly sliced
6 ripe figs (8½ oz / 240 g in total), quartered
5 oz / 150 g soft goat's milk cheese (optional)
Maldon sea salt and freshly ground black pepper

This unusual combination of fresh fruit and roasted vegetables is one of the most popular at Ottolenghi. It wholly depends, though, on the figs being sweet, moist, and perfectly ripe. Go for plump fruit with an irregular shape and a slightly split bottom. Pressing against the skin should result in some resistance but not much. Try to smell the sweetness. The balsamic reduction is very effective here, both for the look and for rounding up the flavors. To save you from making it, you can look for products such as balsamic cream or glaze.

Preheat the oven to 475°F / 240°C.

Wash the sweet potatoes, halve them lengthwise, and then cut each half again similarly into 3 long wedges. Mix with 3 tablespoons of the olive oil, 2 teaspoons salt, and some black pepper. Spread the wedges out, skin side down, on a baking sheet and cook for about 25 minutes, until soft but not mushy. Remove from the oven and leave to cool down.

To make the balsamic reduction, place the balsamic vinegar and sugar in a small saucepan. Bring to a boil, then decrease the heat and simmer for 2 to 4 minutes, until it thickens. Be sure to remove the pan from the heat when the vinegar is still runnier than honey; it will continue to thicken as it cools. Stir in a drop of water before serving if it does become too thick to drizzle.

Arrange the sweet potatoes on a serving platter. Heat the remaining oil in a medium saucepan over medium heat and add the green onions and chile. Fry for 4 to 5 minutes, stirring often to make sure not to burn the chile. Spoon the oil, onions, and chile over the sweet potatoes. Dot the figs among the wedges and then drizzle over the balsamic reduction. Serve at room temperature. Crumble the cheese over the top, if using.

Na'ama's fattoush

scant 1 cup / 200 g Greek
yogurt and ¾ cup plus
2 tbsp / 200 ml whole
milk, or 1⅔ cups /
400 ml buttermilk
(replacing both
yogurt and milk)
2 large stale Turkish
flatbread or naan (9 oz /
250 g in total)
3 large tomatoes (13 oz /
380 g in total), cut into
⅔-inch / 1.5cm dice
3½ oz / 100 g radishes,
thinly sliced
3 Lebanese or mini
cucumbers (9 oz /
250 g in total), peeled
and chopped into
⅔-inch / 1.5cm dice
2 green onions, thinly
sliced
½ oz / 15 g fresh mint
scant 1 oz / 25 g flat-leaf
parsley, coarsely chopped
1 tbsp dried mint
2 cloves garlic, crushed
3 tbsp freshly squeezed
lemon juice
¼ cup / 60 ml olive oil,
plus extra to drizzle
2 tbsp cider or white wine
vinegar
¾ tsp freshly ground
black pepper
1½ tsp salt
1 tbsp sumac or more
to taste, to garnish

Arab salad, chopped salad, Israeli salad—whatever you choose to call it, there is no escaping it. Wherever you go in the city, at any time of the day, a Jerusalemite is most likely to have a plate of freshly chopped vegetables—tomato, cucumber, and onion, dressed with olive oil and lemon juice—served next to whatever else they are having. It's a local affliction, quite seriously. Friends visiting us in London always complain of feeling they ate "unhealthily" because there wasn't a fresh salad served with every meal.

There are plenty of unique variations on the chopped salad but one of the most popular is *fattoush*, an Arab salad that uses grilled or fried leftover pita. Other possible additions include peppers, radishes, lettuce, chile, mint, parsley, cilantro, allspice, cinnamon, and sumac. Each cook, each family, each community has their own variation. A small bone of contention is the size of the dice. Some advocate the tiniest of pieces, only ⅛ inch / 3 mm wide, others like them coarser, up to ¾ inch / 2 cm wide. The one thing that there is no arguing over is that the key lies in the quality of the vegetables. They must be fresh, ripe, and flavorsome, with many hours in the sun behind them.

This fabulous salad is probably Sami's mother's creation; Sami can't recall anyone else in the neighborhood making it. She called it *fattoush*, which is only true to the extent that it includes chopped vegetables and bread. She added a kind of homemade buttermilk and didn't fry her bread, which makes it terribly comforting.

Try to get small cucumbers for this as for any other fresh salad. They are worlds apart from the large ones we normally get in most supermarkets. You can skip the fermentation stage and use only buttermilk instead of the combination of milk and yogurt. For a typical chopped salad, try the Spiced chickpeas and fresh vegetable salad (PAGE 56), *omitting the sugar and the chickpeas.*

If using yogurt and milk, start at least 3 hours and up to a day in advance by placing both in a bowl. Whisk well and leave in a cool place or in the fridge until bubbles form on the surface. What you get is a kind of homemade buttermilk, but less sour.

Tear the bread into bite-size pieces and place in a large mixing bowl. Add your fermented yogurt mixture or commercial buttermilk, followed by the rest of the ingredients, mix well, and leave for 10 minutes for all the flavors to combine.

Spoon the fattoush into serving bowls, drizzle with some olive oil, and garnish generously with sumac.

Baby spinach salad with dates & almonds

1 tbsp white wine vinegar
½ medium red onion,
  thinly sliced
3½ oz / 100 g pitted
  Medjool dates,
  quartered lengthwise
2 tbsp / 30 g unsalted
  butter
2 tbsp olive oil
2 small pitas, about 3½ oz /
  100 g, roughly torn into
  1½-inch / 4cm pieces
½ cup / 75 g whole unsalted
  almonds, coarsely
  chopped
2 tsp sumac
½ tsp chile flakes
5 oz / 150 g baby spinach
  leaves
2 tbsp freshly squeezed
  lemon juice
salt

Pitas are allotted the shortest of shelf lives in Jerusalem. Ideally, you'd eat them within a couple of hours of baking. Crunchy pita croutons make good use of leftover pita. We use them for soups and scatter them over salads and other mezes. They will keep for at least a week in an airtight container. Serve this salad as a starter; its sharp freshness really whets the appetite.

Put the vinegar, onion, and dates in a small bowl. Add a pinch of salt and mix well with your hands. Leave to marinate for 20 minutes, then drain any residual vinegar and discard.

Meanwhile, heat the butter and half the olive oil in a medium frying pan over medium heat. Add the pita and almonds and cook for 4 to 6 minutes, stirring all the time, until the pita is crunchy and golden brown. Remove from the heat and mix in the sumac, chile flakes, and ¼ teaspoon salt. Set aside to cool.

When you are ready to serve, toss the spinach leaves with the pita mix in a large mixing bowl. Add the dates and red onion, the remaining olive oil, the lemon juice, and another pinch of salt. Taste for seasoning and serve immediately.

The humble eggplant

Few ingredients have reached the level of veneration achieved by the humble eggplant or have found their way to almost every table in Jerusalem, for breakfast, lunch, and dinner. Everybody loves to be associated with the eggplant—it's like a little local celebrity. The number of people who claim to have invented baba ghanoush (SEE PAGE 76), or at least elevated it to the level of fine food, is extraordinary.

At the markets in the city, the eggplants come in a wide range of shapes and sizes, from the regular kind, elongated and uniform in size; to zebra—streaked on the outside and pure white on the inside; baby eggplants; globe eggplants; and the *baladi*, a local heirloom variety that is wide, flat, and resembles an open fan.

Eggplants, depending on variety, lend themselves to pickling, stuffing, cooking in sauce, frying, baking, roasting, charring, burning, puréeing, and even cooking in sugar and spice to make a festive jam (Moroccan) or fruit *mostarda* (Aleppine), a type of candied fruit conserved in a spicy syrup. They also marry beautifully with the flavors so typical of the city: tahini, pine nuts, date syrup, tomatoes, chickpeas, potatoes, lemon, garlic, lamb, fresh cheese and yogurt, olive oil, sumac, and cinnamon.

Arabs first brought eggplants to Italy and Spain, but it was the Jews who are said to have introduced them to these cuisines when moving and trading among the Arab Moorish and Christian cultures in the fifteenth and sixteenth centuries. Sephardic Jews have always been identified with eggplants, as were Arabs, even when Europeans were quite suspicious of them and were reluctant to use them, believing that "mad apples," as they were known, induced insanity.

Roasted eggplant with fried onion & chopped lemon

2 large eggplants, halved lengthwise with the stem on (about 1⅔ lb / 750 g in total)
⅔ cup / 150 ml olive oil
4 onions (about 1¼ lb / 550 g in total), thinly sliced
1½ green chiles
1½ tsp ground cumin
1 tsp sumac
1¾ oz / 50 g feta cheese, broken into large chunks
1 medium lemon
1 clove garlic, crushed
salt and freshly ground black pepper

Sharp, salty, and mildly sweet all intermingle here to make a wonderfully rich starter that can be followed by a light and simple main course, like Turkey and zucchini burgers with green onion and cumin (PAGE 200). Good eggplants should be light in weight, with not many seeds inside, and have a tight, shiny skin. Having some moisture in the oven when roasting eggplants prevents them from going dry and crisp as they cook and color. If the oven is pretty full that isn't a problem because of the natural moisture of food. But if you are roasting a single baking sheet of eggplants, we recommend placing a shallow pan of water at the bottom of the oven.

Preheat the oven to 425°F / 220°C.

Score the cut side of each eggplant with a crisscross pattern. Brush the cut sides with 6½ tbsp / 100 ml of the oil and sprinkle liberally with salt and pepper. Place on a baking sheet, cut side up, and roast in the oven for about 45 minutes, until the flesh is golden brown and completely cooked.

While the eggplants are roasting, add the remaining oil to a large frying pan and place over high heat. Add the onions and ½ teaspoon salt and cook for 8 minutes, stirring often, so that parts of the onion get really dark and crisp. Seed and chop the chiles, keeping the whole one separate from the half. Add the ground cumin, sumac, and the whole chopped chile and cook for a further 2 minutes before adding the feta. Cook for a final minute, not stirring much, then remove from the heat.

Use a small serrated knife to remove the skin and pith of the lemon. Coarsely chop the flesh, discarding the seeds, and place the flesh and any juices in a bowl with the remaining ½ chile and the garlic.

Assemble the dish as soon as the eggplants are ready. Transfer the roasted halves to a serving dish and spoon the lemon sauce over the flesh. Warm up the onions a little and spoon over. Serve warm or set aside to come to room temperature.

Za'atar

If there is one smell to match the emblematic image of the Old City of Jerusalem, one odor that encapsulates the soul of this ancient city nestling in the Judean Mountains, it is the smell of *za'atar*. Its scent resides in the aromatic space occupied by herbs like oregano, marjoram, sage, or thyme, but it has a unique characteristic of its own—sharp, warm, and slightly pungent. For us it conjures the most visceral memories of a warm day on the hills. It is almost as one with the smell of goats' dung, smoke from a far-off fire, soil baked in the sun, and—dare we say it—the healthy dose of sweat that is the inevitable result of hiking around Jerusalem. Like other local plants, *za'atar* is full of fragrant, etheric oils that are released when the hardy, dry bushes are trampled underfoot, and so its smell is a cloud that envelops you as you walk.

Za'atar is part and parcel of the Palestinian heritage and the smell of home to anyone who grew up either in Jerusalem or elsewhere in the mountainous regions of the Holy Land. For millennia this pervasive plant, known in English as hyssop, has been picked throughout Palestine and used fresh during the spring and early summer or dried and then rehydrated for use later on in the year.

Typically, the leaves would be used to make a salad with tomatoes, green onion, olive oil, and lemon juice. In Sami's family radishes were served on the side. Another use was mixing the leaves into plain bread dough, along with ground turmeric, to bake into fragrant, light loaves. When Sami and his brothers used to visit his uncle, who lived outside the city, they climbed the rocks surrounding the house to pick large bundles of *za'atar* that grew in between the nooks and crevices.

To most, though, *za'atar* is known in the form of a spice mix consisting of powdered dried hyssop leaves, ground sumac, toasted sesame seeds, and salt. This olive green powder will be familiar to any visitor to East Jerusalem who buys the light, sesame-crusted local Arab bagels. These are almost obligatory (they simply fly off the wooden carts on which they are sold), and are always accompanied by a little pouch made of old newspaper and containing a generous serving of *za'atar* mix. Dip and chew, dip and chew, the combination is fragrant and tasty.

In Palestinian cuisine *za'atar* mix is sprinkled over *labneh* (STRAINED YOGURT, PAGE 302), hummus (PAGE 114), chicken, various

---

ZA'ATAR IS PART AND PARCEL OF THE PALESTINIAN HERITAGE AND THE SMELL OF HOME TO ANYONE WHO GREW UP EITHER IN JERUSALEM OR ELSEWHERE IN THE MOUNTAINOUS REGIONS OF THE HOLY LAND.

salads, and is particularly popular when strewn over a flat piece of dough, covered with tons of olive oil, and then baked to make *manakish*, a hugely popular Levantine flatbread.

Za'atar has now also become central to modern Israeli cuisine. The spice mix is sold in all supermarkets and grocery stores, and cooks sprinkle it liberally to add a certain zest to dishes. Regrettably, *za'atar* has joined the long list of thorny subjects poisoning the fraught relationship between Arabs and Jews, when the Israeli authorities declared the herb an endangered species and banned picking it in the wild. Though a compelling argument was made about preserving the dwindling population of wild *za'atar*, the decree was taken without any form of dialogue with Arabs, who see it as a deliberate violation of their way of life.

Roasted butternut squash & red onion with tahini & za'atar

1 large butternut squash
  (2¼ lb / 1.1 kg in total),
  cut into ¾ by 2½-inch /
  2 by 6cm wedges
2 red onions, cut into
  1¼-inch / 3cm wedges
3½ tbsp / 50 ml olive oil
3½ tbsp light tahini paste
1½ tbsp lemon juice
2 tbsp water
1 small clove garlic,
  crushed
3½ tbsp / 30 g pine nuts
1 tbsp za'atar
1 tbsp coarsely chopped
  flat-leaf parsley
Maldon sea salt and freshly
  ground black pepper

This is a highly versatile dish that is quite simple to prepare but boasts some very substantial flavors. It is ideal as a starter, a vegetarian main course, or as a side to serve with a simple main course such as Lamb shawarma (PAGE 210) or Chicken sofrito, minus the potatoes (PAGE 190). The tahini sauce is quite dominant. Although we love this, you may want to use a little less of it when finishing the dish. Just taste it and decide.

Preheat the oven to 475°F / 240°C.

Put the squash and onion in a large mixing bowl, add 3 tablespoons of the oil, 1 teaspoon salt, and some black pepper and toss well. Spread on a baking sheet with the skin facing down and roast in the oven for 30 to 40 minutes, until the vegetables have taken on some color and are cooked through. Keep an eye on the onions as they might cook faster than the squash and need to be removed earlier. Remove from the oven and leave to cool.

To make the sauce, place the tahini in a small bowl along with the lemon juice, water, garlic, and ¼ teaspoon salt. Whisk until the sauce is the consistency of honey, adding more water or tahini if necessary.

Pour the remaining 1½ teaspoons oil into a small frying pan and place over medium-low heat. Add the pine nuts along with ½ teaspoon salt and cook for 2 minutes, stirring often, until the nuts are golden brown. Remove from the heat and transfer the nuts and oil to a small bowl to stop the cooking.

To serve, spread the vegetables out on a large serving platter and drizzle over the tahini. Sprinkle the pine nuts and their oil on top, followed by the za'atar and parsley.

Fava bean kuku

1 lb / 500 g fava beans,
  fresh or frozen
5 tbsp / 75 ml boiling water
2 tbsp superfine sugar
5 tbsp / 45 g dried
  barberries
3 tbsp heavy cream
¼ tsp saffron threads
2 tbsp cold water
5 tbsp olive oil
2 medium onions, finely
  chopped
4 cloves garlic, crushed
7 large free-range eggs
1 tbsp all-purpose flour
½ tsp baking powder
1 cup / 30 g dill, chopped
½ cup / 15 g mint, chopped
salt and freshly ground
  black pepper

This frittata-like dish is characteristic of the Iranian Jewish cuisine. Barberries, another typical ingredient, are tiny sharp berries. Look for them online or in specialty Middle Eastern and Iranian shops; otherwise, substitute chopped dried sour cherries. Serve this as a starter with Yogurt with cucumber (PAGE 299).

Preheat the oven to 350°F / 180°C. Put the fava beans in a pan with plenty of boiling water. Simmer for 1 minute, drain, refresh under cold water, and set aside.

Pour the 5 tbsp / 75 ml boiling water into a medium bowl, add the sugar, and stir to dissolve. Once this syrup is tepid, add the barberries and leave them for about 10 minutes, then drain.

Bring the cream, saffron, and cold water to a boil in a small saucepan. Immediately remove from the heat and set aside for 30 minutes to infuse.

Heat 3 tablespoons of the olive oil over medium heat in a 10-inch / 25cm nonstick, ovenproof frying pan for which you have a lid. Add the onions and cook for about 4 minutes, stirring occasionally, then add the garlic and cook and stir for a further 2 minutes. Stir in the fava beans and set aside.

Beat the eggs well in a large mixing bowl until frothy. Add the flour, baking powder, saffron cream, herbs, 1½ teaspoons salt, and ½ teaspoon pepper and whisk well. Finally, stir in the barberries and the fava beans and onion mix.

Wipe the frying pan clean, add the remaining olive oil, and place in the oven for 10 minutes to heat well. Pour the egg mix into the hot pan, cover with the lid, and bake for 15 minutes. Remove the lid and bake for another 20 to 25 minutes, until the eggs are just set. Remove from the oven and let rest for 5 minutes, before inverting onto a serving platter. Serve warm or at room temperature.

Raw artichoke & herb salad

2 or 3 large globe
artichokes (1½ lb /
700 g in total)
3 tbsp freshly squeezed
lemon juice
4 tbsp olive oil
2 cups / 40 g arugula
½ cup / 15 g torn mint
leaves
½ cup / 15 g torn cilantro
leaves
1 oz / 30 g pecorino toscano
or romano cheese, thinly
shaved
Maldon sea salt and freshly
ground black pepper

Artichokes are the most extraordinary vegetable; nothing tastes quite as magical. Many cooks tend to be finicky when it comes to artichokes, easily shunning the effort involved in preparing them. In Jerusalem, some housewives buy great numbers of artichokes when they are in season, in early summer, and allocate a couple of hours to trimming and cleaning them, before storing them in the freezer for a rainy day. If you can spare the time, we encourage you to adopt the habit. If you can't, prepare just a couple and make this refreshing salad, the ideal pairing to anything fatty or hearty. Try it with Lamb shawarma (PAGE 210), *Latkes* (PAGE 92), *or Jerusalem mixed grill* (PAGE 174).

Prepare a bowl of water mixed with half of the lemon juice. Remove the stem from 1 artichoke and pull off the tough outer leaves. Once you reach the softer, pale leaves, use a large, sharp knife to cut across the flower so that you are left with the bottom quarter. Use a small, sharp knife or a vegetable peeler to remove the outer layers of the artichoke until the base, or bottom, is exposed. Scrape out the hairy "choke" and put the base in the acidulated water. Discard the rest, then repeat with the other artichoke(s).

Drain the artichokes and pat dry with paper towels. Using a mandoline or large, sharp knife, cut the artichokes into paper-thin slices and transfer to a large mixing bowl. Squeeze over the remaining lemon juice, add the olive oil, and toss well to coat. You can leave the artichoke for up to a few hours if you like, at room temperature. When ready to serve, add the arugula, mint, and cilantro to the artichoke and season with a generous ¼ teaspoon salt and plenty of freshly ground black pepper. Toss gently and arrange on serving plates. Garnish with the pecorino shavings.

Mixed bean salad

String beans are in season in summer and early autumn and are a symbol of the Jewish New Year (Rosh Hashanah), particularly with Sephardic Jews. You would expect the fruit and vegetable market, Machne Yehuda, to be bustling the last two days before Rosh Hashanah, a holiday on which a seminal family meal takes place. Often, though, the market is eerily calm. A taxi driver explained to us that the smart and canny housewives shop well before the holiday, when the prices are low, preparing and cooking whatever can be made in advance, and that only "mugs" go shopping at the last minute, just before the holiday.

10 oz / 280 g yellow beans, trimmed (if unavailable, double the quantity of green beans)

10 oz / 280 g green beans, trimmed

2 red peppers, cut into ¼-inch / 0.5cm strips

3 tbsp olive oil, plus 1 tsp for the peppers

3 cloves garlic, thinly sliced

6 tbsp / 50 g capers, rinsed and patted dry

1 tsp cumin seeds

2 tsp coriander seeds

4 green onions, thinly sliced

⅓ cup / 10 g tarragon, coarsely chopped

⅔ cup / 20 g picked chervil leaves (or a mixture of picked dill and shredded parsley)

grated zest of 1 lemon

salt and freshly ground black pepper

Yellow beans are wonderfully tender. We suggest making an effort to find them, because they make a contribution to the general texture and the look of the dish, but you are perfectly fine substituting as suggested. Serve this salad alongside Polpettone (PAGE 202) *or Roasted chicken with Jerusalem artichoke and lemon* (PAGE 180).

Preheat the oven to 450°F / 220°C.

Bring a large pan with plenty of water to a boil and add the yellow beans. After 1 minute, add the green beans and cook for another 4 minutes, or until the beans are cooked through but still crunchy. Refresh under ice-cold water, drain, pat dry, and place in a large mixing bowl.

Meanwhile, toss the peppers in 1 teaspoon of the oil, spread on a baking sheet, and place in the oven for 5 minutes, or until tender. Remove from the oven and add to the bowl with the cooked beans.

Heat the 3 tablespoons olive oil in a small saucepan. Add the garlic and cook for 20 seconds; add the capers (careful, they spit!) and fry for another 15 seconds. Add the cumin and coriander seeds and continue frying for another 15 seconds. The garlic should have turned golden by now. Remove from the heat and pour the contents of the pan immediately over the beans. Toss and add the green onions, herbs, lemon zest, a generous ¼ teaspoon salt, and black pepper. Serve, or keep refrigerated for up to a day. Just remember to bring back to room temperature before serving.

Lemony leek meatballs

What is a meat recipe doing in the vegetable section? Well, what makes these fritters so special is how well the flavor of the leeks holds its own against the meat, while the latter is more in the background. This is a reversal of roles when compared with other meatballs. The result is featherlight texture and a sharp lemony flavor.

The recipe was given to us by Tamara Meitlis, who is a fine Turkish Jewish cook and a great friend. It is highly typical of the Jews of Izmir. As with most other Turks, you don't mess about with Tamara's recipes. "Sure, you can do it differently if you like," she tells us with a generous smile, "but only if you want it to come out wrong!" Tamara is right. Sephardic recipes, particularly Turkish, which is a mature and confident cuisine, have been perfected over generations and are best adhered to religiously. When you come to think of it, this is true of most Jerusalem cuisines, and you should really only deviate from a traditional recipe once you have made sure there isn't any senior mama looking over your shoulder.

6 large trimmed leeks
   (about 1¾ lb / 800 g
   in total)
9 oz / 250 g ground beef
scant 1 cup / 90 g bread
   crumbs
2 large free-range eggs
2 tbsp sunflower oil
¾ to 1¼ cups / 200 to
   300 ml chicken stock
⅓ cup / 80 ml freshly
   squeezed lemon juice
   (about 2 lemons)
⅓ cup / 80 g Greek yogurt
1 tbsp finely chopped flat-
   leaf parsley
salt and freshly ground
   black pepper

These make a wonderfully light starter after which you can serve almost anything. As a variation, you can finish them off when frying them in the pan. Just cook them longer, without braising them in the stock, and serve hot with lemon wedges.

Cut the leeks into ¾-inch / 2cm slices and steam them for approximately 20 minutes, until completely soft. Drain and leave to cool, then squeeze out any residual water with a tea towel. Process the leeks in a food processor by pulsing a few times until well chopped but not mushy. Place the leeks in a large mixing bowl, along with the meat, bread crumbs, eggs, 1¼ teaspoons salt, and 1 teaspoon black pepper. Form the mix into flat patties, roughly 2¾ by ¾ inches / 7 by 2 cm—this should make 8. Refrigerate for 30 minutes.

Heat the oil over medium-high heat in a large, heavy-bottomed frying pan for which you have a lid. Sear the patties on both sides until golden brown; this can be done in batches if necessary.

Wipe out the pan with a paper towel and then lay the meatballs on the bottom, slightly overlapping if needed. Pour over enough stock to almost, but not quite cover the patties. Add the lemon juice and ½ teaspoon salt. Bring to a boil, then cover and simmer gently for 30 minutes. Remove the lid and cook for a few more minutes, if needed, until almost all the liquid has evaporated. Remove the pan from the heat and set aside to cool down.

Serve the meatballs just warm or at room temperature, with a dollop of the yogurt and a sprinkle of the parsley.

Kohlrabi salad

Kohlrabi is a weird vegetable. We don't like saying it but it is. It is a cabbage with a swollen stem that looks like a bumpy green or purple apple and with a texture and flavor not dissimilar to a radish or cabbage heart. It is weird because of its look—it is like an alien vegetable, with a round, squat base from which straight leafy stems spew out haphazardly—and because people in the West, Germany excepted, have no clue what to do with it. Perhaps because of its oddity and eccentricity, or maybe because it is so easy to grow and tastes so fresh, people in Israel love it. Jerusalemites mainly use kohlrabi for refreshing and crunchy salads, sometimes in combination with other firm vegetables and fruit, such as fennel, radish, cabbage, and apple. But they also cook with it, adding it to stews and creamy gratins and sometimes even stuff it.

3 medium kohlrabies
   (1⅔ lb / 750 g in total)
⅓ cup / 80 g Greek yogurt
5 tbsp / 70 g sour cream
3 tbsp mascarpone cheese
1 small clove garlic,
   crushed
1½ tsp freshly squeezed
   lemon juice
1 tbsp olive oil
2 tbsp finely shredded
   fresh mint
1 tsp dried mint
about 12 sprigs / 20 g
   baby watercress
¼ tsp sumac
salt and white pepper

This salad was first made in our London West End restaurant, NOPI. It is simple, fresh, and makes for a great way to open or to end a meal. You can also serve it alongside a selection of other seasonal salads or cooked vegetables to make a light meal. Choose kohlrabies that are small and hard with tight-looking skin.

Peel the kohlrabies, cut into ⅔-inch / 1.5cm dice, and put in a large mixing bowl. Set aside and make the dressing.

Put the yogurt, sour cream, mascarpone, garlic, lemon juice, and olive oil in a medium bowl. Add ¼ teaspoon salt and a healthy grind of pepper and whisk until smooth. Add the dressing to the kohlrabi, followed by the fresh and dried mint and half the watercress. Gently stir, then place on a serving dish. Dot the remaining watercress on top and sprinkle with the sumac.

Root vegetable slaw with labneh

3 medium beets
  (1 lb / 450 g in total)
2 medium carrots
  (9 oz / 250 g in total)
½ celery root (10 oz /
  300 g in total)
1 medium kohlrabi
  (9 oz / 250 g in total)
4 tbsp freshly squeezed
  lemon juice
4 tbsp olive oil
3 tbsp sherry vinegar
2 tsp superfine sugar
¾ cup / 25 g cilantro
  leaves, coarsely chopped
¾ cup / 25 g mint leaves,
  shredded
⅔ cup / 20 g flat-leaf
  parsley leaves, coarsely
  chopped
½ tbsp grated lemon zest
scant 1 cup / 200 g labneh
  (store-bought or see
  recipe, page 302)
salt and freshly ground
  black pepper

We make this salad in the winter or early spring, before any of the summer crops are around. It is incredibly fresh, ideal for starting a hearty meal. It is also great served alongside grilled oily fish. The labneh can be substituted with Greek yogurt, well seasoned with some olive oil, crushed garlic, and salt and pepper. It can also be left out all together, if you prefer to keep it light and simple. This recipe was inspired by a dish from Manta Ray, a great restaurant on the beach in Tel Aviv.

Peel all the vegetables and slice them thinly, about 1/16 inch / 2 mm thick. Stack a few slices at a time on top of one another and cut them into matchsticklike strips. Alternatively, use a mandoline or a food processor with the appropriate attachment. Place all the strips in a large bowl and cover with cold water. Set aside while you make the dressing.

Place the lemon juice, olive oil, vinegar, sugar, and 1 teaspoon salt in a small saucepan. Bring to a gentle simmer and stir until the sugar and the salt have dissolved. Remove from the heat.

Drain the vegetable strips and transfer to a paper towel to dry well. Dry the bowl and replace the vegetables. Pour the hot dressing over the vegetables, mix well, and leave to cool. Place in the fridge for at least 45 minutes.

When ready to serve, add the herbs, lemon zest, and 1 teaspoon black pepper to the salad. Toss well, taste, and add more salt if needed. Pile onto serving plates and serve with some labneh on the side.

Fried tomatoes with garlic

3 large cloves garlic,
  crushed
½ small hot chile, finely
  chopped
2 tbsp chopped flat-leaf
  parsley
3 large, ripe but
  firm tomatoes
  (about 1 lb / 450 g
  in total)
2 tbsp olive oil
Maldon sea salt and freshly
  ground black pepper
rustic bread, to serve

These tomatoes, eaten by Palestinians any time of the day when tomatoes are in season, are not an earth-shattering revelation, but they are quietly and surprisingly fantastic when served with simply grilled fish (GRILLED FISH SKEWERS WITH HAWAYEJ AND PARSLEY, PAGE 226), *simple rice* (BASMATI RICE AND ORZO, PAGE 103), *or other grain dishes with a clear savory note* (MEJADRA, PAGE 120). *To keep it simple, serve them with a thick slice of good bread. Adjust the cooking time and temperature to the softness of the tomatoes: a soft tomato should be cooked over higher heat for a shorter time. In any case, use only good, flavorsome tomatoes.*

Mix the garlic, chile, and chopped parsley in a small bowl and set aside. Top and tail the tomatoes and slice vertically into slices about ⅔ inch / 1.5 cm thick.

Heat the oil in a large frying pan over medium heat. Add the tomato slices, season with salt and pepper, and cook for about 1 minute, then turn over, season again with salt and pepper, and sprinkle with the garlic mixture. Continue to cook for another minute or so, shaking the pan occasionally, then turn the slices again and cook for a few more seconds, until soft but not mushy.

Turn the tomatoes over onto a serving plate, pour over the juices from the pan, and serve immediately, accompanied with the bread.

Puréed beets with yogurt & za'atar

The beet is one of very few vegetables with a strong presence in the cuisine of almost every group in Jerusalem: it colors pickling juices on the Arab table (SEE PAGE 307) and is used in most meze selections; it is the base for Ashkenazic borscht and *hamitsa*, a refreshing cold version of the soup; and it forms the basis for another soup, of Iraqi Jewish and Kurdish origin, where the famous semolina *kubbeh* is served (PAGE 162).

Beets also cross cultural lines with the flexibility of an acrobat. On Yotam's tour of the city while filming a documentary about Jerusalem food, he met Michal Baranes and Yakub Barhum. They are a mixed couple, she is Jewish with Moroccan ancestry and he is a Muslim from the Arab village of Ein Raffa, on the outskirts of the city. At their restaurant, Michal, the chef, does some cross-cultural fireworks with her food, featuring elements from her Moroccan heritage, alongside very current Israeli themes and many traditional Palestinian dishes she learns from her cooks, who are mostly local. One of Michal's most useful tools is *chrein*, the horseradish and beet relish used in practically every Ashkenazic household. She puts it in her prawn "falafel"—minced prawns and *chrein*, rolled in panko crumbs and deep-fried—making scrumptious fish cakes that look like falafel but taste nothing like it.

---

scant 2 lb / 900 g medium beets (about 1 lb / 500 g in total after cooking and peeling)
2 cloves garlic, crushed
1 small red chile, seeded and finely chopped
rounded 1 cup / 250 g Greek yogurt
1½ tbsp date syrup
3 tbsp olive oil, plus extra to finish the dish
1 tbsp za'atar
salt

TO GARNISH

2 green onions, thinly sliced
2 tbsp / 15 g toasted hazelnuts, coarsely crushed
2 oz / 60 g soft goat's milk cheese, crumbled

You will be surprised how well beet works with chile and za'atar. *Its sweetness takes on a seriously savory edge that makes it one of the most popular salads among Ottolenghi's customers. You can serve it as a dip or a starter, with bread, or as part of a meze. If the beet is watery and the dip ends up runny and doesn't hold its shape, consider adding a little mashed potato to help thicken it. Date syrup can be replaced with maple syrup.*

Preheat the oven to 400°F / 200°C.

Wash the beets and place in a roasting pan. Put them in the oven and cook, uncovered, until a knife slides easily into the center, about 1 hour. Once they are cool enough to handle, peel the beets and cut each one into about 6 pieces. Allow to cool down.

Place the beets, garlic, chile, and yogurt in a food processor and blend to a smooth paste. Transfer to a large mixing bowl and stir in the date syrup, olive oil, za'atar, and 1 teaspoon salt. Taste and add more salt if you like.

Transfer the mixture to a flat serving plate and use the back of a spoon to spread it around the plate. Scatter the green onions, hazelnuts, and cheese on top and finally drizzle with a bit of oil. Serve at room temperature.

Swiss chard fritters

14 oz / 400 g Swiss chard
   leaves, white stalks
   removed
1 oz / 30 g flat-leaf parsley
⅔ oz / 20 g cilantro
⅔ oz / 20 g dill
1½ tsp grated nutmeg
½ tsp sugar
3 tbsp all-purpose flour
2 cloves garlic, crushed
2 large free-range eggs
3 oz / 80 g feta cheese,
   broken into small pieces
4 tbsp / 60 ml olive oil
1 lemon, cut into 4 wedges
salt and freshly ground
   black pepper

The intense green color of these fritters, originally Turkish, is paralleled by a wonderfully concentrated "green" flavor of chard and herbs. They are a truly marvelous way to start a meal. Spinach makes a good substitute for the chard: increase the quantity by 50 percent and just wilt it in a pan instead of boiling it.

Bring a large pan of salted water to a boil, add the chard, and simmer for 5 minutes. Drain the leaves and squeeze them well until completely dry. Place in a food processor along with the herbs, nutmeg, sugar, flour, garlic, eggs, generous ¼ teaspoon salt, and some black pepper. Blitz until smooth and then fold the feta through the mix by hand.

Pour 1 tablespoon of the oil into a medium frying pan. Place over medium-high heat and spoon in a heaping tablespoon of mixture for each fritter. Press down gently to get a fritter 2¾ inches / 7 cm wide and ⅜ inch / 1 cm thick. You should be able to fit about 3 fritters at a time. Cook the fritters for 3 to 4 minutes in total, turning once, until they have taken on some color. Transfer to paper towels, then keep each batch warm while you cook the remaining mixture, adding the remaining oil as needed. Serve at once with the lemon wedges.

Spiced chickpeas & fresh vegetable salad

½ cup / 100 g dried
   chickpeas
1 tsp baking soda
2 small cucumbers
   (10 oz / 280 g in total)
2 large tomatoes
   (10½ oz / 300 g in total)
8½ oz / 240 g radishes
1 red pepper, seeded and
   ribs removed
1 small red onion, peeled
⅔ oz / 20 g cilantro leaves
   and stems, coarsely
   chopped
½ oz / 15 g flat-leaf parsley,
   coarsely chopped
6 tbsp / 90 ml olive oil
grated zest of 1 lemon,
   plus 2 tbsp juice
1½ tbsp sherry vinegar
1 clove garlic, crushed
1 tsp superfine sugar
1 tsp ground cardamom
1½ tsp ground allspice
1 tsp ground cumin
Greek yogurt (optional)
salt and freshly ground
   black pepper

The inspiration for this salad didn't come directly from Jerusalem, but rather from Morito, a wonderful London tapas bar owned and run by Samantha and Samuel Clark, whose food is inspired by southern Spain, North Africa, and the Middle East, very much echoing the same voices that can be heard in Jerusalem's kitchens. The combination of the cold and fresh salad with the warm chickpeas is surprisingly enticing. You can serve this dish as it is, with just a thick, fresh pita. Still, a plate of Hummus (PAGE 114) alongside, or perhaps Fried cauliflower with tahini (PAGE 60), would complement it fantastically well. The salad also works on its own without the chickpeas (just omit the sugar).

Soak the dried chickpeas overnight in a large bowl with plenty of cold water and the baking soda. The next day, drain, place in a large saucepan, and cover with water twice the volume of the chickpeas. Bring to a boil and simmer, skimming off any foam, for about an hour, until completely tender, then drain.

Cut the cucumber, tomato, radish, and pepper into ⅔-inch / 1.5cm dice; cut the onion into ¼-inch / 0.5cm dice. Mix everything together in a bowl with the cilantro and parsley.

In a jar or sealable container, mix 5 tbsp / 75 ml of the olive oil, the lemon juice and zest, vinegar, garlic, and sugar and mix well to form a dressing, then season to taste with salt and pepper. Pour the dressing over the salad and toss lightly.

Mix together the cardamom, allspice, cumin, and ¼ teaspoon salt and spread on a plate. Toss the cooked chickpeas in the spice mixture in a few batches to coat well. Heat the remaining olive oil in a frying pan over medium heat and lightly fry the chickpeas for 2 to 3 minutes, gently shaking the pan so they cook evenly and don't stick. Keep warm.

Divide the salad among four plates, arranging it in a large circle, and spoon the warm spiced chickpeas on top, keeping the edge of the salad clear. You can drizzle some Greek yogurt on top to make the salad creamy.

Chermoula eggplant with bulgur *&* yogurt

Historically, bulgur was generally the rural people's food in the Middle East, while rice was for more affluent city folk. Still, bulgur—boiled wheat that has been dried and cracked or ground—was staple to many Palestinians. Today, this differentiation is less relevant, with bulgur gaining popularity with everybody, particularly for salads and mezes.

Chermoula is a powerful North African paste that is brushed over fish and vegetables, giving them the perfumed aroma of preserved lemon, mixed with heat and spice. Here, the eggplants flavored with chermoula, *drizzled with cold yogurt, make a luscious way to start any meal. Combine it with the sweet and salty bulgur salad and you have a modest vegetarian feast.*

---

2 cloves garlic, crushed
2 tsp ground cumin
2 tsp ground coriander
1 tsp chile flakes
1 tsp sweet paprika
2 tbsp finely chopped preserved lemon peel (store-bought or see recipe, page 303)
⅔ cup / 140 ml olive oil, plus extra to finish
2 medium eggplants
1 cup / 150 g fine bulgur
⅔ cup / 140 ml boiling water
⅓ cup / 50 g golden raisins
3½ tbsp / 50 ml warm water
⅓ oz / 10 g cilantro, chopped, plus extra to finish
⅓ oz / 10 g mint, chopped
⅓ cup / 50 g pitted green olives, halved
⅓ cup / 30 g sliced almonds, toasted
3 green onions, chopped
1½ tbsp freshly squeezed lemon juice
½ cup / 120 g Greek yogurt
salt

Preheat the oven to 400°F / 200°C.

To make the chermoula, mix together in a small bowl the garlic, cumin, coriander, chile, paprika, preserved lemon, two-thirds of the olive oil, and ½ teaspoon salt.

Cut the eggplants in half lengthwise. Score the flesh of each half with deep, diagonal crisscross scores, making sure not to pierce the skin. Spoon the chermoula over each half, spreading it evenly, and place on a baking sheet cut side up. Put in the oven and roast for 40 minutes, or until the eggplants are completely soft.

Meanwhile, place the bulgur in a large bowl and cover with the boiling water.

Soak the raisins in the warm water. After 10 minutes, drain the raisins and add them to the bulgur, along with the remaining oil. Add the herbs, olives, almonds, green onions, lemon juice, and a pinch of salt and stir to combine. Taste and add more salt if necessary.

Serve the eggplants warm or at room temperature. Place ½ eggplant, cut side up, on each individual plate. Spoon the bulgur on top, allowing some to fall from both sides. Spoon over some yogurt, sprinkle with cilantro, and finish with a drizzle of oil.

Fried cauliflower with tahini

This dish is usually served in the context of a large meze assortment, laid out on the table at the beginning of a substantial meal. This type of dining is now familiar in the West and has become quite popular—the communal tables in Ottolenghi provide good evidence—but it is hard to overstate how deeply rooted it is in the culture and the temperament of Jerusalem and the wider region.

For Jerusalemites, Arabs and Jews alike, the idea of dining alone is abhorrent. Eating is a celebration, a feast, it is about breaking bread and about conviviality, it is about abundance and sharing. As no one is particularly fussy about decorum and good table manners, the meal is always destined to turn into a lively gorge, with everybody sharing everything, happy to dig into one another's plates, to grab and move plates around until truly satisfied. It is not a particularly orderly or calm way to eat, but it is certainly a very happy one.

---

2 cups / 500 ml sunflower oil

2 medium heads cauliflower (2¼ lb / 1 kg in total), divided into small florets

8 green onions, each divided into 3 long segments

¾ cup / 180 g light tahini paste

2 cloves garlic, crushed

¼ cup / 15 g flat-leaf parsley, chopped

¼ cup / 15 g chopped mint, plus extra to finish

⅔ cup / 150 g Greek yogurt

¼ cup / 60ml freshly squeezed lemon juice, plus grated zest of 1 lemon

1 tsp pomegranate molasses, plus extra to finish

about ¾ cup / 180 ml water

Maldon sea salt and freshly ground black pepper

For many in the West who have been brought up on cauliflower cheese and other similar dairy-heavy dishes, it is hard to fathom different, sharper, and fresher treatments of cauliflower. This salad keeps the creamy element that helps make cauliflower comforting but without tasting in any way greasy or unctuous. It will keep in the fridge for a day. Just remember to bring it back to room temperature and reseason before serving.

Heat the sunflower oil in a large saucepan placed over medium-high heat. Using a pair of metal tongs or a metal spoon, carefully place a few cauliflower florets at a time into the oil and cook them for 2 to 3 minutes, turning them over so they color evenly. Once golden brown, use a slotted spoon to lift the florets into a colander to drain. Sprinkle with a little salt. Continue in batches until you finish all the cauliflower. Next, fry the green onions in batches but for only about 1 minute. Add to the cauliflower. Allow both to cool down a little.

Pour the tahini paste into a large mixing bowl and add the garlic, chopped herbs, yogurt, lemon juice and zest, pomegranate molasses, and some salt and pepper. Stir well with a wooden spoon as you add the water. The tahini sauce will thicken and then loosen up as you add water. Don't add too much, just enough to get a thick, yet smooth, pourable consistency, a bit like honey.

Add the cauliflower and green onions to the tahini and stir well. Taste and adjust the seasoning. You may also want to add more lemon juice.

To serve, spoon into a serving bowl and finish with a few drops of pomegranate molasses and some mint.

Roasted cauliflower & hazelnut salad

1 head cauliflower, broken
  into small florets
  (1½ lb / 660 g in total)
5 tbsp olive oil
1 large celery stalk,
  cut on an angle into
  ¼-inch / 0.5cm slices
  (⅔ cup / 70 g in total)
5 tbsp / 30 g hazelnuts,
  with skins
⅓ cup / 10 g small flat-leaf
  parsley leaves, picked
⅓ cup / 50 g pomegranate
  seeds (from about
  ½ medium pomegranate)
generous ¼ tsp ground
  cinnamon
generous ¼ tsp
  ground allspice
1 tbsp sherry vinegar
1½ tsp maple syrup
salt and freshly ground
  black pepper

Cauliflower, raw or lightly cooked, is a useful salad ingredient, above all in winter when there isn't a great variety of fresh vegetables available. It soaks up flavors particularly effectively and benefits from anything sweet and sharp. This salad, which will go well with the Chicken sofrito (PAGE 190) or with Grilled fish skewers with hawayej and parsley (PAGE 226), is inspired by a recipe from a brilliant Australian chef and food writer, Karen Martini.

Preheat the oven to 425°F / 220°C.

Mix the cauliflower with 3 tablespoons of the olive oil, ½ teaspoon salt, and some black pepper. Spread out in a roasting pan and roast on the top oven rack for 25 to 35 minutes, until the cauliflower is crisp and parts of it have turned golden brown. Transfer to a large mixing bowl and set aside to cool down.

Decrease the oven temperature to 325°F / 170°C. Spread the hazelnuts on a baking sheet lined with parchment paper and roast for 17 minutes.

Allow the nuts to cool a little, then coarsely chop them and add to the cauliflower, along with the remaining oil and the rest of the ingredients. Stir, taste, and season with salt and pepper accordingly. Serve at room temperature.

Shakshuka

Shakshuka is Tunisian in origin but has become hugely popular in Jerusalem and all over Israel as substantial breakfast or lunch fare. Tunisian cuisine has a passionate love affair with eggs and this particular version of *shakshuka* is the seasonal variant for the summer and early autumn. Potatoes are used during the winter and eggplants in spring.

---

2 tbsp olive oil

2 tbsp Pilpelchuma (page 302) or harissa (store-bought or see recipe, page 301)

2 tsp tomato paste

2 large red peppers, cut into ¼-inch / 0.5cm dice (2 cups / 300 g in total)

4 cloves garlic, finely chopped

1 tsp ground cumin

5 large, very ripe tomatoes, chopped (5 cups / 800 g in total); canned are also fine

4 large free-range eggs, plus 4 egg yolks

½ cup / 120 g labneh (store-bought or see recipe, page 302) or thick yogurt

salt

Having published recipes for shakshuka *once or twice before, we are well aware of the risk of repeating ourselves. Still, we are happy to add another version of this splendid dish, seeing how popular it is and how convenient it is to prepare. This time the focus is on tomato and spice. But we encourage you to play around with different ingredients and adjust the amount of heat to your taste. Serve with good white bread and nothing else.*

Heat the olive oil in a large frying pan over medium heat and add the pilpelchuma or harissa, tomato paste, peppers, garlic, cumin, and ¾ teaspoon salt. Stir and cook over medium heat for about 8 minutes to allow the peppers to soften. Add the tomatoes, bring to a gentle simmer, and cook for a further 10 minutes until you have quite a thick sauce. Taste for seasoning.

Make 8 little dips in the sauce. Gently break the eggs and carefully pour each into its own dip. Do the same with the yolks. Use a fork to swirl the egg whites a little bit with the sauce, taking care not to break the yolks. Simmer gently for 8 to 10 minutes, until the egg whites are set but the yolks are still runny (you can cover the pan with a lid if you wish to hasten the process). Remove from the heat, leave for a couple of minutes to settle, then spoon into individual plates and serve with the labneh or yogurt.

Butternut squash & tahini spread

1 very large butternut
  squash (about 2½ lb /
  1.2 kg), peeled and cut
  into chunks (7 cups /
  970 g in total)
3 tbsp olive oil
1 tsp ground cinnamon
5 tbsp / 70 g light tahini
  paste
½ cup / 120 g Greek yogurt
2 small cloves garlic,
  crushed
1 tsp mixed black and
  white sesame seeds
  (or just white, if you don't
  have black)
1½ tsp date syrup
2 tbsp chopped cilantro
  (optional)
salt

Date syrup, which we use here to add intensity, is a popular natural sweetener with wonderful richness and treacly depth. Use it for salad and vegetable dressings, to sweeten stews, or to drizzle over porridge in the morning. It is available from health food stores and Middle Eastern groceries but can be substituted with maple syrup or molasses.

This dip seems to be fantastically popular with anyone who tries it. There is something about the magical combination of tahini and pumpkin or squash that we always tend to come back to (SEE ALSO ROASTED BUTTERNUT SQUASH, PAGE 36). Serve as a starter with bread or as part of a meze selection.

Preheat the oven to 400°F / 200°C.

Spread the squash out in a medium roasting pan. Pour over the olive oil and sprinkle on the cinnamon and ½ teaspoon salt. Mix together well, cover the pan tightly with aluminum foil, and roast in the oven for 70 minutes, stirring once during the cooking. Remove from the oven and leave to cool.

Transfer the squash to a food processor, along with the tahini, yogurt, and garlic. Roughly pulse so that everything is combined into a coarse paste, without the spread becoming smooth; you can also do this by hand using a fork or potato masher.

Spread the butternut in a wavy pattern over a flat plate and sprinkle with the sesame seeds, drizzle over the syrup, and finish with the cilantro, if using.

Georgia

Walnuts, plums, beets, herbs, eggplants, pomegranates, and grapes are some key ingredients of Georgian cuisine, which is influenced by Russian, Persian, and Turkish cultures. Georgian legend tells that when God was handing out land to the peoples of the world, the Georgians were too busy eating, drinking, and feasting. When they finally arrived it was too late and no land was left. The Georgians had told God they had been toasting his health and invited him to join them. He had such a good time at their table that he eventually decided to give them the land he had been saving for himself.

―――

GEORGIAN LEGEND TELLS THAT WHEN GOD WAS HANDING OUT LAND TO THE PEOPLES OF THE WORLD, THE GEORGIANS WERE TOO BUSY EATING, DRINKING, AND FEASTING.

―――

Jews from Georgia settled in Jerusalem in the late nineteenth century, just outside the Old City walls, building a small neighborhood near Damascus Gate. They brought with them their rich and colorful food, which fitted perfectly with the local cuisine and produce available. *Pkhali*, a crushed walnut sauce that can be spooned over various vegetables such as eggplants, spinach, and beets, bears a resemblance to *muhammara*, a local crushed walnut salad. Their beet salads were often similar to *salatet banjar*, the Palestinian version made of sliced cooked beets, garlic, olive oil, lemon juice, and chopped parsley. Sadly, as is too often the case in this city, this culinary brotherhood was not enough. The Georgian neighborhood was completely decimated during the 1929 Palestinian revolt, the first of many uprisings protesting against the growing presence of Jewish settlers in Palestine. Still, Georgians managed to thrive in other parts of the city and over the years made their mark on the local food.

Spicy beet, leek & walnut salad

**4 medium beets
(1⅓ lb / 600 g in total
after cooking and
peeling)**
**4 medium leeks, cut into
4-inch / 10cm segments
(4 cups / 360 g in total)**
**½ oz / 15 g cilantro,
coarsely chopped**
1¼ cups / 25 g arugula
**⅓ cup / 50 g pomegranate
seeds (optional)**

DRESSING

**1 cup / 100 g walnuts,
coarsely chopped**
**4 cloves garlic, finely
chopped**
¼ tsp chile flakes
**¼ cup / 60 ml cider
vinegar**
2 tbsp tamarind water
½ tsp walnut oil
2½ tbsp peanut oil
1 tsp salt

This gutsy salad is inspired by Georgian cuisine (SEE PAGE 71). *The beets and leeks can be cooked well ahead of time, even a day in advance. We keep the two elements of the salad separate until serving, so the beets don't color the leeks red. This is not necessary if such an aesthetic consideration is not top of your priority list. Beets of other colors— golden, white, or striped—are also good.*

Preheat the oven to 425°F / 220°C.

Wrap the beets individually in aluminum foil and roast them in the oven for 1 to 1½ hours, depending on their size. Once cooked, you should be able to stick a small knife through to the center easily. Remove from the oven and set aside to cool.

Once cool enough to handle, peel the beets, halve them, and cut each half into wedges ⅜ inch / 1 cm thick at the base. Put in a medium bowl and set aside.

Place the leeks in a medium pan with salted water, bring to a boil, and simmer for 10 minutes, until just cooked; it's important to simmer them gently and not to overcook them so they don't fall apart. Drain and refresh under cold water, then use a very sharp serrated knife to cut each segment into 3 smaller pieces and pat dry. Transfer to a bowl, separate from the beets, and set aside.

While the vegetables are cooking, mix together all the dressing ingredients and leave to one side for at least 10 minutes for all the flavors to come together.

Divide the walnut dressing and the cilantro equally between the beets and the leeks and toss gently. Taste both and add more salt if needed.

To put the salad together, spread most of the beets on a serving platter, top with some arugula, then most of the leeks, then the remaining beets, and finish with more leeks and arugula. Sprinkle over the pomegranate seeds, if using, and serve.

Charred okra with tomato, garlic & preserved lemon

Okra in the Middle East is smaller and much less sinewy than the type we usually get in Britain. It is very popular in Jerusalem, where it is normally cooked with tomato, onion, and garlic, often served with fresh cilantro. Tamarind syrup and lemon juice are also popular accompaniments.

When okra was in season, Sami's grandmother used to thread it, like a necklace, onto a long string, hang it in a cool place, and leave it to dry. This would later be rehydrated when cooking it in *yachne*, a Palestinian meat and tomato stew, where it imparted a glorious flavor and thickened the sauce.

10½ oz / 300 g baby or very small okra

2 tbsp olive oil, plus more if needed

4 cloves garlic, thinly sliced

⅔ oz / 20 g preserved lemon peel (store-bought or see recipe, page 303), cut into ⅜-inch / 1cm wedges

3 small tomatoes (7 oz / 200 g in total), cut into 8 wedges, or halved cherry tomatoes

1½ tsp chopped flat-leaf parsley

1½ tsp chopped cilantro

1 tbsp freshly squeezed lemon juice

Maldon sea salt and freshly ground black pepper

For this quick stir-fry, a robust yet not too heavy starter, try to get small okra in markets or Asian grocers. Another alternative, available from some Middle Eastern shops or small supermarkets, is prepared frozen okra, usually from Egypt; it has great flavor and texture.

Using a small, sharp fruit knife, trim the okra pods, removing the stem just above the pod so as not to expose the seeds.

Place a large, heavy-bottomed frying pan over high heat and leave for a few minutes. When almost red hot, throw in the okra in two batches and dry-cook, shaking the pan occasionally, for 4 minutes per batch. The okra pods should have the occasional dark blister.

Return all the charred okra to the pan and add the olive oil, garlic, and preserved lemon. Stir-fry for 2 minutes, shaking the pan. Reduce the heat to medium and add the tomatoes, 2 tablespoons water, the chopped herbs, lemon juice, and ½ teaspoon salt and some black pepper. Stir everything together gently, so that the tomatoes do not break up, and continue to cook for 2 to 3 minutes, until the tomatoes are warmed through. Transfer to a serving dish, drizzle with more olive oil, add a sprinkle of salt, and serve.

Baba ghanoush?

Burning an eggplant is probably the most effective tool of the Jerusalemite cook, as it is of many others throughout the region. Over the years we have cooked dozens of salads based on this super-popular technique. The eggplant pulp can be used in many contexts—stews, soups (BURNT EGGPLANT AND MOGRABIEH SOUP, PAGE 141), with roasted meat or fish (FISH AND CAPER KEBABS, PAGE 221)—but essentially it is in the department of salad and dips that it comes into its glorious own. The variations are numerous and depend on regions and cultures. You would think that everybody would live together in tolerant, yet smoky harmony. Not quite.

Yotam recently appeared on a BBC radio program to talk about and cook his baba ghanoush, a hugely popular Levantine dish that consists of burnt eggplant, mashed and mixed with various seasonings. To stir things up a bit, he was confronted with someone who had a very different idea about baba ghanoush. Rana Jawad, the courageous Lebanese BBC correspondent who went undercover in Tripoli during the final months of Gaddafi's reign, wasn't on the show to talk about food but was given a spoonful of the salad. She loved it but strongly protested against calling it baba ghanoush. "If it doesn't have tahini in it, it isn't the real thing," she said. Yotam was happy to concede.

We are not sure what Rana would have said had she seen the deconstructed baba ghanoush that the Jerusalemite chef Ezra Kedem cooked for Yotam. He spread the flesh of a baby eggplant on a plate beautifully and then dotted it with all the other salad elements, tahini included, but without stirring or mixing it. In any case, it seemed clear that everybody was agreed: baba ghanoush has to have tahini.

Then, another turn of events. When we went to talk to Nawal Abu Ghosh, an expert on Arab Israeli food who has written a comprehensive book about it, she insisted that baba ghanoush has no tahini in it whatsoever—just cubed vegetables, lemon juice, garlic, and olive oil—and that if you add tahini, it is just called eggplant salad. Go figure!

Burnt eggplant with garlic, lemon
& pomegranate seeds

**4 large eggplants
(3¼ lb / 1.5 kg before
cooking; 2½ cups /
550 g after burning
and draining the flesh)
2 cloves garlic, crushed
grated zest of 1 lemon and
2 tbsp freshly squeezed
lemon juice
5 tbsp olive oil
2 tbsp chopped flat-leaf
parsley
2 tbsp chopped mint
seeds of ½ large
pomegranate (scant
½ cup / 80 g in total)
salt and freshly ground
black pepper**

*This salad has the most wonderful smoky aroma and works well with
grilled meat or fish, as well as with other dips and salads to kick-start a
passionate Levantine feast. But in order to get the full smoky flavor, you
really need to stick to the instructions and allow the eggplants to burn well.
If you want to turn it into a "real" baba ghanoush, whatever that may be*
(SEE PAGE 76), *drizzle on some light tahini paste at the end.*

If you have a gas range, line the base with aluminum foil to protect
it, keeping only the burners exposed. Place the eggplants directly on
four separate gas burners with medium flames and roast for 15 to
18 minutes, until the skin is burnt and flaky and the flesh is soft.
Use metal tongs to turn them around occasionally. Alternatively,
score the eggplants with a knife in a few places, about ¾ inch / 2 cm
deep, and place on a baking sheet under a hot broiler for about an
hour. Turn them around every 20 minutes or so and continue to
cook even if they burst and break.

Remove the eggplants from the heat and allow them to cool down
slightly. Once cool enough to handle, cut an opening along each
eggplant and scoop out the soft flesh, dividing it with your hands
into long thin strips. Discard the skin. Drain the flesh in a colander
for at least an hour, preferably longer, to get rid of as much water as
possible.

Place the eggplant pulp in a medium bowl and add the garlic, lemon
zest and juice, olive oil, ½ teaspoon salt, and a good grind of black
pepper. Stir and allow the eggplant to marinate at room temperature
for at least an hour.

When you are ready to serve, mix in most of the herbs and taste for
seasoning. Pile high on a serving plate, scatter on the pomegranate
seeds, and garnish with the remaining herbs.

Parsley & barley salad

We started off calling this Barley and feta tabbouleh, but the longer we spent with our recipes and sources the more we realized how strongly people feel about the names given to dishes. This is understandable in a place where so much is always at stake.

Still, this recipe is very much inspired by the concept of tabbouleh (PAGE 85). It was first cooked for Yotam by Tami Rosenbaum, mother of Yoni, his childhood best friend. Tami is a fantastic cook. She comes from a Yekke family (German Jews), and had a "proper," not particularly Middle Eastern upbringing. Tami studied cookery at secondary school, again receiving traditional training. When Yotam used to visit Yoni as a child, it was the only home of any of his friends where bread rolls—sweet and savory—were baked regularly; schnitzels were made from veal and stuffed with bacon; and all the children played musical instruments seriously—just like back home in Germany. Despite all that, even Tami's food was not immune to local Middle Eastern influences, and many dishes she cooks today manage to fuse together the two worlds in a very delicious way.

"Serious" Jerusalem dishes—those substantial, slow-cooked ones that everybody adores but at the same time is also slightly terrified of due to how heavy and sleep-inducing they can be (SEE CHICKEN WITH CARAMELIZED ONION AND CARDAMOM RICE, PAGE 184, OR TURNIP AND VEAL "CAKE," PAGE 156)—must always be accompanied by a sharp, fresh salad such as this one. The herbs and lemon juice cleanse the palate and give a certain sense of lightness, balancing out any overdose of carbs and unctuous meat. You can also serve it alongside other vegetable-based meze dishes. The barley can be replaced with spelt, farro, or wheat berries, with cooking times varying.

scant ¼ cup / 40 g pearl barley
5 oz / 150 g feta cheese
5½ tbsp olive oil
1 tsp za'atar
½ tsp coriander seeds, lightly toasted and crushed
¼ tsp ground cumin
scant 3 oz / 80 g flat-leaf parsley, leaves and fine stems
4 green onions, finely chopped (⅓ cup / 40 g in total)
2 cloves garlic, crushed
⅓ cup / 40 g cashew nuts, lightly toasted and coarsely crushed
1 green pepper, seeded and cut into ⅜-inch / 1cm dice
½ tsp ground allspice
2 tbsp freshly squeezed lemon juice
salt and freshly ground black pepper

Place the pearl barley in a small saucepan, cover with plenty of water, and boil for 30 to 35 minutes, until tender but with a bite. Pour into a fine sieve, shake to remove all the water, and transfer to a large bowl.

Break the feta into rough pieces, about ¾ inch / 2 cm in size, and mix in a small bowl with 1½ tablespoons of the olive oil, the za'atar, the coriander seeds, and the cumin. Gently mix together and leave to marinate while you prepare the rest of the salad.

Chop the parsley finely and place in a bowl with the green onions, garlic, cashew nuts, pepper, allspice, lemon juice, the remaining olive oil, and the cooked barley. Mix together well and season to taste. To serve, divide the salad among four plates and top with the marinated feta.

Chunky zucchini & tomato salad

8 pale green zucchini
  or regular zucchini
  (about 2¼ lb / 1 kg
  in total)
5 large, very ripe tomatoes
  (1¾ lb / 800 g in total)
3 tbsp olive oil, plus extra
  to finish
2⅓ cups / 300 g Greek
  yogurt
2 cloves garlic, crushed
2 red chiles, seeded and
  chopped
grated zest of 1 medium
  lemon and 2 tbsp freshly
  squeezed lemon juice
1 tbsp date syrup, plus
  extra to finish (see
  page 69)
2 cups / 200 g walnuts,
  coarsely chopped
2 tbsp chopped mint
⅔ oz / 20 g flat-leaf
  parsley, chopped
salt and freshly ground
  black pepper

This is a variation on mafghoussa, *a popular Palestinian salad or spread. The vegetables for* mafghoussa *were traditionally grilled on the ambers in the* tabun, *the clay oven often found outdoors in village homes. The original recipe calls for grilled tomatoes and zucchini, garlic, buttermilk, and chopped parsley. We added a bit of this and a bit of that so it is a little richer, a perfect meal opener, accompanied with bread. You can cook your vegetables on a grill instead of a griddle pan.*

Preheat the oven to 425°F / 220°C. Place a ridged griddle pan over high heat.

Trim the zucchini and cut them in half lengthwise. Halve the tomatoes as well. Brush the zucchini and tomatoes with olive oil on the cut side and season with salt and pepper.

By now the griddle pan should be piping hot. Start with the zucchini. Place a few of them on the pan, cut side down, and cook for 5 minutes; the zucchini should be nicely charred on one side. Now remove the zucchini and repeat the same process with the tomatoes. Place the vegetables in a roasting pan and put in the oven for about 20 minutes, until the zucchini are very tender.

Remove the pan from the oven and allow the vegetables to cool down slightly. Chop them coarsely and leave to drain in a colander for 15 minutes.

Whisk together the yogurt, garlic, chile, lemon zest and juice, and molasses in a large mixing bowl. Add the chopped vegetables, walnuts, mint, and most of the parsley and stir well. Season with ¾ teaspoon salt and some pepper.

Transfer the salad to a large, shallow serving plate and spread it out. Garnish with the remaining parsley. Finally, drizzle over some date syrup and olive oil.

Tabbouleh

"If you want to find a good husband, you'd better learn how to chop your parsley properly," Sami's mother sternly cautioned his sister when she was a teenager. Indeed tabbouleh, as is not always understood in the West, is all about parsley. It is a key ingredient—both in this salad and in Palestinian cuisine in general—and it must be treated with respect and great deftness, as implied by Sami's mum.

Tabbouleh probably hails from Lebanon and Syria, but has become such an essential part of the Palestinian heritage that nobody seems to remember any more. A good tabbouleh is based on plenty of fresh flat-leaf parsley and mint, carefully shredded by hand to prevent bruising, well seasoned and sharp, mixed with some tomato and al dente bulgur wheat. The exact proportions of parsley to bulgur vary. The Lebanese use the least amount of bulgur, just a tiny quantity of grain dotted sparingly among the parsley. The Palestinians add a little more. Other elements need to be added carefully. Whichever way, this is, essentially, a parsley salad, not a bulgur salad.

⅓ cup / 30 g fine bulgur wheat

2 large tomatoes, ripe but firm (10½ oz / 300 g in total)

1 shallot, finely chopped (3 tbsp / 30 g in total)

3 tbsp freshly squeezed lemon juice, plus a little extra to finish

4 large bunches flat-leaf parsley (5½ oz / 160 g in total)

2 bunches mint (1 oz / 30 g in total)

2 tsp ground allspice

1 tsp baharat spice mix (store-bought or see recipe, page 299)

⅓ cup / 80 ml top-quality olive oil

seeds of about ½ large pomegranate (⅓ cup / 70 g in total), optional

salt and freshly ground black pepper

If you can't get fine bulgur wheat, or if the pack doesn't mention the grade, soak it in boiling water for 5 minutes, then drain and leave to dry in a fine sieve. Tabbouleh is traditionally eaten scooped up with small romaine lettuce leaves. These can be arranged on a platter at the start of a meal and everybody helps themselves. It also goes well next to most meat and fish dishes.

Put the bulgur in a fine sieve and run under cold water until the water coming through looks clear and most of the starch has been removed. Transfer to a large mixing bowl.

Use a small serrated knife to cut the tomatoes into slices ¼ inch / 0.5 cm thick. Cut each slice into ¼-inch / 0.5cm strips and then into dice. Add the tomatoes and their juices to the bowl, along with the shallot and lemon juice and stir well.

Take a few sprigs of parsley and pack them together tightly. Use a large, very sharp knife to trim off most of the stems and discard. Now use the knife to move up the stems and leaves, gradually "feeding" the knife in order to shred the parsley as finely as you can and trying to avoid cutting pieces wider than 1/32 inch / 1 mm. Add to the bowl.

Pick the mint leaves off the stems, pack a few together tightly, and shred them finely as you did the parsley; don't chop them up too much as they tend to discolor. Add to the bowl.

Finally, add the allspice, baharat, olive oil, pomegranate, if using, and some salt and pepper. Taste, and add more salt and pepper if you like, possibly a little bit of lemon juice, and serve.

Roasted potatoes with caramel & prunes

This is our little tribute to *tzimmes*, a common Polish Ashkenazic sweet stew of carrots and dried fruit that in most of its local manifestations, we have to admit, is pretty gross. However, when done properly, with beef flank pieces, marrowbones, goose fat, cinnamon, honey, and lemon juice, it is one of the most delectable wintery stews you can make. A lesser-known Lithuanian version is made with potatoes instead of carrots.

We first published this recipe a few years back for a Guardian *Christmas booklet. It is perfectly suited to such seminal family feasts, where the eating carries on for hours and the cooking isn't too much work. Serve it with roasted beef or chicken and Kohlrabi salad* (PAGE 46). *Vegetarians can substitute the goose fat with sunflower oil.*

2¼ lb / 1 kg floury potatoes, such as russet
½ cup / 120 ml goose fat
5 oz / 150 g whole soft Agen prunes, pitted
scant ½ cup / 90 g superfine sugar
3½ tbsp / 50 ml iced water
salt

Preheat the oven to 475°F / 240°C.

Peel the potatoes, leave the small ones whole and halve the larger ones, so you end up with pieces of around 2 oz / 60 g. Rinse under cold water, then place the potatoes in a large pan with plenty of fresh cold water. Bring to a boil, and simmer for 8 to 10 minutes. Drain the potatoes well, then shake the colander to roughen their edges.

Place the goose fat in a roasting pan and heat in the oven until smoking, about 8 minutes. Carefully take the pan out of the oven and add the boiled potatoes to the hot fat with metal tongs, rolling them around in the fat as you do so. Gently place the pan on the highest rack of the oven and cook for 50 to 65 minutes, or until the potatoes are golden and crunchy on the outside. Turn them over from time to time while they are cooking.

Once the potatoes are almost ready, take the tray out of the oven and tip it over a heatproof bowl to remove most of the fat. Add ½ teaspoon salt and the prunes and stir gently. Return to the oven for another 5 minutes.

During this time, make the caramel. Put the sugar in a clean, heavy-bottomed saucepan and place over low heat. Without stirring, watch the sugar turn a rich caramel color. Make sure to keep your eyes on the sugar at all times. As soon as you reach this color, remove the pan from the heat. Holding the pan at a safe distance from your face, quickly pour the iced water into the caramel to stop it from cooking. Return to the heat and stir to remove any sugar lumps.

Before serving, stir the caramel into the potatoes and prunes. Transfer to a serving bowl and eat at once.

Swiss chard with tahini, yogurt
& buttered pine nuts

2¾ lb / 1.3 kg Swiss chard
2½ tbsp / 40 g unsalted
  butter
2 tbsp olive oil, plus extra
  to finish
scant 5 tbsp / 40 g pine
  nuts
2 small cloves garlic, sliced
  very thinly
¼ cup / 60 ml dry white
  wine
sweet paprika, to garnish
  (optional)
salt and freshly ground
  black pepper

TAHINI &
YOGURT SAUCE

3½ tbsp / 50 g light
  tahini paste
4½ tbsp / 50 g Greek
  yogurt
2 tbsp freshly squeezed
  lemon juice
1 clove garlic, crushed
2 tbsp water

Chard leaves are some of the most popular greens in Jerusalem. They have a fantastic sharp aroma and tend to hold their texture when cooked. We love stuffing them and sautéing them with herbs and various spices. Garlic is essential! Paired with tahini and yogurt, they make a remarkable side dish—sharp, full of flavor, and yet not so dominant that they overshadow most main courses. Try this dish next to Mejadra (PAGE 120) or Lamb shawarma (PAGE 210).

Start with the sauce. Place all the ingredients in a medium bowl, add a pinch of salt, and stir well with a small whisk until you get a smooth, semistiff paste. Set aside.

Use a sharp knife to separate the white chard stalks from the green leaves and cut both into slices ¾ inch / 2 cm wide, keeping them separate. Bring a large pan of salted water to a boil and add the chard stalks. Simmer for 2 minutes, add the leaves, and cook for a further minute. Drain and rinse well under cold water. Allow the water to drain and then use your hands to squeeze the chard until it is completely dry.

Put half the butter and the 2 tablespoons olive oil in a large frying pan and place over medium heat. Once hot, add the pine nuts and toss them in the pan until golden, about 2 minutes. Use a slotted spoon to remove them from the pan, then throw in the garlic. Cook for about a minute, until it starts to become golden. Carefully (it will spit!) pour in the wine. Leave for a minute or less, until it reduces to about one-third. Add the chard and the rest of the butter and cook for 2 to 3 minutes, stirring occasionally, until the chard is completely warm. Season with ½ teaspoon salt and some black pepper.

Divide the chard among individual serving bowls, spoon some tahini sauce on top, and scatter with the pine nuts. Finally, drizzle with olive oil and sprinkle with some paprika, if you like.

Sabih

This isn't a Jerusalem dish. It was developed by Iraqi Jews settling in the 1950s in the city of Ramat Gan, near Tel Aviv. It incorporates so many elements, though, that it perfectly epitomizes the jumble of cuisines of the region. The simply fried eggplant slices are a mainstay of both Arab and Sephardic cooking. Tahini has a similar lineage. The *zhoug* (PAGE 301) is a Jewish Yemeni chile paste that has become the Israeli equivalent to ketchup. The savory mango pickle the Iraqis brought with them reflects Indian influence. Hard-boiled egg is another Sephardic basic, and the chopped salad, well, that's as Arab and as Israeli as can be (PAGE 29).

2 large eggplants
(about 1⅔ lb / 750 g
in total)

about 1¼ cups / 300 ml
sunflower oil

4 slices good-quality white
bread, toasted, or fresh
and moist mini pitas

1 cup / 240 ml Tahini sauce
(page 298)

4 large free-range eggs,
hard-boiled, peeled, and
cut into ⅜-inch / 1cm
thick slices or quartered

about 4 tbsp Zhoug
(page 301)

amba or savory mango
pickle (optional)

salt and freshly ground
black pepper

CHOPPED SALAD

2 medium ripe tomatoes,
cut into ⅜-inch / 1cm dice
(about 1 cup / 200 g
in total)

2 mini cucumbers, cut into
⅜-inch / 1cm dice (about
1 cup / 120 g in total)

2 green onions,
thinly sliced

1½ tbsp chopped flat-leaf
parsley

2 tsp freshly squeezed
lemon juice

1½ tbsp olive oil

This mumbo-jumbo served in or on a pita is one of the most exciting street foods you can come across. If you can't get a thick, fresh pita from a Middle Eastern grocer, don't bother with the supermarket brands and use toasted bread instead. While you are there, buy a savory mango pickle if you can. Sweet mango pickles or mango chutneys are not really suitable.

Use a vegetable peeler to peel away strips of eggplant skin from top to bottom, leaving the eggplants with alternating strips of black skin and white flesh, zebralike. Cut both eggplants widthwise into slices 1 inch / 2.5 cm thick. Sprinkle them on both sides with salt, then spread them out on a baking sheet and let stand for at least 30 minutes to remove some water. Use paper towels to wipe them.

Heat the sunflower oil in a wide frying pan. Carefully—the oil spits—fry the eggplant slices in batches until nice and dark, turning once, 6 to 8 minutes total. Add oil if needed as you cook the batches. When done, the eggplant pieces should be completely tender in the center. Remove from the pan and drain on paper towels.

Make the chopped salad by mixing together all the ingredients and seasoning with salt and pepper to taste.

Just before serving, place 1 slice of bread or pita on each plate. Spoon 1 tablespoon of the tahini sauce over each slice, then arrange the eggplant slices on top, overlapping. Drizzle over some more tahini but without completely covering the eggplant slices. Season each egg slice with salt and pepper and arrange over the eggplant. Drizzle some more tahini on top and spoon over as much zhoug as you like; be careful, it's hot! Spoon over mango pickle as well, if you like. Serve the vegetable salad on the side, spooning some on top of every serving if desired.

Latkes

5½ cups / 600 g peeled
  and grated fairly waxy
  potatoes such as
  Yukon Gold
2¾ cups / 300 g peeled and
  grated parsnips
⅔ cup / 30 g chives, finely
  chopped
4 egg whites
2 tbsp cornstarch
5 tbsp / 80 g unsalted butter
6½ tbsp / 100 ml sunflower
  oil
salt and freshly ground
  black pepper
sour cream, to serve

We would like to thank our friend Helen Goh, a true perfectionist if ever there was one, for perfecting this Ashkenazic Hanukkah specialty for us. Don't save latkes just for holidays though; they are truly marvelous and a good way to start any meal, or to accompany roasted beef. Latkes are also often served sweet. To do this, remove the chive and reduce the salt. Serve warm with sour cream and sprinkled with superfine sugar.

Rinse the potato in a large bowl of cold water. Drain in a colander, squeeze out any excess water, and then spread the potato out on a clean kitchen towel to dry completely.

In a large bowl, mix together the potato, parsnip, chives, egg whites, cornstarch, 1 teaspoon salt, and plenty of black pepper.

Heat half the butter and half the oil in a large frying pan over medium-high heat. Use your hands to pick out portions of about 2 tablespoons of the latke mix, squeeze firmly to remove some of the liquid, and shape into thin patties about ⅜ inch / 1 cm thick and 3¼ inches / 8 cm in diameter. Carefully place as many latkes as you can comfortably fit in the pan, push them down gently, and level them with the back of a spoon. Fry over medium-high heat for 3 minutes on each side. The latkes need to be completely brown on the outside. Remove the fried latkes from the oil, place on paper towels, and keep warm while you cook the rest. Add the remaining butter and oil as needed. Serve at once with sour cream on the side.

BEANS
& GRAINS

Falafel

Falafel and hummus are the ultimate daily grub in Muslim Jerusalem. As a little boy, Sami used to be sent out to the shops every morning to buy breakfast for his older brothers: hummus and freshly fried falafel balls. He'd take an empty plate to Abu Shukri, a famous hummus spot in the Old City, and the man himself would spread the warm paste over the plate and, with much attention, garnish it with herbs, spices, and pickled cucumber. The warm falafel and fresh pitas were carried alongside in a brown paper bag. Sami would charge his brothers "a little something" for the task, which he always spent in the sweet shop.

And that was not the end of it. Fresh falafel was sold as a snack—stuffed into pita with hummus, tahini sauce, fiery red chile sauce, and chopped salad—throughout the day. Sami would often come back from school with a stained uniform and no appetite for lunch after slyly indulging in one on the way home. Na'ama wasn't happy.

Over on the west side of the city, Yotam had a pretty similar experience: school-day end, a massive falafel sandwich, tahini-stained shirt, no appetite, angry mother.

In west Jerusalem, as in the rest of Israel, it was Yemeni Jews arriving in the country in the first half of the twentieth century who set up falafel shops and introduced the street food to Jewish society for the first time. The iconic Israeli "mana falafel," the pita pocket stuffed with falafel, french fries, salad, and other goodies, emerged when the Yemenis began to flavor falafel with *hawayej* (PAGE 226) and *zhoug* (PAGE 301).

Don't be alarmed about not boiling the chickpeas before they are blitzed into a falafel mix. This is part of the process. When frying falafel, it is important that they get just the right amount of time in the oil. If you don't have an appropriate thermometer, assess the temperature of the oil by frying one falafel ball as instructed, making sure it takes the specified amount of time to cook through completely but without burning on the outside. Serve hot with pita bread, Tahini sauce (PAGE 298), *chopped tomato and cucumber salad* (SPICED CHICKPEAS AND FRESH VEGETABLE SALAD, PAGE 56), *Zhoug* (PAGE 301), *and pickles* (PICKLED TURNIP AND BEET, PAGE 307).

1¼ cups / 250 g dried chickpeas

½ medium onion, finely chopped (½ cup / 80 g in total)

1 clove garlic, crushed

1 tbsp finely chopped flat-leaf parsley

2 tbsp finely chopped cilantro

¼ tsp cayenne pepper

½ tsp ground cumin

½ tsp ground coriander

¼ tsp ground cardamom

½ tsp baking powder

3 tbsp water

1½ tbsp all-purpose flour

about 3 cups / 750 ml sunflower oil, for deep-frying

½ tsp sesame seeds, for coating

salt

Place the chickpeas in a large bowl and cover with cold water at least twice their volume. Set aside to soak overnight.

The next day, drain the chickpeas well and combine them with the onion, garlic, parsley, and cilantro. For the best results, use a meat grinder for the next part. Put the chickpea mixture once through the machine, set to its finest setting, then pass it through the machine for a second time. If you don't have a meat grinder, use a food processor. Blitz the mix in batches, pulsing each for 30 to 40 seconds, until it is finely chopped, but not mushy or pasty, and holds itself together. Once processed, add the spices, baking powder, ¾ teaspoon salt, flour, and water. Mix well by hand until smooth and uniform. Cover the mixture and leave it in the fridge for at least 1 hour, or until ready to use.

Fill a deep, heavy-bottomed medium saucepan with enough oil to come 2¾ inches / 7 cm up the sides of the pan. Heat the oil to 350°F / 180°C.

With wet hands, press 1 tablespoon of the mixture in the palm of your hand to form a patty or a ball the size of a small walnut, about a scant 1 oz / 25 g (you can also use a wet ice-cream scoop for this).

Sprinkle the balls evenly with sesame seeds and deep-fry them in batches for 4 minutes, until well browned and cooked through. It is important they really dry out on the inside, so make sure they get enough time in the oil. Drain in a colander lined with paper towels and serve at once.

Wheat berries & Swiss chard with pomegranate molasses

This recipe was given to us with much love by our friend Anat Teitelbaum, a passionate Jerusalem cook who personifies some of the most wonderful things about this city. Anat does all her shopping in Machne Yehuda market, where she knows every street vendor and every restaurant owner. She is familiar with her ingredients and makes the most out of them, with great confidence and only when they are in season. Just like us, she likes big flavors and simple cooking techniques, and she is happy to pick and choose from all the different cuisines around her. This dish, with its deep sweet and sour flavors and with its marvelous earthiness, is typical Anat and typical Jerusalem.

1⅓ lb / 600 g Swiss chard or rainbow chard
2 tbsp olive oil
1 tbsp unsalted butter
2 large leeks, white and pale green parts, thinly sliced (3 cups / 350 g in total)
2 tbsp light brown sugar
about 3 tbsp pomegranate molasses
scant 1¼ cups / 200 g hulled or unhulled wheat berries
2 cups / 500 ml chicken stock
salt and freshly ground black pepper
Greek yogurt, to serve

This potent dish is great eaten on its own as a light supper, or can be served with plainly cooked chicken or burgers. Try it with the Turkey and zucchini burgers with green onion and cumin (PAGE 200), leaving out the sauce. Wheat berries, hulled (aka peeled wheat) and unhulled, are available online or from Middle Eastern and Turkish groceries. Pearl barley is an okay substitute but doesn't take as long to cook, so you won't get that deep flavor that comes from the caramelizing of the sugars. Brands of pomegranate molasses vary, so we suggest assessing the flavor of the dish at the end and adding more if needed.

Separate the chard's white stalks from the green leaves using a small, sharp knife. Slice the stalks into ⅜-inch / 1cm slices and the leaves into ¾-inch / 2cm slices.

Heat the oil and butter in a large heavy-bottomed pan. Add the leeks and cook, stirring, for 3 to 4 minutes. Add the chard stalks and cook for 3 minutes, then add the leaves and cook for a further 3 minutes. Add the sugar, 3 tablespoons pomegranate molasses, and the wheat berries and mix well. Add the stock, ¾ teaspoon salt, and some black pepper, bring to a gentle simmer, and cook over low heat, covered, for 60 to 70 minutes. The wheat should be al dente at this point.

Remove the lid and, if needed, increase the heat and allow any remaining liquid to evaporate. The base of the pan should be dry and have a bit of burnt caramel on it. Remove from the heat.

Before serving, taste and add more molasses, salt, and pepper if needed; you want it sharp and sweet, so don't be shy with your molasses. Serve warm, with a dollop of Greek yogurt.

Balilah

On the corner of the souk in the Old City stood the very popular *balilah* man. He had large piles of freshly cooked chickpeas on his stall, steaming and beautifully decorated with parsley and lemon. Like a magician, he used to whip the *balilah* into a newspaper cone in a flash and serve it to the eager customer.

Balilah is a popular Palestinian street food consisting of fresh chickpeas seasoned with cumin and lemon juice and it makes the most gratifying snack. Curiously, in the Jewish Orthodox neighborhood of Me'ah She'arim, a cheap and cheerful snack called *arbes* is sold. It is just like *balilah*, only seasoned with black pepper instead of cumin. It, too, is highly popular.

---

1 cup / 200 g dried
   chickpeas
1 tsp baking soda
1 cup / 60 g chopped
   flat-leaf parsley
2 green onions,
   thinly sliced
1 large lemon
3 tbsp olive oil
2½ tsp ground cumin
salt and freshly ground
   black pepper

Balilah can be eaten warm, not hot, or at room temperature as a little between-meal snack. It is also delicious served next to grilled chicken or fish, or can be turned into a salad by adding some leaves, feta, and diced tomatoes.

The night before, put the chickpeas in a large bowl and cover with cold water at least twice their volume. Add the baking soda and leave at room temperature to soak overnight.

Drain the chickpeas and place them in a large saucepan. Cover with plenty of cold water and place over high heat. Bring to a boil, skim the surface of the water, then decrease the heat and simmer for 1 to 1½ hours, until the chickpeas are very soft but still retain their shape.

While the chickpeas are cooking, put the parsley and green onions in a large mixing bowl. Peel the lemon by topping and tailing it, placing on a board, and running a small sharp knife along its curves to remove the skin and white pith. Discard the skin, pith, and seeds and coarsely chop the flesh. Add the flesh and all of the juices to the bowl.

Once the chickpeas are ready, drain and add them to the bowl while they are still hot. Add the olive oil, cumin, ¾ teaspoon salt, and a good grind of pepper. Mix well. Allow to cool down until just warm, taste for seasoning, and serve.

Basmati rice & orzo

Just like the Palestinians (SEE PAGE 184), rice is the basic grain for most Sephardic communities, excluding North Africans. Although the cooking methods and accompanying ingredients vary greatly, with Iranians developing the most complex method and best texture, rice is an essential element in every Friday night dinner. Mixing chickpeas with rice (or bulgur) is common practice among Sephardim (SEE PAGE 106), as it makes the rice, served next to stews and long-cooked dishes, more interesting in look and texture. Many other substantial elements—vermicelli (see below), potatoes, lentils, nuts—could also be included. Bukharan Jews, a substantial community in Jerusalem, make a pilaf with plenty of spices (ginger, clove, cardamom, cinnamon), lots of mint, raisins, and peas. It is a luxurious and rich dish, appropriate for a previously wealthy Jewish community that had built its own neighborhood when its members started coming to Palestine in the late nineteenth and early twentieth century, wearing unusual embroidered clothes, adorned with jewelry. Later on, after the Russian Revolution, many lost their wealth and the neighborhood lost much of its past glory, but the food remains as spectacular and vibrant.

1⅓ cups / 250 g basmati
  rice
1 tbsp melted ghee or
  unsalted butter
1 tbsp sunflower oil
scant ½ cup / 85 g orzo
2½ cups / 600 ml chicken
  stock
1 tsp salt

Long-grain rice, cooked simply with plain vermicelli noodles, is common all over the Levant and Turkey. Its neutral flavor and playful textures make an effective background for various stews, soups, and salads. Our version uses orzo—tiny rice-shaped pasta—but you can use vermicelli. Just don't fry them as long, as they burn quickly. Try this and you may not want to cook plain rice ever again.

Wash the basmati rice well, then place in a large bowl and cover with plenty of cold water. Allow it to soak for 30 minutes, then drain.

Heat the ghee and oil over medium-high heat in a medium heavy-bottomed saucepan for which you have a lid. Add the orzo and sauté for 3 to 4 minutes, until the grains turn dark golden. Add the stock, bring to a boil, and cook for 3 minutes. Add the drained rice and salt, bring to a gentle boil, stir once or twice, cover the pan, and simmer over very low heat for 15 minutes. Don't be tempted to uncover the pan; you'll need to allow the rice to steam properly.

Turn off the heat, remove the lid, and quickly cover the pan with a clean tea towel. Place the lid back on top of the towel and leave for 10 minutes. Fluff the rice with a fork before serving.

Saffron rice with barberries, pistachio & mixed herbs

This dish is inspired by *shirin polo*, a celebration rice dish of the Iranian Jewish community. The original includes candied orange peel, sour cherries, cranberries, and almonds and is often served at weddings. We use barberries, an Iranian mainstay, to give a sweet-and-sour effect, but our rice is by no means very sweet. You could easily add cranberries, sliced dried apricots, or even chopped dates if you want to emphasize the sweetness. This would be very much in line with the sensibilities of Iraqi, Iranian, and North African Jews, who love mixing sweet with savory.

Alternatively, make a simplified version of *baghali polo*, another inspired Iranian rice dish, by simply leaving out the barberries and pistachios and adding skinned, cooked fava beans.

2½ tbsp / 40 g unsalted butter

2 cups / 360 g basmati rice, rinsed under cold water and drained well

2⅓ cups / 560 ml boiling water

1 tsp saffron threads, soaked in 3 tbsp boiling water for 30 minutes

¼ cup / 40 g dried barberries, soaked for a few minutes in boiling water with a pinch of sugar

1 oz / 30 g dill, coarsely chopped

⅔ oz / 20 g chervil, coarsely chopped

⅓ oz / 10 g tarragon, coarsely chopped

½ cup / 60 g slivered or crushed unsalted pistachios, lightly toasted

salt and freshly ground white pepper

Barberries are tiny, jewel-like dried sweet-and-sour Iranian berries that we have started using a bit obsessively recently. It is hard not to. Their intense sharpness accentuates the other flavors in the dish and adds wonderful "drama." They are available online, or from Iranian and some Middle Eastern groceries. If you can't get them, consider substituting currants soaked in a little lemon juice. Serve this rice with roasted chicken or Turkey and zucchini burgers with green onion and cumin (PAGE 200).

Melt the butter in a medium saucepan and stir in the rice, making sure the grains are well coated in butter. Add the boiling water, 1 teaspoon salt, and some white pepper. Mix well, cover with a tightly fitting lid, and leave to cook over very low heat for 15 minutes. Don't be tempted to uncover the pan; you'll need to allow the rice to steam properly.

Remove the rice pan from the heat—all the water will have been absorbed by the rice—and pour the saffron water over one side of the rice, covering about one-quarter of the surface and leaving the majority of it white. Cover the pan immediately with a tea towel and reseal tightly with the lid. Set aside for 5 to 10 minutes.

Use a large spoon to remove the white part of the rice into a large mixing bowl and fluff it up with a fork. Drain the barberries and stir them in, followed by the herbs and most of the pistachios, leaving a few to garnish. Mix well. Fluff the saffron rice with a fork and gently fold it into the white rice. Don't overmix—you don't want the white grains to be stained by the yellow. Taste and adjust the seasoning. Transfer the rice to a shallow serving bowl and scatter the remaining pistachios on top. Serve warm or at room temperature.

Basmati & wild rice with chickpeas, currants & herbs

⅓ cup / 50 g wild rice
2½ tbsp olive oil
rounded 1 cup / 220 g
 basmati rice
scant 1½ cups / 330 ml
 boiling water
2 tsp cumin seeds
1½ tsp curry powder
1½ cups / 240 g cooked
 and drained chickpeas
 (canned are fine)
¾ cup / 180 ml sunflower
 oil
1 medium onion, thinly
 sliced
1½ tsp all-purpose flour
⅔ cup / 100 g currants
2 tbsp chopped flat-leaf
 parsley
1 tbsp chopped cilantro
1 tbsp chopped dill
salt and freshly ground
 black pepper

This Sephari-inspired dish can be the centerpiece of a festive vegetarian meal, or served alongside Chicken sofrito (PAGE 190) or Panfried mackerel with golden beet and orange salsa (PAGE 222).

Start by putting the wild rice in a small saucepan, cover with plenty of water, bring to a boil, and leave to simmer for about 40 minutes, until the rice is cooked but still quite firm. Drain and set aside.

To cook the basmati rice, pour 1 tablespoon of the olive oil into a medium saucepan with a tightly fitting lid and place over high heat. Add the rice and ¼ teaspoon salt and stir as you warm up the rice. Carefully add the boiling water, decrease the heat to very low, cover the pan with the lid, and leave to cook for 15 minutes.

Remove the pan from the heat, cover with a clean tea towel and then the lid, and leave off the heat for 10 minutes.

While the rice is cooking, prepare the chickpeas. Heat the remaining 1½ tbsp olive oil in a small saucepan over high heat. Add the cumin seeds and curry powder, wait for a couple seconds, and then add the chickpeas and ¼ teaspoon salt; make sure you do this quickly or the spices may burn in the oil. Stir over the heat for a minute or two, just to heat the chickpeas, then transfer to a large mixing bowl.

Wipe the saucepan clean, pour in the sunflower oil, and place over high heat. Make sure the oil is hot by throwing in a small piece of onion; it should sizzle vigorously. Use your hands to mix the onion with the flour to coat it slightly. Take some of the onion and carefully (it may spit!) place it in the oil. Fry for 2 to 3 minutes, until golden brown, then transfer to paper towels to drain and sprinkle with salt. Repeat in batches until all the onion is fried.

Finally, add both types of rice to the chickpeas and then add the currants, herbs, and fried onion. Stir, taste, and add salt and pepper as you like. Serve warm or at room temperature.

Barley risotto with marinated feta

1 cup / 200 g pearl barley
2 tbsp / 30 g unsalted butter
6 tbsp / 90 ml olive oil
2 small celery stalks, cut
  into ¼-inch / 0.5cm dice
2 small shallots, cut into
  ¼-inch / 0.5cm dice
4 cloves garlic, cut into
  ¹⁄₁₆-inch / 2mm dice
4 thyme sprigs
½ tsp smoked paprika
1 bay leaf
4 strips lemon peel
¼ tsp chile flakes
one 14-oz / 400g can
  chopped tomatoes
scant 3 cups / 700 ml
  vegetable stock
1¼ cups / 300 ml passata
  (sieved crushed tomatoes)
1 tbsp caraway seeds
10½ oz / 300 g feta cheese,
  broken into roughly
  ¾-inch / 2cm pieces
1 tbsp fresh oregano leaves
salt

This vegetarian main course is a dish everybody loves, particularly children. Unlike the proper Italian risotto, ours does not require the exact precision and meticulous preparation, but still tastes sensational.

Rinse the pearl barley well under cold water and leave to drain.

Melt the butter and 2 tablespoons of the olive oil in a very large frying pan and cook the celery, shallots, and garlic over gentle heat for 5 minutes, until soft. Add the barley, thyme, paprika, bay leaf, lemon peel, chile flakes, tomatoes, stock, passata, and salt. Stir to combine. Bring the mixture to a boil, then reduce to a very gentle simmer and cook for 45 minutes, stirring frequently to make sure the risotto does not catch on the bottom of the pan. When ready, the barley should be tender and most of the liquid absorbed.

Meanwhile, toast the caraway seeds in a dry pan for a couple of minutes. Then lightly crush them so that some whole seeds remain. Add them to the feta with the remaining 4 tablespoons / 60 ml olive oil and gently mix to combine.

Once the risotto is ready, check the seasoning and then divide it among four shallow bowls. Top each with the marinated feta, including the oil, and a sprinkling of oregano leaves.

Conchiglie with yogurt, peas & chile

Cooking or serving pasta in hot yogurt sauce may sound slightly out of the ordinary, but the Palestinian classic *shishbarak*—ravioli-like dumplings stuffed with meat—is prepared in just such a manner. Turkish and Armenian *manti* are similar examples. The yogurt gives a delightful creaminess, without the heaviness of cream, and we urge you to try it as an alternative to the familiar Italian sauces.

Turkey and Syria produce many types of dried chile flakes, known throughout the region, varying greatly in sweetness, acidity, smokiness, heat, and earthiness. Each has its own unique aroma and identifiable tinge, and we like playing around with them in flavoring many of our dishes. We particularly like Urfa chile, dark purple and almost musky in flavor; Aleppo chile, burgundy color and fruity; or the more general Kirmizi biber, literally translating from Turkish as "red pepper," which is easier to find and covers a range of Turkish products. Look for all of them in Middle Eastern and Turkish shops, or online. If you can't get them, use regular chile flakes with a tiny amount of smoked paprika.

2½ cups / 500 g Greek yogurt
⅔ cup / 150 ml olive oil
4 cloves garlic, crushed
1 lb / 500 g fresh or thawed frozen peas
1 lb / 500 g conchiglie pasta
scant ½ cup / 60 g pine nuts
2 tsp Turkish or Syrian chile flakes (or less, depending on how spicy they are)
1⅔ cups / 40 g basil leaves, coarsely torn
8 oz / 240 g feta cheese, broken into chunks
salt and freshly ground white pepper

Put the yogurt, 6 tablespoons / 90 ml of the olive oil, the garlic, and ⅔ cup / 100 g of the peas in a food processor. Blitz to a uniform pale green sauce and transfer to a large mixing bowl.

Cook the pasta in plenty of salted boiling water until al dente. As the pasta cooks, heat the remaining olive oil in a small frying pan over medium heat. Add the pine nuts and chile flakes and fry for 4 minutes, until the nuts are golden and the oil is deep red. Also, heat the remaining peas in some boiling water, then drain.

Drain the cooked pasta into a colander, shake well to get rid of the water, and add the pasta gradually to the yogurt sauce; adding it all at once may cause the yogurt to split. Add the warm peas, basil, feta, 1 teaspoon salt, and ½ teaspoon white pepper. Toss gently, transfer to individual bowls, and spoon over the pine nuts and their oil.

Hummus wars

Political and nationalistic discussions about hummus—where it started and how; who was the first to crush chickpeas and mix them with sesame paste and when—are almost compulsive. No one enjoys them anymore, but no one is ready to concede, either.

Generally, most people agree that it was Levantine or Egyptian Arabs who first made hummus, though even this is debatable. In an article published in a local paper, the celebrated Jewish author Meir Shalev interpreted a certain biblical passage as evidence that Jews ate hummus in biblical times. But when push comes to shove, nobody seriously challenges the Palestinian hegemony in making hummus, even though both they and the Jews like calling it their own. The arguments never cease. And even if the question of authorship is somehow set aside, you are still left with who makes the best hummus now? And here we need to start again—is it Ta'ami in west Jerusalem or Lina in the Old City? Pinati or Abu Hassan?

Jews in particular, and even more specifically Jewish men, never tire of arguments about the absolute, the one and only, the most fantastic *hummusia*. A *hummusia* is a simple eatery that specializes in hummus, and is normally open from breakfast until late afternoon. It is, like the English fish-and-chips shop, a savored local treasure. Yet, typically, it carries with it much stronger sentiments. The *hummusia* fetish is so powerful that even the best of friends may easily turn against each other if they suddenly find themselves in opposite hummus camps. The discussions and lively arguments can carry on for hours, going into the minutest of details regarding consistency (some like it smooth and fluffy, others a little chunky and spicy), temperature (some like it warm, others ambient), and the perfect condiments (cooked chickpeas, rehydrated dried fava beans, spice paste, or nothing at all). Still, the hummus debate is fun.

As mentioned, it is also a source of identity—personal or national—which can easily turn into an issue of confused identity. A typical story is that of a *hummusia* in the Arab village of Abu Gosh, about 6 miles / 10 kilometers west of Jerusalem.

Abu Shukri was for years considered one of the best *hummusia* in the country, only rivaled by the famous Abu Hassan in Jaffa or Said's in Acre (or Akko). One day, across the unpaved dirt road, another *hummusia* opened, with a little sign hanging over the door saying, "We moved here. This is the real Abu Shukri." The newcomer, believe it or not, was Abu Shukri's son-in-law, an ex-waiter. The outrage! The next day the old restaurant hung a sign on its door: "We didn't move anywhere. This is the real Abu Shukri." A large banner appeared across the road not long afterward: "The real real, one and only, original Abu Shukri." You can probably imagine what followed. In the end, after years of fierce rivalry and many confused diners mistaking one Abu Shukri for the other, a big food corporation selling packed hummus in supermarkets decided to run a TV campaign to promote its own brand. It culminated in a big reconciliation event between the two Abu Shukris and was labeled "The End of Hummus Wars."

Basic hummus

1¼ cups / 250 g dried chickpeas
1 tsp baking soda
6½ cups / 1.5 liters water
1 cup plus 2 tbsp / 270 g light tahini paste
4 tbsp freshly squeezed lemon juice
4 cloves garlic, crushed
6½ tbsp / 100 ml ice-cold water
salt

Our basic hummus recipe is supersmooth and rich in tahini, just as we like it, and can be kept in the fridge for up to three days and used simply spread over a plate, drizzled with olive oil, and eaten with a pita or bread. However, the two recipes that follow turn hummus into an altogether different thing, an exciting centerpiece of a seriously substantial meal, as it is mostly enjoyed in Jerusalem. If you prefer to stick to the basic recipe, you can vary it by folding in cooked and crushed chickpeas for texture, adding some ground cumin, and adjusting the amount of lemon juice and tahini to your taste.

The night before, put the chickpeas in a large bowl and cover them with cold water at least twice their volume. Leave to soak overnight.

The next day, drain the chickpeas. Place a medium saucepan over high heat and add the drained chickpeas and baking soda. Cook for about 3 minutes, stirring constantly. Add the water and bring to a boil. Cook, skimming off any foam and any skins that float to the surface. The chickpeas will need to cook between 20 and 40 minutes, depending on the type and freshness, sometimes even longer. Once done, they should be very tender, breaking up easily when pressed between your thumb and finger, almost but not quite mushy.

Drain the chickpeas. You should have roughly 3⅔ cups / 600 g now. Place the chickpeas in a food processor and process until you get a stiff paste. Then, with the machine still running, add the tahini paste, lemon juice, garlic, and 1½ teaspoons salt. Finally, slowly drizzle in the iced water and allow it to mix for about 5 minutes, until you get a very smooth and creamy paste.

Transfer the hummus to a bowl, cover the surface with plastic wrap, and let it rest for at least 30 minutes. If not using straightaway, refrigerate until needed. Make sure to take it out of the fridge at least 30 minutes before serving.

Hummus kawarma (lamb) with lemon sauce

Basic hummus (page 114), reserving 4 tbsp of the cooked chickpeas to garnish

chopped flat-leaf parsley, to garnish

2 tbsp pine nuts, toasted in the oven or fried in a little unsalted butter

KAWARMA

10½ oz / 300 g neck fillet of lamb, finely chopped by hand

¼ tsp freshly ground black pepper

¼ tsp freshly ground white pepper

1 tsp ground allspice

½ tsp ground cinnamon

good pinch of freshly grated nutmeg

1 tsp crushed dried za'atar or oregano leaves

1 tbsp white wine vinegar

1 tbsp chopped mint

1 tbsp chopped flat-leaf parsley

1 tsp salt

1 tbsp unsalted butter or ghee

1 tsp olive oil

LEMON SAUCE

⅓ oz / 10 g flat-leaf parsley, finely chopped

1 green chile, finely chopped

4 tbsp freshly squeezed lemon juice

2 tbsp white wine vinegar

2 cloves garlic, crushed

¼ tsp salt

Hummus kawarma is the Lebanese name given to freshly made hummus, topped with fried chopped lamb. It is a small meal or a starter in a bowl and one of the most sensational things you can put in your mouth. Have it with Na'ama's fattoush (PAGE 29) or a similar salad and pita. Ground lamb can be used instead of chopping the meat by hand, but it won't have quite the same gratifying texture. This dish also works well without lamb—just the hummus, chickpeas, lemon sauce, and pine nuts.

To make the kawarma, place all the ingredients apart from the butter or ghee and oil in a medium bowl. Mix well, cover, and allow the mixture to marinate in the fridge for 30 minutes.

Just before you are ready to cook the meat, place all the ingredients for the lemon sauce in a small bowl and stir well.

Heat the butter or ghee and the olive oil in a large frying pan over medium-high heat. Add the meat in two or three batches and stir as you fry each batch for 2 minutes. The meat should be light pink in the middle.

Divide the hummus among 6 individual shallow bowls, leaving a slight hollow in the center of each. Spoon the warm kawarma into the hollow and scatter with the reserved chickpeas. Drizzle generously with the lemon sauce and garnish with some parsley and the pine nuts.

See picture on previous page

Musabaha (warm chickpeas with hummus) & toasted pita

1¼ cups / 250 g dried
  chickpeas
1 tsp baking soda
1 tbsp ground cumin
4½ tbsp / 70 g light tahini
  paste
3 tbsp freshly squeezed
  lemon juice
1 clove garlic, crushed
2 tbsp ice-cold water
4 small pitas (4 oz / 120 g
  in total)
2 tbsp olive oil
2 tbsp chopped flat-leaf
  parsley
1 tsp sweet paprika
salt and freshly ground
  black pepper

TAHINI SAUCE

5 tbsp / 75 g light tahini
  paste
¼ cup / 60 ml water
1 tbsp freshly squeezed
  lemon juice
½ clove garlic, crushed

LEMON SAUCE

⅓ oz / 10 g flat-leaf parsley,
  finely chopped
1 green chile, finely
  chopped
4 tbsp freshly squeezed
  lemon juice
2 tbsp white wine vinegar
2 cloves garlic, crushed
¼ tsp salt

Traditionally, this dish is served for breakfast along with various pickles, fresh radishes, and green onion or white onion wedges. You can serve it for a weekend brunch. The dried pita is used to scoop up the musabaha *for eating.*

Follow the Basic hummus recipe (PAGE 114) for the method of soaking and cooking the chickpeas, but cook them a little less; they should have a little resistance left in them but still be fully cooked. Drain the cooked chickpeas, reserving ⅓ cup / 80 ml of the cooking water, and measure them. You should end up with roughly 3½ cups / 600 g of cooked chickpeas. Mix three-quarters of the chickpeas (2⅔ cups / 450 g) with the reserved cooking water, the cumin, ½ teaspoon salt, and ¼ teaspoon pepper. Keep the mixture warm.

Place the remaining chickpeas (1 cup / 150 g) in a small food processor and process until you get a stiff paste. Then, with the machine still running, add the tahini paste, lemon juice, garlic, and ½ teaspoon salt. Finally, slowly drizzle in the iced water and mix for about 3 minutes, until you get a very smooth and creamy paste. Leave the hummus to one side.

While the chickpeas are cooking, you can prepare the other elements of the dish. For the tahini sauce, put all the ingredients and a pinch of salt in a small bowl. Mix well and add a little more water if needed to get a consistency slightly runnier than honey.

Next, mix together all the ingredients for the lemon sauce, and set aside.

Finally, open up the pitas, tearing the two sides apart. Place under a hot broiler for 2 minutes, until golden and completely dry. Allow to cool down before breaking into odd-shaped pieces.

Divide the hummus among four individual shallow bowls; don't level it or press it down, you want the height. Spoon over the warm chickpeas, followed by the tahini sauce, the lemon sauce, and a drizzle of olive oil. Garnish with the parsley and a sprinkle of paprika and serve, accompanied with the toasted pita pieces.

Mejadra

This ancient dish, popular throughout the Arab world, is also one of our most loved. The fried onion, with its sweet oiliness and slight crunch, is the secret. When Sami's family would go out on a day trip to Jericho, they would take a large pot of *mejadra* for the picnic. The lentils were divided among small bowls and topped with a spoonful of fresh yogurt sauce. Dessert was a huge watermelon that Sami's dad chilled in a small stream running into the Jordan River.

1¼ cups / 250 g green or
  brown lentils
4 medium onions
  (1½ lb / 700 g before
  peeling)
3 tbsp all-purpose flour
about 1 cup / 250 ml
  sunflower oil
2 tsp cumin seeds
1½ tbsp coriander seeds
1 cup / 200 g basmati rice
2 tbsp olive oil
½ tsp ground turmeric
1½ tsp ground allspice
1½ tsp ground cinnamon
1 tsp sugar
1½ cups / 350 ml water
salt and freshly ground
  black pepper

The two of us can spend many pointless hours discussing what makes the best comfort food and why, but never seem to reach any kind of serious conclusion. Mejadra, however, is where the dispute ends. When served alongside Yogurt with cucumber (PAGE 299) *or just plain Greek yogurt, the sweetly spiced rice and lentils strewn with soft fried onion is as comforting as it gets in Jerusalem. It is best served warm but is also fine at room temperature.*

Place the lentils in a small saucepan, cover with plenty of water, bring to a boil, and cook for 12 to 15 minutes, until the lentils have softened but still have a little bite. Drain and set aside.

Peel the onions and slice thinly. Place on a large flat plate, sprinkle with the flour and 1 teaspoon salt, and mix well with your hands. Heat the sunflower oil in a medium heavy-bottomed saucepan placed over high heat. Make sure the oil is hot by throwing in a small piece of onion; it should sizzle vigorously. Reduce the heat to medium-high and carefully (it may spit!) add one-third of the sliced onion. Fry for 5 to 7 minutes, stirring occasionally with a slotted spoon, until the onion takes on a nice golden brown color and turns crispy (adjust the temperature so the onion doesn't fry too quickly and burn). Use the spoon to transfer the onion to a colander lined with paper towels and sprinkle with a little more salt. Do the same with the other two batches of onion; add a little extra oil if needed.

Wipe the saucepan in which you fried the onion clean and put in the cumin and coriander seeds. Place over medium heat and toast the seeds for a minute or two. Add the rice, olive oil, turmeric, allspice, cinnamon, sugar, ½ teaspoon salt, and plenty of black pepper. Stir to coat the rice with the oil and then add the cooked lentils and the water. Bring to a boil, cover with a lid, and simmer over very low heat for 15 minutes.

Remove from the heat, lift off the lid, and quickly cover the pan with a clean tea towel. Seal tightly with the lid and set aside for 10 minutes.

Finally, add half the fried onion to the rice and lentils and stir gently with a fork. Pile the mixture in a shallow serving bowl and top with the rest of the onion.

One-pot wonders

Maqluba (PAGE 127) is a one-pot meal of rice, vegetables, and meat turned on its head. Literally translating to "upside down," it is made with fried cauliflower or eggplant, often with carrots and potatoes, all of which are usually fried, and includes meat such as chicken, lamb, goat, or beef. Sami's mum used to prepare this dish for dinner and at the same time she'd fry more vegetables than needed. The next day she would warm them up, add garlic and lemon, and serve them for lunch with homemade flatbread, tahini, and pickles. It's the nicest thing to have as a child—a sandwich of garlicky, lemony, warm fried vegetables.

Normally, women with children had their hands full with the general family requirements and the running of the house. The need to prepare a delicious and hearty meal that would feed an entire family inexpensively, with little fuss or washing up, is the general idea behind *maqluba*, as it is behind the Ashkenazi *tchulnt*, the Sephardi *dafina*, and the Iraqi-Jewish *tebit*. While they may each be arranged differently in the pot, require specific cooking times, and incorporate different combinations of meat, cereals, legumes, and vegetables, essentially all of them feed many mouths from a single pot.

THE FAMOUS, SLOW-COOKED DISHES OF BOTH ASHKENAZIM AND SEPHARDIM ARE FINE EXAMPLES OF NECESSITY CREATING CULINARY ARTISTRY.

In Jewish communities, this is also a solution to the Shabbat's challenges, where copious quantities of food have to be prepared by Friday afternoon and last the entire weekend. The famous, slow-cooked dishes of both Ashkenazim and Sephardim are fine examples of necessity creating culinary artistry. Their iconic standing in Jewish culture reflects the amount of love and thought put into them. The challenge is to make a dish that is appealing and diverse even though it has been cooked, or has started its cooking, many hours before. The solutions are so creative and varied that Israeli food writer Sherry Ansky has even dedicated a whole book to *tchulnt*, or *hamin* as it is also called. Each community has managed to include its staple ingredients in the famous one-pot meal to uncanny degrees of harmony and deliciousness. Among others, chickpeas and all types of dried beans are included, wheat, rice or barley, kosher sausages, various fritters, all types of meat, eggs, noodles, potatoes, zucchini, and stuffed vegetables of every description.

Maqluba

2 medium eggplants
(1½ lb / 650 g in total),
cut into ¼-inch / 0.5cm
slices

1⅔ cups / 320 g basmati
rice

6 to 8 boneless chicken
thighs, with the skin on,
about 1¾ lb / 800 g in
total

1 large onion, quartered
lengthwise

10 black peppercorns

2 bay leaves

4 cups / 900 ml water

sunflower oil, for frying

1 medium cauliflower
(1 lb / 500 g), divided
into large florets

melted butter, for greasing
the pan

3 to 4 medium ripe
tomatoes (12 oz / 350 g
in total), cut into
¼-inch / 0.5cm thick
slices

4 large cloves garlic, halved

1 tsp ground turmeric

1 tsp ground cinnamon

1 tsp ground allspice

¼ tsp freshly ground black
pepper

1 tsp baharat spice mix
(store-bought or see
recipe, page 299)

3½ tbsp / 30 g pine nuts,
fried in 1 tbsp / 15 g ghee
or unsalted butter until
golden

Yogurt with cucumber
(page 299), to serve

salt

Even if this massive savory cake doesn't manage to keep its shape—and to assist with that, Sami swears, all members of the family must place the palms of their hands on the inverted pot and wait the specified three minutes—you are still in for a hearty celebration of flavors.

Place the eggplant slices on paper towels, sprinkle on both sides with salt, and leave for 20 minutes to lose some of the water.

Wash the rice and soak in plenty of cold water and 1 teaspoon salt for at least 30 minutes.

Meanwhile, heat a large saucepan over medium-high heat and sear the chicken for 3 to 4 minutes on each side, until golden brown (the chicken skin should produce enough oil to cook it; if needed, add a little sunflower oil). Add the onion, peppercorns, bay leaves, and water. Bring to a boil, then cover and cook over low heat for 20 minutes. Remove the chicken from the pan and set it aside. Strain the stock and reserve for later, skimming the fat.

While the chicken is cooking, heat a saucepan or Dutch oven, preferably nonstick and roughly 9½ inches / 24 cm in diameter and 5 inches / 12 cm deep, over medium-high heat. Add enough sunflower oil to come about ¾ inch / 2 cm up the sides of the pan. When you start seeing little bubbles surfacing, carefully (it may spit!) place some of the cauliflower florets in the oil and fry until golden brown, up to 3 minutes. Use a slotted spoon to transfer the first batch to paper towels and sprinkle with salt. Repeat with the remaining cauliflower.

Pat the eggplant slices dry with paper towels and fry them similarly in batches.

Remove the oil from the pan and wipe the pan clean. If it isn't a nonstick pan, line the bottom with a circle of parchment paper cut to the exact size and brush the sides with some melted butter. Now you are ready to layer the maqluba.

Start by arranging the slices of tomato in one layer, overlapping, followed by the eggplant slices. Next, arrange the cauliflower pieces and chicken thighs. Drain the rice well and spread it over the final layer and scatter the garlic pieces on top. Measure out a scant 3 cups / 700 ml of the reserved chicken stock and mix in all the spices, plus 1 teaspoon salt. Pour this over the rice and then gently press it down with your hands, making sure all the rice is covered with stock. Add a little extra stock or water if needed.

Recipe continued on next page

Put the pan over medium heat and bring to a simmer; the stock doesn't need to simmer vigorously but you do need to make sure that it boils properly before covering the pan with a lid, decreasing the heat to low, and cooking over low heat for 30 minutes. Don't be tempted to uncover the pan; you'll need to allow the rice to steam properly. Remove the pan from the heat, take off the lid, and quickly place a clean tea towel over the pan, then seal with the lid again. Leave to rest for 10 minutes.

Once ready, remove the lid, invert a large round serving plate or platter over the open pan, and carefully but quickly invert the pan and plate together, holding both sides firmly. Leave the pan on the plate for 2 to 3 minutes, then slowly and carefully lift it off. Garnish with the pine nuts and serve with the Yogurt with cucumber.

Couscous with tomato and onion

3 tbsp olive oil
1 medium onion, finely
  chopped (1 cup / 160 g
  in total)
1 tbsp tomato paste
½ tsp sugar
2 very ripe tomatoes, cut
  into ¼-inch / 0.5cm dice
  (1¾ cups / 320 g in total)
scant 1 cup / 150 g couscous
scant 1 cup / 220 ml boiling
  chicken or vegetable stock
2½ tbsp / 40 g unsalted
  butter
salt and freshly ground
  black pepper

This wonderfully comforting couscous is based on a dish Sami's mother cooked for him when he was a child (SEE PAGE 8). All we did was add a crust, similar to Iranian tadik, *which is a famous rice dish cooked in such a way that a crispy crust forms at the bottom of the pot; this crunchy bit is everybody's favorite. Good-quality stock is important here. Serve with Grilled fish skewers with hawayej and parsley (PAGE 226), Turkey and zucchini burgers with green onion and cumin (PAGE 200), or just with salad as a light vegetarian meal.*

Pour 2 tablespoons of the olive oil into a nonstick pan about 8½ inches / 22 cm in diameter and place over medium heat. Add the onion and cook for 5 minutes, stirring often, until it has softened but not colored. Stir in the tomato paste and sugar and cook for 1 minute. Add the tomatoes, ½ teaspoon salt, and some black pepper and cook for 3 minutes.

Meanwhile, put the couscous in a shallow bowl, pour over the boiling stock, and cover with plastic wrap. Set aside for 10 minutes, then remove the cover and fluff the couscous with a fork. Add the tomato sauce and stir well.

Wipe the pan clean and heat the butter and the remaining 1 tablespoon olive oil over medium heat. When the butter has melted, spoon the couscous into the pan and use the back of the spoon to pat it down gently so it is all packed in snugly. Cover the pan, reduce the heat to its lowest setting, and allow the couscous to steam for 10 to 12 minutes, until you can see a light brown color around the edges. Use an offset spatula or a knife to help you peer between the edge of the couscous and the side of the pan: you want a really crisp edge all over the base and sides.

Invert a large plate on top of the pan and quickly invert the pan and plate together, releasing the couscous onto the plate. Serve warm or at room temperature.

Pictured opposite

SOUPS

Watercress & chickpea soup with rose water & ras el hanout

2 medium carrots (9 oz / 250 g in total), cut into ¾-inch / 2cm dice
3 tbsp olive oil
2½ tsp ras el hanout
½ tsp ground cinnamon
1½ cups / 240 g cooked chickpeas, fresh or canned
1 medium onion, thinly sliced
2½ tbsp / 15 g peeled and finely chopped fresh ginger
2½ cups / 600 ml vegetable stock
7 oz / 200 g watercress
3½ oz / 100 g spinach leaves
2 tsp superfine sugar
1 tsp rose water
salt
Greek yogurt, to serve (optional)

Ras el hanout, *a spice blend brought to Jerusalem by North African Jews, consists mainly of sweet and hot spices, toasted and ground. There isn't one definitive recipe; every spice shop in North Africa (*hanout *means "shop" in Arabic) has its own signature blend with a typical set of secret components. Home cooks buy the blend or try to emulate it themselves. In any case, the name stuck, signifying a sweet-and-heady mix. Commercial varieties available in the UK are fine, but feel free to enhance them with your own additions. If your* ras el hanout *doesn't contain cinnamon, make sure you add some as we do here. If you don't like rose water, leave it out.*

Preheat the oven to 425°F / 220°C.

Mix the carrots with 1 tablespoon of the olive oil, the ras el hanout, cinnamon, and a generous pinch of salt and spread flat in a roasting pan lined with parchment paper. Place in the oven for 15 minutes, then add half the chickpeas, stir well, and cook for another 10 minutes, until the carrot softens but still has a bite.

Meanwhile, place the onion and ginger in a large saucepan. Sauté with the remaining olive oil for about 10 minutes over medium heat, until the onion is completely soft and golden. Add the remaining chickpeas, stock, watercress, spinach, sugar, and ¾ teaspoon salt, stir well, and bring to a boil. Cook for a minute or two, just until the leaves wilt.

Using a food processor or blender, blitz the soup until smooth. Add the rose water, stir, taste, and add more salt or rose water if you like. Set aside until the carrot and chickpeas are ready, then reheat to serve.

To serve, divide the soup among four bowls and top with the hot carrot and chickpeas and, if you like, about 2 teaspoons yogurt per portion.

From top: Cannellini bean & lamb soup (page 135), Hot yogurt & barley soup (page 134), Watercress & chickpea soup with rose water & ras el hanout

Seafood & fennel soup

2 tbsp olive oil

4 cloves garlic, thinly sliced

2 fennel bulbs (10½ oz / 300 g in total), trimmed and cut into thin wedges

1 large waxy potato (7 oz / 200 g in total), peeled and cut into ⅔-inch / 1.5cm cubes

scant 3 cups / 700 ml fish stock (or chicken or vegetable stock, if preferred)

½ medium preserved lemon (½ oz / 15 g in total), store-bought or see recipe, page 303

1 red chile, sliced (optional)

6 tomatoes (14 oz / 400 g in total), peeled and cut into quarters

1 tbsp sweet paprika

good pinch of saffron

4 tbsp finely chopped flat-leaf parsley

4 fillets sea bass (about 10½ oz / 300 g in total), skin on, cut in half

14 mussels (about 8 oz / 220 g in total)

15 clams (about 4½ oz / 140 g in total)

10 tiger prawns (about 8 oz / 220 g in total), in their shells or peeled and deveined

3 tbsp arak, ouzo, or Pernod

2 tsp chopped tarragon (optional)

salt and freshly ground black pepper

You don't see lots of seafood in Jerusalem. The distance from the sea and kosher rules (SEE PAGE 231) make it a rare find. However, many of Jerusalem's culinary inventions aren't necessarily "natural" to its surroundings or population. The restaurant Machenyuda, which became famous for its little Kilner jars of polenta topped with asparagus and truffle, is the current trendsetter. Just as influential in the 1990s was Occianus (Ocean), where Eyal Shani, the enfant terrible of Israeli cooking, made his name. Shani's prawns grilled over orange-tree charcoal and his ingredients foraged in the Judean mountains, combined with his fiery and eccentric ways, made him *the* voice of modern Israeli cuisine.

This is our interpretation of a Tunisian fish soup, with embellishments that take it way out of the realm of traditional, kosher cooking. Of all Jewish communities, it is the Tunisians who make the most extensive and creative use of fresh fish (PANFRIED SEA BASS WITH HARISSA AND ROSE, PAGE 219, AND FRICASSEE SALAD, PAGE 227). *Tunisian Jews traditionally had fish most days of the week and served it over couscous. This soup would, obviously, not appear on a traditional Tunisian Jewish table but it would still taste wonderful when spooned over couscous (just reduce the soup a little so it turns slightly thicker).*

Place the olive oil and garlic in a wide, low-rimmed frying pan and cook over medium heat for 2 minutes without coloring the garlic. Stir in the fennel and potato and cook for a further 3 to 4 minutes. Add the stock and preserved lemon, season with ¼ teaspoon salt and some black pepper, bring to a boil, then cover and cook over low heat for 12 to 14 minutes, until the potatoes are cooked. Add the chile (if using), tomatoes, spices, and half the parsley and cook for a further 4 to 5 minutes.

Add up to another 1¼ cups / 300 ml of water at this point, simply as much as is needed to be able just to cover the fish to poach it, and bring to a simmer again. Add the sea bass and shellfish, cover the pan, and allow to boil quite fiercely for 3 to 4 minutes, until the shellfish open and the prawns turn pink.

Using a slotted spoon, remove the fish and shellfish from the soup. If it is still a bit watery, allow the soup to boil for a few more minutes to reduce. Add the arak and taste for seasoning.

Finally, return the shellfish and fish to the soup to reheat them. Serve at once, garnished with the remainder of the parsley and the tarragon, if using.

Pistachio soup

2 tbsp boiling water
¼ tsp saffron threads
1⅔ cups / 200 g shelled
  unsalted pistachios
2 tbsp / 30 g unsalted
  butter
4 shallots, finely chopped
  (3½ oz / 100 g in total)
scant 1 oz / 25 g ginger,
  peeled and finely
  chopped
1 leek, finely chopped
  (1¼ cups / 150 g in total)
2 tsp ground cumin
scant 3 cups / 700 ml
  chicken stock
⅓ cup / 80 ml freshly
  squeezed orange juice
1 tbsp freshly squeezed
  lemon juice
salt and freshly ground
  black pepper
sour cream, to serve

Don't be too quick to judge. This soup, traditional of the Iranian Jewish community, only reveals its true glory at the very last stage, when fresh orange juice is stirred through it. Serve small portions; it's quite rich. If you don't want to skin the pistachios, don't; it will only affect the color.

Preheat the oven to 350°F / 180°C. Pour the boiling water over the saffron threads in a small cup and leave to infuse for 30 minutes.

To remove the pistachio skins, blanch the nuts in boiling water for 1 minute, drain, and while still hot, remove the skins by pressing the nuts between your fingers. Not all the skins will come off as with almonds—this is fine as it won't affect the soup—but getting rid of some skin will improve the color, making it a brighter green. Spread the pistachios out on a baking sheet and roast in the oven for 8 minutes. Remove and leave to cool.

Heat the butter in a large saucepan and add the shallots, ginger, leek, cumin, ½ teaspoon salt, and some black pepper. Sauté over medium heat for 10 minutes, stirring often, until the shallots are completely soft. Add the stock and half of the saffron liquid. Cover the pan, lower the heat, and let the soup simmer for 20 minutes.

Place all but 1 tablespoon of the pistachios in a large bowl along with half of the soup. Use a handheld blender to blitz until smooth and then return this to the saucepan. Add the orange and lemon juice, reheat, and taste to adjust the seasoning.

To serve, coarsely chop up the reserved pistachios. Transfer the hot soup into bowls and top with a spoonful of sour cream. Sprinkle with the pistachios and drizzle with the remaining saffron liquid.

Couscous & Co.

It is extremely characteristic of Jerusalem's position at the heart of so many Middle Eastern and North African cuisines that it is impossible to untangle and unravel the distinct name and characteristics of certain ingredients. Take little pasta balls— we are not even sure by what name to introduce them—most commonly known in the West as couscous.

Well, there is indeed couscous, tiny semolina balls that in the past were only freshly rolled by women, steamed, and served with soups and *tagines*, and are now sold dried and packaged and are also used for making salads and as a general side dish. Couscous is relatively new to Jerusalem, gaining popularity mostly since the arrival of large numbers of North African Jews in the 1950s and 1960s, particularly from Morocco. Still, it has spread deep roots and is extremely popular in Jewish culture. Many Jerusalem women continue to roll their own couscous, which can be found in restaurants around the city.

The local Palestinian equivalent to couscous is called *maftoul*. *Maftoul* are less even in shape, larger than couscous and are also either made at home or sold dried. Similar to couscous, *maftoul* is served with stews and soups, often steamed, and reserved for special occasions (SEE ALSO PAGE 141).

Israeli couscous, *ptitim*, also made of wheat, is another variation on the theme. This is also substantially larger than couscous and was thought up during the 1950s' food shortages by the then prime minister, David Ben-Gurion, as an industrial solution for feeding the vast number of newly arrived immigrants. It has taken root in Israeli culture and is particularly liked by children when cooked with onion and tomato (SEE PAGE 8).

The spread of "Israeli couscous" in the West, from comfort food in its early years to top chefs' latest trendy ingredient, caused some resentment among Palestinians, whose *maftoul* isn't very different from *ptitim*, and among Lebanese, whose *mograbieh*, or Lebanese couscous, is similar to and only a bit larger than *ptitim*. *Mograbieh*, which literally means "from North Africa," clearly affirms its origin and source of inspiration through its name, while "Israeli couscous," claim the critics, does the exact opposite.

Burnt eggplant & mograbieh soup

5 small eggplants
   (about 2½ lb / 1.2 kg
   in total)
sunflower oil, for frying
1 onion, sliced
   (about 1 cup / 125 g
   in total)
1 tbsp cumin seeds,
   freshly ground
1½ tsp tomato paste
2 large tomatoes
   (12 oz / 350 g in total),
   skinned and diced
1½ cups / 350 ml chicken
   or vegetable stock
1⅔ cups / 400 ml water
4 cloves garlic, crushed
2½ tsp sugar
2 tbsp freshly squeezed
   lemon juice
⅓ cup / 100 g mograbieh,
   or alternative, such as
   maftoul, fregola, or giant
   couscous (see page 139)
2 tbsp shredded basil,
   or 1 tbsp chopped dill,
   optional
salt and freshly ground
   black pepper

Mograbieh, *and to a lesser degree* maftoul, *are available from some Middle Eastern groceries and online* (SEE MORE ON MOGRABIEH AND MAFTOUL ON PAGE 139). *Giant or Israeli couscous are widely available and so is* fregola, *the Sardinian equivalent. Whichever you choose for making this wonderfully hefty soup, check the package for cooking times, making sure the little pasta balls are just al dente. Follow the soup with something light, like the Fava bean kuku* (PAGE 39) *or Panfried mackerel with golden beet and orange salsa* (PAGE 222).

Start by burning three of the eggplants. To do this, follow the instructions for Burnt eggplant with garlic, lemon, and pomegranate seeds (PAGE 79).

Cut the remaining eggplants into ⅔-inch / 1.5cm dice. Heat about ⅔ cup / 150 ml oil in a large saucepan over medium-high heat. When it is hot, add the eggplant dice. Fry for 10 to 15 minutes, stirring often, until colored all over; add a little more oil if needed so there is always some oil in the pan. Remove the eggplant, place in a colander to drain, and sprinkle with salt.

Make sure you have about 1 tablespoon oil left in the pan, then add the onion and cumin and sauté for about 7 minutes, stirring often. Add the tomato paste and cook for another minute before adding the tomatoes, stock, water, garlic, sugar, lemon juice, 1½ teaspoons salt, and some black pepper. Simmer gently for 15 minutes.

Meanwhile, bring a small saucepan of salted water to a boil and add the mograbieh or alternative. Cook until al dente; this will vary according to brand but should take 15 to 18 minutes (check the packet). Drain and refresh under cold water.

Transfer the burnt eggplant flesh to the soup and blitz to a smooth liquid with a handheld blender. Add the mograbieh and fried eggplant, keeping some to garnish at the end, and simmer for another 2 minutes. Taste and adjust the seasoning. Serve hot, with the reserved mograbieh and fried eggplant on top and garnished with basil or dill, if you like.

Tomato & sourdough soup

Yotam's mother, Ruth, who kindly gave us this recipe, is in many ways a typical Jewish Jerusalem cook. She was born to a Yekke family, German Jews who settled in the city just before the Second World War. Growing up, she spoke German at home and ate sweet-spiced red cabbage, potatoes, and sausages. Outside, she would experience some Arab food—it tasted thoroughly exotic to her—and the food of various Jewish immigrants, particularly from Poland and eastern Europe. She would also experience the beginnings of what later developed into a pretty defined Israeli cuisine, particularly as it was prepared in the kibbutzim—the famous chopped cucumber and tomato salad, tahini sauce, and olives.

Ruth married Michael, of Italian background, and so a whole new culinary world was opened up for her. She also got to travel a bit, mainly to Europe and the United States, and being an open person, she was always seeking new influences, new cuisines to try.

Growing up, Yotam remembers Ruth daringly trying all kinds of dishes. She made Spanish gazpachos, Italian zabagliones, and Malaysian curries. She cooked beef bourguignon; roast beef, English style; and sweet-and-sour chicken. She also cooked many specialties of her German heritage. What you could hardly find in her kitchen were many local Palestinian ingredients. Yotam can't remember ever seeing a tub of tahini in the house or a bag of bulgur. Still, over the years, Arab food gained respectability in Israeli culture and people started daring to go beyond the obligatory visit to a Palestinian joint for a kebab skewer and a plate of hummus when visiting the Old City. Ruth, like many other Israeli cooks, began to get to know what was happening in her neighbors' kitchens and what was laid on their tables. Instead of feeling exotic, ingredients like *za'atar* made their way into the daily food repertoire, until they felt like they had always been there.

Today, like many other Jewish cooks, Ruth is comfortable with her European culinary heritage, but her style has changed and the ingredients she uses are much more local. In her larder you can now find *freekeh* and tahini sitting next to fusilli and a jar of rollmops. On her spice shelf are sumac, cumin, and organic Swiss bouillon powder. And you can even catch her, once in a while, burning a little eggplant.

---

2 tbsp olive oil, plus extra
  to finish
1 large onion, chopped
  (1⅔ cups / 250 g in total)
1 tsp cumin seeds
2 cloves garlic, crushed
3 cups / 750 ml vegetable
  stock
4 large ripe tomatoes,
  chopped (4 cups / 650 g
  in total)
one 14-oz / 400g can
  chopped Italian tomatoes
1 tbsp superfine sugar
1 slice sourdough bread
  (1½ oz / 40 g in total)
2 tbsp chopped cilantro,
  plus extra to finish
salt and freshly ground
  black pepper

This modest list of ingredients yields the most delicate soup. It is truly wonderful.

Heat the oil in a medium saucepan and add the onion. Sauté for about 5 minutes, stirring often, until the onion is translucent. Add the cumin and garlic and fry for 2 minutes. Pour in the stock, both types of tomato, sugar, 1 teaspoon salt, and a good grind of black pepper.

Bring the soup to a gentle simmer and cook for 20 minutes, adding the bread, torn into chunks, halfway through the cooking. Finally, add the cilantro and then blitz, using a blender, in a few pulses so that the tomatoes break down but are still a little coarse and chunky. The soup should be quite thick; add a little water if it is too thick at this point. Serve, drizzled with oil and scattered with fresh cilantro.

Clear chicken soup with knaidlach

Knaidlach, matzo meal dumplings served in chicken or beef broth, appear on most Jewish tables in Jerusalem and around the world at Pesach (Passover) and often also at Rosh Hashanah. Believe it or not, Sami, with not a Jewish bone in his body, is renowned for his *knaidlach*. So much so that he has personally disclosed to many respectable North London housewives his hush-hush tips for making this ultimate Ashkenazic festive delicacy, which he has perfected over time.

Knaidlach need to be light, but not too fluffy, with just enough flavor to bring out the qualities of the broth, the real pride of the housewife.

Chicken soup is deeply engrained in Jewish culture, famous for its mythological healing qualities. It is the basis for the Ashkenazic Shabbat and holiday meals, with every woman having her own "secret" recipe.

It is said that former Israeli prime minister Golda Meir was a good cook, and that even while she held the office in the 1970s, she never had a dedicated cook in the prime minister's residence. Instead, she did the cooking herself or it was done by one of only two staff members. Golda was a daring eater and would try whatever she was offered around the world. Still, at home it was a typical Ashkenazic affair. Her chicken soup with *knaidlach* was her grandchildren's favorite.

The knaidlach *take a while to make so are better started a day in advance. You can stop at the batter stage, or once they are shaped, cooked, and cooled. In both cases, keep in the fridge till the next day. The soup can also be made a day ahead and chilled.*

You can opt for making the soup only. If you do, return the chicken meat to the finished soup to warm up, and serve the soup with the chicken pieces and some cooked egg vermicelli. If you do make the knaidlach, *serve the chicken warm over well-seasoned cooked rice or bulgur wheat (but not during Pesach!) with a drizzle of olive oil and a sprinkle of toasted pine nuts, coarse sea salt, black pepper, and chopped parsley.*

---

1 free-range chicken, about
  4½ lb / 2 kg, divided into
  quarters, with all the
  bones, plus giblets if you
  can get them and any
  extra wings or bones you
  can get from the butcher
1½ tsp sunflower oil
1 cup / 250 ml dry white
  wine
2 carrots, peeled and cut
  into ¾-inch / 2cm slices
  (2 cups / 250 g in total)
4 celery stalks (about
  10½ oz / 300 g in total),
  cut into 2½-inch / 6cm
  segments
2 medium onions (about
  12 oz / 350 g in total),
  cut into 8 wedges
1 large turnip (7 oz /
  200 g), peeled, trimmed,
  and cut into 8 segments
scant 2 oz / 50 g bunch
  flat-leaf parsley
scant 2 oz / 50 g bunch
  cilantro
5 thyme sprigs
1 small rosemary sprig
¾ oz / 20 g dill, plus
  extra to garnish
3 bay leaves
3½ oz / 100 g fresh ginger,
  thinly sliced
20 black peppercorns
5 allspice berries
salt

KNAIDLACH
(MAKES 12 TO 15)

2 extra-large eggs
2½ tbsp / 40 g margarine
  or chicken fat, melted
  and allowed to cool a bit
2 tbsp finely chopped
  flat-leaf parsley
⅔ cup / 75 g matzo meal
4 tbsp soda water
salt and freshly ground
  black pepper

To make the knaidlach, whisk the eggs in a medium bowl until frothy. Whisk in the melted margarine, then ½ teaspoon salt, some black pepper, and the parsley. Gradually, stir in the matzo meal, followed by the soda water, and stir to a uniform paste. Cover the bowl and chill the batter until cold and firm, at least an hour or two and up to 1 day ahead.

Line a baking sheet with plastic wrap. Using your wet hands and a spoon, shape the batter into balls the size of small walnuts and place on the baking sheet.

Drop the matzo balls into a large pot of gently boiling salted water. Cover partially with a lid and decrease the heat to low. Simmer gently until tender, about 30 minutes.

Using a slotted spoon, transfer the knaidlach onto a clean baking sheet where they can cool down, and then be chilled for up to a day. Or, they can go straight into the hot soup.

For the soup, trim any excess fat off the chicken and discard. Pour the oil into a very large saucepan or Dutch oven and sear the chicken pieces over high heat on all sides, 3 to 4 minutes. Remove from the pan, discard the oil, and wipe the pan. Add the wine and let it bubble away for a minute. Return the chicken, cover with water, and bring to a very gentle simmer. Simmer for about 10 minutes, skimming away the scum. Add the carrots, celery, onions, and turnip. Tie all the herbs into a bundle with string and add to the pot. Add the bay leaves, ginger, peppercorns, allspice, and 1½ teaspoons salt and then pour in enough water to cover everything well.

Bring the soup back to a very gentle simmer and cook for 1½ hours, skimming occasionally and adding water as needed to keep everything well covered. Lift the chicken from the soup and remove the meat from the bones. Keep the meat in a bowl with a little broth to keep it moist, and refrigerate; reserve for another use. Return the bones to the pot and simmer for another hour, adding just enough water to keep the bones and vegetables covered. Strain the hot soup and discard the herbs, vegetables, and bones. Warm the cooked knaidlach in the soup. Once they are hot, serve the soup and knaidlach in shallow bowls, sprinkled with dill.

Spicy freekeh soup with meatballs

MEATBALLS

14 oz / 400 g ground beef, lamb, or a combination of both

1 small onion (5 oz / 150 g in total), finely diced

2 tbsp finely chopped flat-leaf parsley

½ tsp ground allspice

¼ tsp ground cinnamon

3 tbsp all-purpose flour

2 tbsp olive oil

salt and freshly ground black pepper

SOUP

2 tbsp olive oil

1 large onion (9 oz / 250 g in total), chopped

3 cloves garlic, crushed

2 carrots (9 oz / 250 g in total), peeled and cut into ⅜-inch / 1cm cubes

2 celery stalks (5 oz / 150 g in total), cut into ⅜-inch / 1cm cubes

3 large tomatoes (12 oz / 350 g in total), chopped

2½ tbsp / 40 g tomato paste

1 tbsp baharat spice mix (store-bought or see recipe, page 299)

1 tbsp ground coriander

1 cinnamon stick

1 tbsp superfine sugar

1 cup / 150 g cracked freekeh

2 cups / 500 ml beef stock

2 cups / 500 ml chicken stock

3¼ cups / 800 ml hot water

⅓ oz / 10 g cilantro, chopped

1 lemon, cut into 6 wedges

Palestinians, like many others in the region, used to harvest some of their wheat while the grains were still green and not completely dry. These were then set on fire in order to burn the chaff and straw. The village women would then get together in large groups to beat the wheat and collect the green grains. The result of this process is *freekeh*, or green wheat, a highly popular cereal with a hint of smokiness. It imparts a brilliant aroma when added to soups or stews but can also be cooked like rice or bulgur.

Today, *freekeh* is produced and sold commercially, whole or cracked; when cracked, it looks like bulgur wheat but is green. We use it for making pilafs, in salads, and for serving with lamb or chicken (POACHED CHICKEN WITH SWEET SPICED FREEKEH, PAGE 182). Its earthy flavor and slightly coarse texture go particularly well with sweet spices.

In our first book, we published a recipe for the Moroccan soup harira, *a traditional meal for breaking the Ramadan fast. It proved very popular with our readers, who particularly mentioned the deep and comforting aromas, broken by a surprising sharpness of lemon juice and plenty of spices. This is a Palestinian version on the theme and it does the same job. It is warming, hearty, sweet, and substantial. Look for* freekeh *online or in Middle Eastern groceries. Bulgur is an acceptable substitute; it won't take as long to cook however; 20 to 25 minutes should be enough.*

Start with the meatballs. In a large bowl, mix together the meat, onion, parsley, allspice, cinnamon, ½ teaspoon salt, and ¼ teaspoon pepper. Using your hands, mix well, then form the mixture into Ping-Pong-size balls and roll them in the flour; you will get about 15. Heat the olive oil in a large Dutch oven and fry the meatballs over medium heat for a few minutes, until golden brown on all sides. Remove the meatballs and set aside.

Wipe out the pan with paper towels and add the olive oil for the soup. Over medium heat, fry the onion and garlic for 5 minutes. Stir in the carrots and celery and cook for 2 minutes. Add the tomatoes, tomato paste, spices, sugar, 2 teaspoons salt, and ½ teaspoon pepper and cook for 1 more minute. Stir in the freekeh and cook for 2 to 3 minutes. Add the stocks, hot water, and meatballs. Bring to a boil, lower the heat, and simmer very gently for a further 35 to 45 minutes, stirring occasionally, until the freekeh is plump and tender. The soup should be quite thick. Reduce or add a little water as needed. Finally, taste and adjust the seasoning.

Ladle the hot soup into serving bowls and sprinkle with the cilantro. Serve the lemon wedges on the side.

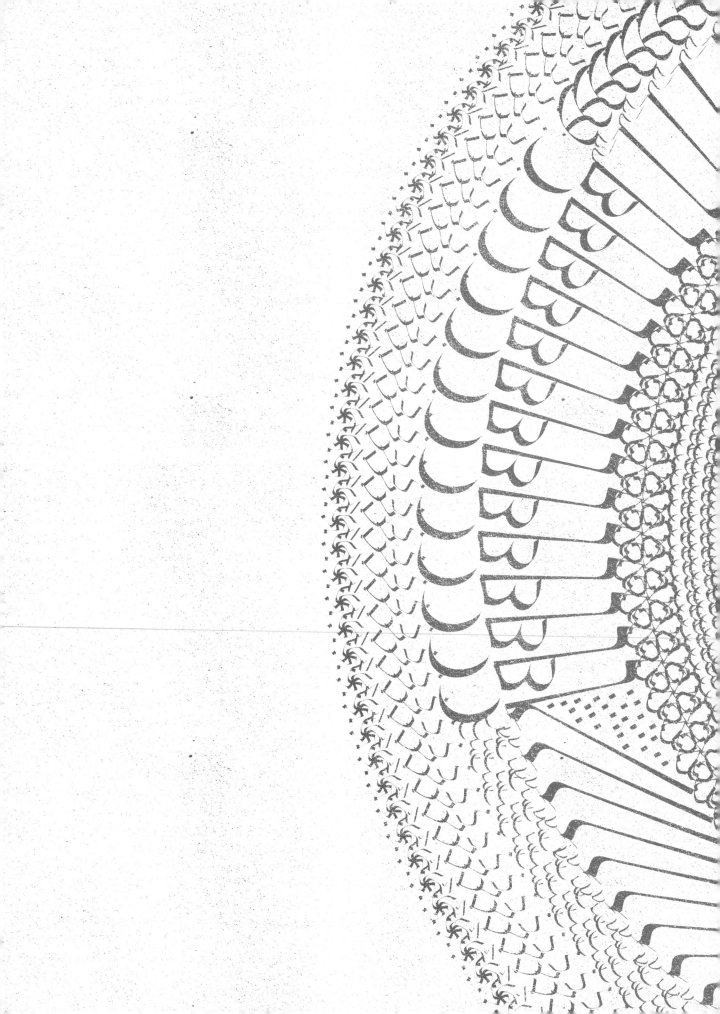

STUFFED

Stuffed

When Henry Kissinger visited Jerusalem in 1974 for one of his peace missions, the chef at the city's top restaurant at the time, Mishkenot Sha'ananim, prepared a special platter with six items, each representing a stop on the secretary of state's tour: Morocco, Egypt, Syria, Jordan, Lebanon, and Israel. Food writer Rina Valero, who recounts the story, mentions the six dishes on what became known as the Kissinger Platter: *kubbeh*, stuffed vine leaves, stuffed prunes wrapped in goose breast, filo stuffed with chicken liver and veal, cigars stuffed with foie gras, and pears stuffed with walnuts and raisins. This selection reflects well the local fascination with all things stuffed. It is a unique phenomenon that doesn't apply only to top-end restaurants. Absolutely every single one of the city's numerous cultures has at least one major dish that involves stuffing, often many more, and a few cuisines, like the Kurdish Jewish, have become identified with a particular set of dishes that involve stuffing. *Ma'amul* cookies (PAGE 288), much-loved Palestinian staples, are based on a pastry shell stuffed with great deftness with a filling that is loaded with flavor. Numerous versions of *mahshi*, stuffed vegetables, can be found throughout the region and are much admired by everybody.

EGGPLANTS, POTATOES, ZUCCHINI, BEETS, TOMATOES, ONIONS, PEPPERS, TURNIPS, CHARD, AND VINE AND CABBAGE LEAVES ARE AMONG THE POPULAR ONES. BUT ANYTHING GOES, REALLY.

In the days before women went out to work, and still to a lesser degree today, groups of women, Jewish as well as Palestinian, would work together at home stuffing vegetables. This requires dexterity and patience, particularly hollowing out carrots and zucchini, for which there is a specialized tool, but they are made with much pride. The stuffing usually consists of seasoned rice with or without the addition of ground meat, and the cooking liquid is either water or tomato based. The Arab version is served with yogurt and sometimes dried yogurt (*kishk*) is added to the cooking liquid. Trotters or a whole sheep's head can be added to the pot for flavor.

Still seeing so many foods in Jerusalem being stuffed, filled, or rolled today is a bit of a miracle. Stuffing is an activity suitable for old times, when people had more time and less money; when women spent hours at home but could afford much less. What stuffing does is stretch your meat or rice much further, with a result that is impressive to look at because of its complexity but is also very delicious. It also includes meat, veg, and carb in one pot, which saves the cook much cleaning up and having to flavor the separate components.

For Jews there is also the benefit of cooking for Shabbat. Their stuffed vegetables are slowly cooked on Friday and can be left on a warm platter or served cold. Sephardim also stuff vegetables for special events and holidays. The stuffed vegetables are sometimes dipped in egg, fried, and then stewed on the stove top or in the oven. Eggplants, potatoes, zucchini, beets, tomatoes, onions, peppers, turnips, chard, and vine and cabbage leaves are among the popular ones. But anything goes, really. Dried apricots and other fruit can be added to the stuffing or the sauce—we've even seen apricot jam (!)—as well as tamarind. This mixture of sweet and sour is typical Jerusalem.

Polish Jews stuff cabbage, a result of the interaction during the seventeenth century with the Ottoman Empire. They stuff their cabbage with beef and rice and cook it in stock. Hungarian Jews stuff peppers and cook them in a sweet tomato and paprika sauce.

But stuffing doesn't end with vegetables. *Shishbarak*, little dumplings, a bit like tortellini, stuffed with meat and cooked in yogurt, are an Arab specialty. The various Ashkenazic and Sephardic cuisines all have their own versions of dumplings that are still highly popular today.

Kubbeh—bulgur or semolina dumplings, normally stuffed with meat—are a mainstay of Palestinians (SEE PAGE 159), who fry them, and Kurdish Jews, who cook them in various soups (KUBBEH HAMUSTA, PAGE 162).

Hollowed-out carrots ready to stuff for sale in a market.

Lamb-stuffed quince
with pomegranate & cilantro

14 oz / 400 g ground lamb

1 clove garlic, crushed

1 red chile, chopped

⅔ oz / 20 g cilantro, chopped, plus 2 tbsp, to garnish

scant ½ cup / 50 g bread crumbs

1 tsp ground allspice

2 tbsp finely grated fresh ginger

2 medium onions, finely chopped (1⅓ cups / 220 g in total)

1 large free-range egg

4 quince (2¾ lb / 1.3 kg in total)

juice of ½ lemon, plus 1 tbsp freshly squeezed lemon juice

3 tbsp olive oil

8 cardamom pods

2 tsp pomegranate molasses

2 tsp sugar

2 cups / 500 ml chicken stock

seeds of ½ pomegranate

salt and freshly ground black pepper

This is a stunning dish that we always go back to. We regularly teach a simplified version in our Saturday morning classes at Leiths cookery school in London. There, we don't stuff the quince but just dice it and cook it in the sauce with the meat filling shaped into meatballs. We recommend doing that if you don't have the time or the inclination to stuff the quince (it is a pretty hardy fruit!). You could use hard pears as an alternative. Another variation is based on a Persian dish, khoresht beh, which calls for lamb or beef cubes, chopped onion, cinnamon, nutmeg, sliced quince, lemon juice, and sugar. All these are cooked together very slowly to make a sweet and sharp stew.

Place the lamb in a mixing bowl along with the garlic, chile, cilantro, bread crumbs, allspice, half of the ginger, half of the onion, egg, ¾ teaspoon salt, and some pepper. Mix well with your hands and set aside.

Peel the quince and halve them lengthwise. Put them in a bowl of cold water with the juice of the ½ lemon so that they do not turn brown. Use a melon baller or small spoon to remove the seeds and then hollow out the quince halves so that you are left with a ⅖-inch / 1.5cm shell. Keep the scooped-out flesh. Fill the hollows with the lamb mix, using your hands to push it down.

Heat the olive oil in a large frying pan for which you have a lid. Place the reserved quince flesh in a food processor, blitz to chop well, and then transfer the mixture to the pan along with the remaining onion, ginger, and the cardamom pods. Sauté for 10 to 12 minutes, until the onion has softened. Add the molasses, the 1 tablespoon lemon juice, sugar, stock, ½ teaspoon salt, and some black pepper and mix well. Add the quince halves to the sauce, with the meat stuffing facing upward, lower the heat to a gentle simmer, cover the pan, and cook for about 30 minutes. At the end the quince should be completely soft, the meat well cooked, and the sauce thick. Lift the lid and simmer for a minute or two to reduce the sauce if needed.

Serve warm or at room temperature, sprinkled with the cilantro and pomegranate seeds.

Turnip & veal "cake"

1²⁄₃ cups / 300 g basmati rice

14 oz / 400 g ground veal, lamb, or beef

½ cup / 30 g chopped flat-leaf parsley

1½ tsp baharat spice mix (store-bought or see recipe, page 299)

½ tsp ground cinnamon

½ tsp chile flakes

2 tbsp olive oil

10 to 15 medium turnips (3¼ lb / 1.5 kg in total)

about 1²⁄₃ cups / 400 ml sunflower oil

scant 2 cups / 300 g chopped tomatoes, canned are fine

1½ tbsp tamarind paste

¾ cup plus 2 tbsp / 200 ml chicken stock, hot

1 cup / 250 ml water

1½ tbsp superfine sugar

2 thyme sprigs, leaves picked

salt and freshly ground black pepper

After about an hour of serious struggling with various kitchen utensils and a host of small, sharp tools—and with turnip shells breaking up or cracking all over the place—we finally gave up trying to hollow out turnips for a popular Palestinian dish where they are stuffed with rice and cooked in tomato sauce. Instead, we came up with this layered dish that saves much hassle and time but also leaves us full of admiration and awe for generations of housewives and mothers who prepared these regularly and without a single grumble. Similar to Maqluba (PAGE 127), this is a meal in a pot. It is sweet and sour with a very clear aroma of all the spices. Turnips can be substituted with potatoes, if you prefer. Serve it with seasoned Greek yogurt or Yogurt with cucumber (PAGE 299).

Wash the rice and drain well. Place in a large mixing bowl and add the meat, parsley, baharat, cinnamon, 2 teaspoons salt, ½ teaspoon pepper, chile, and olive oil. Mix well and set aside.

Peel the turnips and cut them into slices ³⁄₈ inch / 1 cm thick. Heat enough sunflower oil over medium-high heat to come ¾ inch / 2 cm up the sides of a large frying pan. Fry the turnip slices in batches for 3 to 4 minutes per batch, until golden. Transfer to a plate lined with paper towels, sprinkle with a little salt, and allow to cool down.

Put the tomatoes, tamarind, stock, water, sugar, 1 teaspoon salt, and ½ teaspoon pepper in a large mixing bowl. Whisk well. Pour about one-third of this liquid into a medium, heavy-bottomed saucepan (9½ inches / 24 cm in diameter). Arrange one-third of the turnip slices inside. Add half the rice mixture and level. Arrange another layer of turnips, followed by the second half of the rice. Finish with the last of the turnips, pressing down softly with your hands. Pour the remaining tomato liquid over the turnip and rice layers and sprinkle with the thyme. Gently slide a spatula down the sides of the pot to allow the juices to flow to the bottom.

Place over medium heat and bring to a boil. Lower the heat to an absolute minimum, cover, and simmer for 1 hour. Take off the heat, uncover, and allow to rest for 10 to 15 minutes before serving. Unfortunately, it is impossible to invert the cake onto a plate as it doesn't hold its shape, so it must be spooned out.

Stuffed onions

4 large onions (2 lb / 900 g
  in total, peeled weight)
about 1⅔ cups / 400 ml
  vegetable stock
1½ tbsp pomegranate
  molasses
salt and freshly ground
  black pepper

STUFFING

1½ tbsp olive oil
1 cup / 150 g finely chopped
  shallots
½ cup / 100 g short-grain
  rice
¼ cup / 35 g pine nuts,
  crushed
2 tbsp chopped fresh mint
2 tbsp chopped flat-leaf
  parsley
2 tsp dried mint
1 tsp ground cumin
⅛ tsp ground clove
¼ tsp ground allspice
¾ tsp salt
½ tsp freshly ground
  black pepper
4 lemon wedges (optional)

As a result of the long cooking and the sharp sweetness of the pomegranate molasses, these onions have a surprisingly deep, yet fresh flavor. Serve them at the start of a meat-centered meal, or alongside a selection of small vegetable dishes, such as Charred okra with tomato, garlic, and preserved lemon (PAGE 74) *or Fried cauliflower with tahini* (PAGE 60). *Consider a variation based on a Syrian Jewish dish: stuff the onions with ground beef flavored with cinnamon and allspice and braise in a sauce made with water, tamarind, lemon juice, sugar, and a little oil.*

Peel and cut about ¼ inch / 0.5 cm off the tops and tails of the onions, place the trimmed onions in a large saucepan with plenty of water, bring to a boil, and cook for 15 minutes. Drain and set aside to cool down.

To prepare the stuffing, heat the olive oil in a medium frying pan over medium-high heat and add the shallots. Sauté for 8 minutes, stirring often, then add all the remaining ingredients except the lemon wedges. Turn the heat to low and continue to cook and stir for 10 minutes.

Using a small knife, make a long cut from the top of the onion to the bottom, running all the way to its center, so that each layer of onion has only one slit running through it. Start gently separating the onion layers, one after another, until you reach the core. Don't worry if some of the layers tear a little through the peeling; you can still use them.

Hold a layer of onion in one cupped hand and spoon about 1 tablespoon of the rice mixture into one-half of the onion, placing the filling near to one end of the opening. Don't be tempted to fill it up more, as it needs to be wrapped up nice and snug. Fold the empty side of the onion over the stuffed side and roll it up tightly so the rice is covered with a few layers of onion with no air in the middle. Place in a medium frying pan for which you have a lid, seam side down, and continue with the remaining onions and rice mixture. Lay the onions side by side in the pan, so that there is no space to move about. Fill any spaces with parts of the onion that have not been stuffed. Add enough stock so that the onions are three-quarters covered, along with the pomegranate molasses, and season with ¼ teaspoon salt.

Cover the pan and cook on the lowest possible simmer for 1½ to 2 hours, until the liquid has evaporated. Serve warm or at room temperature, with lemon wedges if you like.

The capital of kibbeh

Jerusalem is the world capital of *kibbeh*; if not for quantity then definitely for variety. Most people would happily agree on that. The trouble is they'd find it much harder to agree on what that thing actually is. Food definitions can get terribly complicated in this city, but if you are happy to walk into this trap, it is fascinating. You'll find the most convoluted and intricate mixes when you look into Arabic cuisine and its counterpart, Sephardic cuisine of Jews of the Levant. And nowhere more so than when it comes to *kibbeh*.

Kibbeh, kubbeh, or *kobeba* all mean "the shape of a ball" in Arabic. Indeed, this is how they started. The most familiar variation in the West and in eastern Jerusalem is the Syrian and Lebanese national dish, where ground meat and bulgur wheat are mixed together to make a shell, stuffed with meat flavored with sweet spices and pine nuts, shaped into balls or torpedoes, and deep-fried. They are deliciously crisp and wholesome.

DAINTILY SHAPING THE CASES AS THINLY AS POSSIBLE, WITHOUT THEM TEARING OR BREAKING, USED TO BE THE ULTIMATE INDICATOR OF FEMALE DEXTERITY AND GENERAL DOMESTIC APTITUDE.

Daintily shaping the cases as thinly as possible, without them tearing or breaking, used to be the ultimate indicator of female dexterity and general domestic aptitude. For generations of Jewish and Arab women being able to make nice *kubbeh* was considered one of the basic requirements of a "good" domesticated woman; a test of their refinement and elegance. A less arduous version—why hasn't anyone told the poor women?—is *kibbeh b'siniyah*, where the casing and filling are layered in a dish to form a pie. And then there is the Lebanese *kibbeh nayyeh*, which is like steak tartare, using raw ground meat and bulgur—no trouble at all.

Jews from Iraq, Syria, and Kurdistan have a range of *kibbeh* that are made with ground rice or semolina and cooked in soups or stews (as well as the fried *kibbeh* we described). These are unique to them but have come to be seen as the typical Jewish ethnic food of Jerusalem (KUBBEH HAMUSTA, PAGE 162).

Open kibbeh

scant 1 cup / 125 g fine
  bulgur wheat
scant 1 cup / 200 ml water
6 tbsp / 90 ml olive oil
2 cloves garlic, crushed
2 medium onions, finely
  chopped
1 green chile, finely
  chopped
12 oz / 350 g ground lamb
1 tsp ground allspice
1 tsp ground cinnamon
1 tsp ground coriander
2 tbsp coarsely chopped
  cilantro
scant ½ cup / 60 g pine nuts
3 tbsp coarsely chopped
  flat-leaf parsley
2 tbsp self-rising flour,
  plus a little extra if
  needed
3½ tbsp / 50 g light tahini
  paste
2 tsp freshly squeezed
  lemon juice
1 tsp sumac
salt and freshly ground
  black pepper

This variation of kibbeh *is very nontraditional. It is more of a layered savory cake incorporating the essential elements—bulgur, ground meat, spices, and pine nuts—plus the obligatory tahini dipping sauce, spread on top. Serve it warm or at room temperature as a light meal, alongside a sharp aromatic salad such as Tabbouleh or Na'ama's fattoush* (PAGES 85 AND 29, RESPECTIVELY).

Preheat the oven to 400°F / 200°C. Line an 8-inch / 20cm springform pan with waxed paper.

Place the bulgur in a large bowl and cover it with the water. Leave for 30 minutes.

Meanwhile, heat 4 tablespoons of the olive oil in a large frying pan over medium-high heat. Sauté the garlic, onion, and chile until they are completely soft. Remove everything from the pan, return it to high heat, and add the lamb. Cook for 5 minutes, stirring continuously, until brown.

Return the onion mixture to the pan and add the spices, cilantro, ½ teaspoon salt, a generous grind of black pepper, and most of the pine nuts and parsley, leaving some aside. Cook for a couple of minutes, remove from the heat, taste, and adjust the seasoning.

Check the bulgur to see if all the water has been absorbed. Drain to remove any remaining liquid. Add the flour, 1 tablespoon of the olive oil, ¼ teaspoon salt, and a pinch of black pepper and use your hands to work everything into a pliable mixture that just holds together; add a little bit more flour if the mixture is very sticky. Push firmly onto the bottom of the springform pan so that it is compacted and leveled. Spread the lamb mixture evenly on top and press it down a little. Bake for about 20 minutes, until the meat is quite dark brown and very hot.

While you wait, whisk together the tahini paste with the lemon juice, 3½ tbsp / 50 ml water, and a pinch of salt. You are after a very thick, yet pourable sauce. If needed, add a little extra water.

Remove the kibbeh cake from the oven, spread the tahini sauce evenly on top, sprinkle with the reserved pine nuts and chopped parsley, and return to the oven immediately. Bake for 10 to 12 minutes, until the tahini is just setting and has taken on a little bit of color, and the pine nuts are golden.

Remove from the oven and let cool until warm or at room temperature. Before serving, sprinkle the top with the sumac and drizzle with the remaining oil. Carefully remove the pan sides and cut the kibbeh into slices. Lift them gently so they don't break.

Kubbeh hamusta

Friday lunchtime around Machne Yehuda market is all about *kubbeh* in soup, a tradition of Kurdish and other Jews from Iraq, Syria, and Turkey that has caught on and become the ultimate local comfort food, served in simple dedicated restaurants around the market. Unlike the more familiar fried *kibbeh* using bulgur (PAGE 160), these are normally made with semolina or ground rice, stuffed with meat, and poached in a variety of soups. The principal three are tomato (and often okra), beet, and the sour, green *hamusta*, the most popular soup, made with chard, celery, zucchini, garlic, and lemon juice. All are extremely potent and sharp, typical of Jerusalem.

For Syrian Jews, whose wonderful cuisine is world renowned, the ultimate Shabbat meal is a soup similar to *hamusta*. *Chamot* (or *hamud*) is also made with celery and lemon, only meatballs are added instead of dumplings.

The story of the *kubbeh* soup is another example of necessity breeding culinary ingenuity. Back in Kurdistan, Jews could afford to buy meat only rarely. When they did, they had to buy a whole animal and make the most of it. They cooked their meat for a very long time in vast chunks, adding celery toward the end. Then everything was ground and kept in a very dry place for up to a few months (!), and used sparingly to stuff the *kubbeh* dumplings and cook in a fresh soup.

Making the dumplings for this soup is not the kind of thing we'd embark on when in a hurry or without perfect peace of mind. It is a kind of meditative activity that one can take up on leisurely weekends or when cooking in company. However, there are less time-consuming alternatives that we urge you to try because this soup is quite spectacular. One option is to forget the dumplings and simply add diced potato, celery root, or both, and cook them in the soup. Another is to make small, simple meatballs and poach them in the soup (USE THE RECIPE FOR BEEF MEATBALLS WITH FAVA BEANS AND LEMON, PAGE 196, BUT OMIT THE CAPERS). *This would be our preferred option for balancing work and flavor. If you still want the semolina casing in the soup, make little round semolina balls and cook them next to the meatballs. The stuffed* kubbeh *can be cooked, chilled, and then reheated in the soup.*

1½ tbsp sunflower oil

½ medium onion, very
    finely chopped (½ cup /
    75 g in total)

12 oz / 350 g ground beef

½ tsp ground allspice

1 large clove garlic, crushed

2 pale celery stalks, very
    finely chopped, or an
    equal amount of chopped
    celery leaves (½ cup /
    60 g in total)

salt and freshly ground
    black pepper

KUBBEH CASES

2 cups / 325 g semolina

5 tbsp / 40 g all-purpose
    flour

scant 1 cup / 220 ml hot
    water

SOUP

4 cloves garlic, crushed

5 celery stalks, leaves
    picked and stalks cut
    on an angle into ⅔-inch /
    1.5cm slices (2 cups /
    230 g in total)

10½ oz / 300 g Swiss
    chard leaves, green part
    only, cut into ¾-inch /
    2cm strips

2 tbsp sunflower oil

1 large onion, coarsely
    chopped (1¼ cups /
    200 g in total)

2 quarts / 2 liters
    chicken stock

1 large zucchini, cut into
    ⅜-inch / 1cm cubes
    (1⅔ cups / 200 g in total)

6½ tbsp / 100 ml freshly
    squeezed lemon juice, plus
    extra if needed

lemon wedges, to serve

First, prepare the meat stuffing. Heat the oil in a medium frying pan, and add the onion. Cook over medium heat until translucent, about 5 minutes. Add the beef, allspice, ¾ teaspoon salt, and a good grind of black pepper and stir as you cook for 3 minutes, just to brown. Reduce the heat to medium-low and allow the meat to cook slowly for about 20 minutes, until completely dry, stirring from time to time. At the end, add the garlic and celery, cook for another 3 minutes, and remove from the heat. Taste and adjust the seasoning. Allow to cool down.

While the beef mix is cooking, prepare the kubbeh cases. Mix the semolina, flour, and ¼ teaspoon salt in a large mixing bowl. Gradually add the water, stirring with a wooden spoon and then your hands until you get a sticky dough. Cover with a damp cloth and set aside to rest for 15 minutes.

Knead the dough for a few minutes on a work surface. It must be supple and spreadable without cracking. Add a little water or flour if needed. To make the dumplings, get a bowl of water and wet your hands (make sure your hands are wet throughout the process to prevent sticking). Take a piece of dough weighing about 1 oz / 30 g and flatten it in your palm; you're aiming for disks 4 inches / 10 cm in diameter. Place about 2 teaspoons of the stuffing in the center. Fold the edges over the stuffing to cover and then seal it inside. Roll the kubbeh between your hands to form a ball and then press it down into a round, flat shape about 1¼ inches / 3 cm thick. Place the dumplings on a tray covered with plastic wrap and drizzled with a little water and leave to one side.

For the soup, place the garlic, half the celery, and half the chard in a food processor and blitz to a coarse paste. Heat the oil in a large saucepan over medium heat and sauté the onion for about 10 minutes, until pale golden. Add the celery and chard paste and cook for 3 minutes more. Add the stock, zucchini, the remaining celery and chard, the lemon juice, 1 teaspoon salt, and ½ teaspoon black pepper. Bring to a boil and cook for 10 minutes, then taste and adjust the seasoning. It needs to be sharp, so add another tablespoon of lemon juice if you need to.

Finally, carefully add the kubbeh to the soup—a few at a time, so they don't stick to one another—and simmer gently for 20 minutes. Leave aside for a good half hour for them to settle and soften, then reheat and serve. Accompany with a wedge of lemon for an extra lemony kick.

Ruth's stuffed Romano peppers

8 medium Romano or other sweet peppers
1 large tomato, coarsely chopped (1 cup / 170 g in total)
2 medium onions, coarsely chopped (1²/₃ cups / 250 g in total)
about 2 cups / 500 ml vegetable stock

STUFFING
¾ cup / 140 g basmati rice
1½ tbsp baharat spice mix (store-bought or see recipe, page 299)
½ tsp ground cardamom
2 tbsp olive oil
1 large onion, finely chopped (1⅓ cups / 200 g in total)
14 oz / 400 g ground lamb
2½ tbsp chopped flat-leaf parsley
2 tbsp chopped dill
1½ tbsp dried mint
1½ tsp sugar
salt and freshly ground black pepper

This is Yotam's mother's recipe. It is mellow yet delectable and you don't need much else beside it. Serve with Kohlrabi salad (PAGE 46) and you are sorted. Make sure you have a frying pan or pot wide enough to accommodate all the peppers snugly, in one layer; you can squash them together a little. Otherwise, consider cooking in two separate pans.

Start with the stuffing. Place the rice in a saucepan and cover with lightly salted water. Bring to a boil and then cook for 4 minutes. Drain, refresh under cold water, and set aside.

Dry-fry the spices in a frying pan. Add the olive oil and onion and fry for about 7 minutes, stirring often, until the onion is soft. Pour this, along with the rice, meat, herbs, sugar, and 1 teaspoon salt into a large mixing bowl. Use your hands to mix everything together well.

Starting from the stalk end, use a small knife to cut lengthwise three-quarters of the way down each pepper, without removing the stalk, creating a long opening. Without forcing the pepper open too much, remove the seeds and then stuff each pepper with an equal amount of the mixture.

Place the chopped tomato and onion in a very large frying pan for which you have a tight-fitting lid. Arrange the peppers on top, close together, and pour in just enough stock so that it comes ⅛ inch / 1 cm up the sides of the peppers. Season with ½ teaspoon salt and some black pepper. Cover the pan with a lid and simmer over the lowest possible heat for an hour. It is important that the filling is just steamed, so the lid must fit tightly; make sure there is always a little bit of liquid at the bottom of the pan. Serve the peppers warm, not hot, or at room temperature.

Stuffed eggplant with lamb & pine nuts

Elran Shrefler, the youngest of Ezra and Rachela Shrefler's nine children, together with his brothers runs Azura. This restaurant in the heart of Machne Yehuda market serves Jerusalemites traditional Kurdish recipes with a Turkish influence, the cuisine of Ezra's birthplace. A member of the Slow Food movement, Elran starts work at four every morning and cooks all his food in massive pots on small oil-burning stoves, just as his family has done for generations. His food, long-cooked stews and hearty soups, is ready for the first customers who arrive at around 8 a.m. (!). It is essentially real fast food—after the long hours of slow cooking, it takes seconds to plate and serve. Elran showed us how to make his stuffed eggplant, Turkish style, which is our favorite dish at Azura. This is our interpretation.

In their book, *The Flavor of Jerusalem*, Joan Nathan and Judy Stacey Goldman give a slightly unorthodox recipe for stuffed eggplant with calves' liver and apples. This is the creation of Reverend William Gardiner-Scott, who, in the 1970s, was head of St. Andrew's, the only Presbyterian church in Jerusalem. The church was erected in 1927 to commemorate the capture of Jerusalem by the British during the First World War. This is one of only a few culinary marks the Brits have left behind.

---

4 medium eggplants
  (about 2½ lb / 1.2 kg),
  halved lengthwise
6 tbsp / 90 ml olive oil
1½ tsp ground cumin
1½ tbsp sweet paprika
1 tbsp ground cinnamon
2 medium onions (12 oz /
  340 g in total), finely
  chopped
1 lb / 500 g ground lamb
7 tbsp / 50 g pine nuts
⅔ oz / 20 g flat-leaf parsley,
  chopped
2 tsp tomato paste
3 tsp superfine sugar
⅔ cup / 150 ml water
1½ tbsp freshly squeezed
  lemon juice
1 tsp tamarind paste
4 cinnamon sticks
salt and freshly ground
  black pepper

These are deliciously hearty and best served with some bread or simple rice (BASMATI RICE AND ORZO, PAGE 103) *and some pickles on the side* (PICKLED TURNIP AND BEET, PAGE 307).

Preheat the oven to 425°F / 220°C.

Place the eggplant halves, skin side down, in a roasting pan large enough to accommodate them snugly. Brush the flesh with 4 tablespoons of the olive oil and season with 1 teaspoon salt and plenty of black pepper. Roast for about 20 minutes, until golden brown. Remove from the oven and allow to cool slightly.

While the eggplants are cooking, you can start making the stuffing by heating the remaining 2 tablespoons olive oil in a large frying pan. Mix together the cumin, paprika, and ground cinnamon and add half of this spice mix to the pan, along with the onions. Cook over medium-high heat for about 8 minutes, stirring often, before adding the lamb, pine nuts, parsley, tomato paste, 1 teaspoon of the sugar, 1 teaspoon salt, and some black pepper. Continue to cook and stir for another 8 minutes, until the meat is cooked.

Place the remaining spice mix in a bowl and add the water, lemon juice, tamarind, the remaining 2 teaspoons sugar, the cinnamon sticks, and ½ teaspoon salt; mix well.

Reduce the oven temperature to 375°F / 195°C. Pour the spice mix into the bottom of the eggplant roasting pan. Spoon the lamb mixture on top of each eggplant. Cover the pan tightly with aluminum foil, return to the oven, and roast for 1½ hours, by which point the eggplants should be completely soft and the sauce thick; twice during the cooking, remove the foil and baste the eggplants with the sauce, adding some water if the sauce dries out. Serve warm, not hot, or at room temperature.

Stuffed artichokes with peas & dill

14 oz / 400 g leeks,
  trimmed and cut into
  ¼-inch / 0.5cm slices
9 oz / 250 g ground beef
1 large free-range egg
1 tsp ground allspice
1 tsp ground cinnamon
2 tsp dried mint
12 medium globe
  artichokes or thawed
  frozen artichoke
  bottoms (see
  introduction)
6 tbsp / 90 ml freshly
  squeezed lemon juice,
  plus juice of ½ lemon if
  using fresh artichokes
⅓ cup / 80 ml olive oil
all-purpose flour, for
  coating the artichokes
about 2 cups / 500 ml
  chicken or vegetable
  stock
1⅓ cups / 200 g frozen
  peas
⅓ oz / 10 g dill, coarsely
  chopped
salt and freshly ground
  black pepper

Thrifty Jerusalem cooks make good use of the abundance of spring vegetables and preserve fava beans, young vine leaves, and artichokes at the height of their season. The artichokes are trimmed and their hearts are frozen, ready to be used when needed (SEE PAGE 41). *Increasingly, though, prepared frozen artichoke bottoms are available in supermarkets and they are pretty good. Look for them in Middle Eastern stores and you will save yourself a lot of work. Serve these as a main course with Basmati rice and orzo* (PAGE 103).

Blanch the leeks in boiling water for 5 minutes. Drain, refresh, and squeeze out the water.

Coarsely chop the leeks and place in a mixing bowl along with the meat, egg, spices, mint, 1 teaspoon salt, and plenty of pepper. Stir well.

If you are using fresh artichokes, prepare a bowl with water and the juice of ½ lemon. Remove the stalk from the artichoke and pull off the tough outer leaves. Once you reach the softer, pale leaves, use a large sharp knife to cut across the flower so that you are left with the bottom quarter. Use a small, sharp knife or a vegetable peeler to remove the outer layers of the artichoke until the base, or bottom, is exposed. Scrape out the hairy "choke" and put the base in the acidulated water. Discard the rest, then repeat with the other artichokes.

Put 2 tablespoons of the olive oil in a saucepan wide enough to hold the artichokes lying flat and heat over medium heat. Fill each artichoke bottom with 1 to 2 tablespoons of the beef mixture, pressing the filling in. Gently roll the bottoms in some flour, coating lightly and shaking off the excess. Fry in the hot oil for 1½ minutes on each side. Wipe the pan clean and return the artichokes to the pan, arranging them flat and snugly side by side.

Mix the stock, lemon juice, and the remaining oil and season generously with salt and pepper. Ladle spoonfuls of the liquid over the artichokes until they are almost, but not completely, submerged; you may not need all the liquid. Place a piece of parchment paper over the artichokes, cover the pan with a lid, and simmer over low heat for 1 hour. When they're ready, only about 4 tablespoons liquid should remain. If necessary, remove the lid and paper and reduce the sauce. Set the pan aside until the artichokes are just warm or at room temperature.

When ready to serve, blanch the peas for 2 minutes. Drain and add them and the dill to the pan with the artichokes, season to taste, and mix everything together gently.

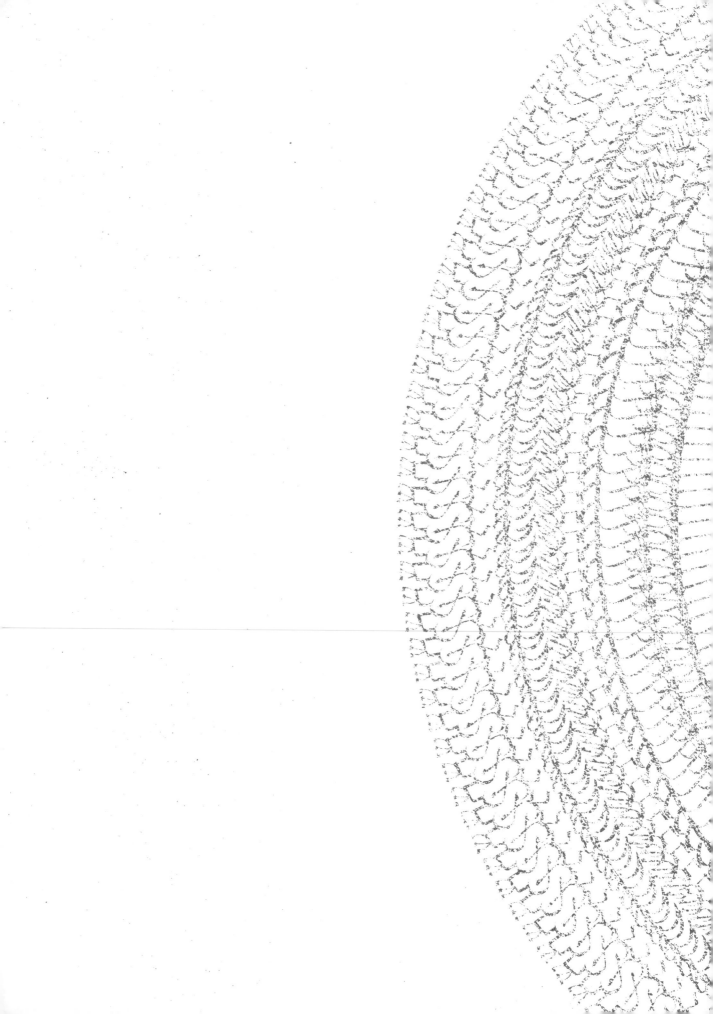

MEAT

Jerusalem mixed grill

Aside from kugel (PAGE 206), few dishes have gained the addition of "Jerusalem" to their name. Despite the misleading name, Jerusalem artichokes aren't named after the city but are welcome here anyway. The *me'orav Yerushalmi*, literally translated as "Jerusalem mixed grill," was invented on Agripas Street near Machne Yehuda market in the late 1960s. Several local steakhouses claim credit for the invention, but according to food writer Sherry Ansky, the original Jerusalem mixed grill was born at Makam steakhouse and almost overnight the chicken innards and onions, all fried in a particular spice mix, became one of the city's most iconic dishes. Today, many specialty steakhouses serve mixed grills to local clientele—mostly taxi drivers, who flock there in the early evening or late at night for the offal delight.

Meanwhile, on the eastern side of Jerusalem, Palestinians have been making their version of the dish for centuries. They stuff the cooked innards in a pita and lightly season them with freshly squeezed lemon juice, hot chile peppers, parsley, and crushed cumin seeds. The dish, in either version, solves the issue of using the cheapest, unloved parts of Jerusalem's most loved meat, the chicken. We adore it.

10½ oz / 300 g boneless chicken breast, cut into ¾-inch / 2cm cubes
7 oz / 200 g chicken hearts, cut in half lengthwise (optional)
4 tbsp olive oil
9 oz / 250 g chicken livers, cleaned and diced
2 large onions, thinly sliced (about 4½ cups / 500 g in total)
1½ tsp ground turmeric
1 tbsp baharat spice mix (store-bought or see recipe, page 299)
salt

Serve the mixed grill as a whole meal with fresh pita, savory mango chutney, Tahini sauce (PAGE 298), *and pickles.*

Put a large cast-iron or other heavy frying pan over medium-high heat and leave for a few minutes, until nearly smoking. Add the chicken breast and leave for a minute, stir once, then cook until browned all over, 2 to 3 minutes. Transfer the pieces to a bowl and set aside.

Put the hearts in the pan and cook, stirring occasionally, until browned but not cooked through, 2 to 3 minutes. Add to the bowl.

Pour a teaspoon of the olive oil into the pan and add the livers. Cook for 2 to 3 minutes, stirring just once or twice, then remove from the pan.

Pour 2 tablespoons of the olive oil into the pan and add half of the onions. Cook, stirring all the time, for 4 to 5 minutes, until the onions soften and slightly char but aren't completely limp. Add the remaining oil to the pan and repeat with the second half of the onions. Return the first batch to the pan, along with the spices and cooked chicken pieces, hearts, and livers. Season with ¾ teaspoon salt and continue to cook for about 3 minutes, scraping the pan as you cook, until the chicken is cooked through. Serve at once.

Braised quail with apricots, currants & tamarind

Tamarhindi, the Arab name for tamarind, literally translates to "Indian date." It arrived in the Levant somewhere around the seventh century, having made its way there from India via Persia, but it never really caught on to become a household staple in the region's cuisine. Apart from Jerusalem, that is, where it is mostly known in its ultrasweet beverage form, sold cold under the scorching summer sun.

---

4 extra-large quail, about
  6½ oz / 190 g each, cut in
  half along the breastbone
  and back
¾ tsp chile flakes
¾ tsp ground cumin
½ tsp fennel seeds, lightly
  crushed
1 tbsp olive oil
1¼ cups / 300 ml water
5 tbsp / 75 ml white wine
⅔ cup / 80 g dried
  apricots, thickly sliced
2½ tbsp / 25 g currants
1½ tbsp superfine sugar
1½ tbsp tamarind paste
2 tbsp freshly squeezed
  lemon juice
1 tsp picked thyme leaves
salt and freshly ground
  black pepper
2 tbsp chopped mixed
  cilantro and flat-leaf
  parsley, to garnish
  (optional)

With its sweet-and-sour combination of meat and dried fruit, this dish is typical of the Sephardic tradition of cooking. It is pretty special and can be placed in the middle of a festive dining table (Christmas, perhaps?) with great pride. Quail can be replaced with boneless chicken thighs. Serve with plain rice, sprinkled with toasted pine nuts or almonds.

Wipe the quail with paper towels and place in a mixing bowl. Sprinkle with the chile flakes, cumin, fennel seeds, ½ teaspoon salt, and some black pepper. Massage well with your hands, then cover and leave to marinate in the fridge for at least 2 hours or overnight.

Heat the oil over medium-high heat in a frying pan that is just large enough to accommodate the birds snugly and for which you have a lid. Brown the birds on all sides for about 5 minutes, to get a nice golden brown color.

Remove the quail from the pan and discard most of the fat, leaving about 1½ teaspoons. Add the water, the wine, apricots, currants, sugar, tamarind, lemon juice, thyme, ½ teaspoon salt, and some black pepper. Return the quail to the pan. The water should come three-quarters up the sides of the birds; if not, add more water. Bring to a boil, cover the pan, and simmer very gently for 20 to 25 minutes, turning the quail over once or twice, until the birds are just cooked.

Lift the quail from the pan and onto a serving platter and keep warm. If the liquid isn't very thick, return it to medium heat and simmer for a few minutes to reduce to a good sauce consistency. Spoon the sauce over the quail and garnish with the cilantro and parsley, if using.

Roasted chicken with clementines & arak

6½ tbsp / 100 ml arak,
  ouzo, or Pernod
4 tbsp olive oil
3 tbsp freshly squeezed
  orange juice
3 tbsp freshly squeezed
  lemon juice
2 tbsp grain mustard
3 tbsp light brown sugar
2 medium fennel bulbs
  (1 lb / 500 g in total)
1 large organic or free-
  range chicken, about
  2¾ lb / 1.3 kg, divided
  into 8 pieces, or the same
  weight in skin-on, bone-in
  chicken thighs
4 clementines, unpeeled
  (14 oz / 400 g in total), cut
  horizontally into ¼-inch /
  0.5cm slices
1 tbsp thyme leaves
2½ tsp fennel seeds, lightly
  crushed
salt and freshly ground
  black pepper
chopped flat-leaf parsley,
  to garnish

All the intense flavors lavished on the poor chicken—arak, mustard, fennel, clementines with their skins, brown sugar—somehow manage to come together in a sweetly comforting dish you will always want to come back to. Serve it with plainly cooked rice or bulgur.

Put the first six ingredients in a large mixing bowl and add 2½ teaspoons salt and 1½ teaspoons black pepper. Whisk well and set aside.

Trim the fennel and cut each bulb in half lengthwise. Cut each half into 4 wedges. Add the fennel to the liquids, along with the chicken pieces, clementine slices, thyme, and fennel seeds. Stir well with your hands, then leave to marinate in the fridge for a few hours or overnight (skipping the marinating stage is also fine, if you are pressed for time).

Preheat the oven to 425°F / 220°C. Transfer the chicken and its marinade to a baking sheet large enough to accommodate everything comfortably in a single layer (roughly a 12 by 14½-inch / 30 by 37cm pan); the chicken skin should be facing up. Once the oven is hot enough, put the pan in the oven and roast for 35 to 45 minutes, until the chicken is colored and cooked through. Remove from the oven.

Lift the chicken, fennel, and clementines from the pan and arrange on a serving plate; cover and keep warm. Pour the cooking liquid into a small saucepan, place over medium-high heat, bring to a boil, and then simmer until the sauce is reduced by one-third, so you are left with about ⅓ cup / 80 ml. Pour the hot sauce over the chicken, garnish with some parsley, and serve.

Roasted chicken with Jerusalem artichoke & lemon

Jerusalem artichokes are well loved in the city but have actually got nothing to do with it; not officially anyway. The name is a distortion of the Italian name of this sunflower tuber, which has an artichoke-like flavor. From *girasole articiocco* to Jerusalem artichoke.

1 lb / 450 g Jerusalem artichokes, peeled and cut lengthwise into 6 wedges ⅔ inch / 1.5 cm thick

3 tbsp freshly squeezed lemon juice

8 skin-on, bone-in chicken thighs, or 1 medium whole chicken, quartered

12 banana or other large shallots, halved lengthwise

12 large cloves garlic, sliced

1 medium lemon, halved lengthwise and then very thinly sliced

1 tsp saffron threads

3½ tbsp / 50 ml olive oil

⅔ cup / 150 ml cold water

1½ tbsp pink peppercorns, lightly crushed

¼ cup / 10 g fresh thyme leaves

1 cup / 40 g tarragon leaves, chopped

2 tsp salt

½ tsp freshly ground black pepper

The combination of saffron and whole lemon slices not only makes for a beautiful-looking dish but also goes exceptionally well with the nutty earthiness of the artichokes. This is easy to prepare. You just need to plan ahead and leave it to marinate properly. Serve it with Mejadra (PAGE 120).

Put the Jerusalem artichokes in a medium saucepan, cover with plenty of water, and add half the lemon juice. Bring to a boil, lower the heat, and simmer for 10 to 20 minutes, until tender but not soft. Drain and leave to cool.

Place the Jerusalem artichokes and all the remaining ingredients, excluding the remaining lemon juice and half of the tarragon, in a large mixing bowl and use your hands to mix everything together well. Cover and leave to marinate in the fridge overnight, or for at least 2 hours.

Preheat the oven to 475°F / 240°C. Arrange the chicken pieces, skin side up, in the center of a roasting pan and spread the remaining ingredients around the chicken. Roast for 30 minutes. Cover the pan with aluminum foil and cook for a further 15 minutes. At this point, the chicken should be completely cooked. Remove from the oven and add the reserved tarragon and lemon juice. Stir well, taste, and add more salt if needed. Serve at once.

Poached chicken with sweet spiced freekeh

One of the most practical and fun ways of preparing meat and starch at the same time forms the basis of many fantastic Palestinian dishes. The technique involves poaching mutton or chicken in water, often flavored with sweet spices, then using the stock to cook a grain—rice, bulgur, *freekeh*, or *maftoul* (a kind of rough couscous). The meat is then served over the grain, topped with clarified butter and nuts, or served with yogurt or tomato sauce.

When we filmed a documentary for the BBC about food in Jerusalem, a family from the neighborhood of Atur, in the east of the city, cooked chicken and lamb together in this way and served it over *maftoul* with a simple yet delicious tomato and chickpea sauce. The incredible thing with all these is the intensity of flavor throughout the dish. Absolutely nothing is wasted.

Mansaf and *kidreh* are two festive examples, using lamb and saffron-flavored rice, served lavishly in a large, round platter. To cook *kidreh*, the rice and meat are arranged in layers in a special brass pot and topped with stock. As it requires long and slow cooking, these pots were often given to the local baker to put in his oven and cook for hours in the residual heat from the bread baking. Maqluba (PAGE 127) is a more everyday affair.

---

1 small free-range chicken, about 3¼ lb / 1.5 kg
2 long cinnamon sticks
2 medium carrots, peeled and cut into slices ¾ inch / 2 cm thick
2 bay leaves
2 bunches flat-leaf parsley (about 2½ oz / 70 g in total)
2 large onions
2 tbsp olive oil
2 cups / 300 g cracked freekeh
½ tsp ground allspice
½ tsp ground coriander
2½ tbsp / 40 g unsalted butter
⅔ cup / 60 g sliced almonds
salt and freshly ground black pepper

This is a hearty dish that is easy to prepare and leaves everybody very satisfied. Serve it with Yogurt with cucumber (PAGE 299). *Freekeh is a wonderfully aromatic smoked green cracked wheat* (FOR MORE INFORMATION, SEE PAGE 148)*; you can find it in Middle Eastern groceries. Bulgur is a good substitute; just reduce the amount of stock by about 10 percent and cook it for only 5 minutes.*

Place the chicken in a large pot, along with the cinnamon, carrots, bay leaves, 1 bunch of parsley, and 1 teaspoon salt. Quarter 1 onion and add it to the pot. Add cold water to almost cover the chicken; bring to a boil and simmer, covered, for 1 hour, occasionally skimming any oil and froth away from the surface.

About halfway through the cooking of the chicken, slice the second onion thinly and place it in a medium saucepan with the olive oil. Fry over medium-low heat for 12 to 15 minutes, until the onion turns golden brown and soft. Add the freekeh, allspice, coriander, ½ teaspoon salt, and some black pepper. Stir well and then add 2½ cups / 600 ml of the chicken broth. Turn the heat up to medium-high. As soon as the broth boils, cover the pan and lower the heat. Simmer gently for 20 minutes, then remove from the heat and leave covered for 20 minutes more.

Remove the leaves from the remaining parsley bunch and chop them up, not too fine. Add most of the chopped parsley to the cooked freekeh, mixing it in with a fork.

Lift the chicken out of the broth and place it on a cutting board. Carefully carve off the breasts and slice them thinly at an angle; remove the meat from the legs and thighs. Keep the chicken and the freekeh warm.

When ready to serve, place the butter, almonds, and some salt in a small frying pan and fry until golden. Spoon the freekeh onto individual serving dishes or one platter. Top with the leg and thigh meat, then arrange the breast slices neatly on top. Finish with the almonds and butter and a sprinkle of parsley.

Chicken with caramelized onion & cardamom rice

Although rice has never been grown locally, it has become a staple Palestinian grain and definitely the basic ingredient in all ceremonial meals (people of lesser means and from the countryside often had to make do with bulgur, which costs less).

Cooking meat with rice and water in one pot is a good way of introducing a good meaty flavor to the rice while keeping things relatively simple—no stock is needed and only one pot is used. Bukharan Jews (from Uzbekistan) have a more sophisticated version than the one below, called *plov*, which is at the center of all Bukharan celebrations. There, the chicken and rice are layered more carefully so that when the pan is inverted at the end, the chicken that was perfectly fried on the bottom now crowns the top of the elaborate creation.

---

3 tbsp / 40 g sugar

scant 3 tbsp / 40 ml water

2½ tbsp / 25 g barberries (or currants; see page 105)

4 tbsp olive oil

2 medium onions, thinly sliced (2 cups / 250 g in total)

2¼ lb / 1 kg skin-on, bone-in chicken thighs, or 1 whole chicken, quartered

10 cardamom pods

rounded ¼ tsp whole cloves

2 long cinnamon sticks, broken in two

1⅔ cups / 300 g basmati rice

2¼ cups / 550 ml boiling water

1½ tbsp / 5 g flat-leaf parsley leaves, chopped

½ cup / 5 g dill leaves, chopped

¼ cup / 5 g cilantro leaves, chopped

⅓ cup / 100 g Greek yogurt, mixed with 2 tbsp olive oil (optional)

salt and freshly ground black pepper

This chicken and rice casserole is the definition of comfort food. For an Aleppine variation, replace the chicken with 2-inch / 5cm pieces of good stewing beef. Boil it in some water with the spices until tender, 1 to 2 hours. Add liquid as needed to total 2 cups / 500 ml before adding the rice and onion. At the end, you can also stir in some cooked and skinned fava beans.

Put the sugar and water in a small saucepan and heat until the sugar dissolves. Remove from the heat, add the barberries, and set aside to soak. If using currants, you do not need to soak them in this way.

Meanwhile, heat half the olive oil in a large sauté pan for which you have a lid over medium heat, add the onion, and cook for 10 to 15 minutes, stirring occasionally, until the onion has turned a deep golden brown. Transfer the onion to a small bowl and wipe the pan clean.

Place the chicken in a large mixing bowl and season with 1½ teaspoons each salt and black pepper. Add the remaining olive oil, cardamom, cloves, and cinnamon and use your hands to mix everything together well. Heat the frying pan again and place the chicken and spices in it. Sear for 5 minutes on each side and remove from the pan (this is important as it part-cooks the chicken). The spices can stay in the pan, but don't worry if they stick to the chicken. Remove most of the remaining oil as well, leaving just a thin film at the bottom. Add the rice, caramelized onion, 1 teaspoon salt, and plenty of black pepper. Drain the barberries and add them as well. Stir well and return the seared chicken to the pan, pushing it into the rice.

Pour the boiling water over the rice and chicken, cover the pan, and cook over very low heat for 30 minutes. Take the pan off the heat, remove the lid, quickly place a clean tea towel over the pan, and seal again with the lid. Leave the dish undisturbed for another 10 minutes. Finally, add the herbs and use a fork to stir them in and fluff up the rice. Taste and add more salt and pepper if needed. Serve hot or warm with yogurt if you like.

Chopped liver

"Liver-flavor eggplant" is a weird-sounding, yet popular invention, which is probably one of the best products to expose the unique, often paradoxical history of the city over the last sixty years.

During the days of rationing, in the 1950s, Ashkenazic Jews couldn't afford to make one of their most loved dishes, chopped liver, second only to gefilte fish in its iconic value. A creative solution was found using eggplants, a cheap and abundant local ingredient, that was "made" to taste like the real thing. Still, over the years this dish, using an ingredient their eastern European Ashkenazic ancestors would have thought was a UFO, has become a hit with many and is now sold everywhere, enjoying particular popularity in Orthodox neighborhoods. The liver has turned into an eggplant within two generations, with the origins of the dish still carried on in the name.

6½ tbsp / 100 ml melted goose or duck fat
2 large onions, sliced (about 3 cups / 400 g in total)
14 oz / 400 g chicken livers, cleaned and broken down into roughly 1¼-inch / 3cm chunks
5 extra-large free-range eggs, hard boiled
4 tbsp dessert wine
1 tsp salt
½ tsp freshly ground black pepper
2 to 3 green onions, thinly sliced
1 tbsp chopped chives

Our "real" chicken liver is a fantastic way to start a meal. Serve it with little toasts or with slices of good white bread.

Place two-thirds of the goose fat in a large frying pan and fry the onions over medium heat for 10 to 15 minutes, stirring occasionally, until dark brown. Remove the onions from the pan, pushing them down a little as you do so, so that you are left with some fat in the pan. Add a little fat if needed. Add the livers and cook them for up to 10 minutes, stirring from time to time, until they are properly cooked in the middle—no blood should be coming out at this stage.

Mix the livers with the onion before chopping them together. The best way to do this is with a meat grinder, processing the mixture twice to get the right texture. If you don't have a meat grinder, a food processor is also fine. Blitz the onions and liver in two or three batches so the machine bowl isn't very full. Pulse for 20 to 30 seconds, then check, making sure the liver and onions have turned into a uniformly smooth, yet still "bumpy" paste. Transfer everything into a large mixing bowl.

Peel the eggs, then grate two of them roughly and another two finely and add them to the liver mixture. Add the remaining fat, the dessert wine, and the salt and pepper and fold everything together gently. Transfer the mix to a nonmetallic flat dish and cover the surface tightly with plastic wrap. Leave it to cool down, then store in the fridge for at least 2 hours to firm up a little.

To serve, finely chop the remaining egg. Spoon the chopped liver onto individual serving plates, garnish with the chopped egg, and sprinkle with the green onions and chives.

Snow on high ground

Only Jaffa and Jericho oranges were sold in Jerusalem when we were growing up. The city sits at quite a high altitude and therefore gets very cold in winter, while its air is dry throughout the year—not good for oranges, which need shelter and warmer temperatures.

We Jerusalemites are blessed, or not, depending on whom you ask, with a central European kind of climate: distinctly hot summers and cold winters. In Jerusalem we had central heating in homes and in classrooms, a completely foreign notion to most people in other parts of the country. Driving into Jericho or Tel Aviv, you felt like you had arrived in a tropical land: humid air, lush vegetation, and kids with no winter coats. Our perk, though, was snow.

——

GOSH, WE WERE OUT IN A NANOSECOND, THROWING SNOWBALLS, MAKING SNOWMEN, AND CONSTRUCTING MAKESHIFT SLIDES— A VERY SMALL PRICE TO PAY FOR NO ORANGE ORCHARDS.

——

Jerusalem is the only big city in Israel (though not in Palestine) to get snow. It didn't come every year, perhaps every other, and only settled occasionally, but, boy, we loved it, and milked it. The night before a cold-weather front was about to hit, we used to huddle around the radio and wait for the hugely anticipated news of "snow on high ground." And the cherry on this fluffy white cake would be an announcement that schools were closed for the day. Gosh, we were out in a nanosecond, throwing snowballs, making snowmen, and constructing makeshift slides—a very small price to pay for no orange orchards.

Saffron chicken & herb salad

1 orange
2½ tbsp / 50 g honey
½ tsp saffron threads
1 tbsp white wine vinegar
1¼ cups / about 300 ml
   water
2¼ lb / 1 kg skinless,
   boneless chicken breast
4 tbsp olive oil
2 small fennel bulbs, thinly
   sliced
1 cup / 15 g picked cilantro
   leaves
⅔ cup / 15 g picked basil
   leaves, torn
15 picked mint leaves, torn
2 tbsp freshly squeezed
   lemon juice
1 red chile, thinly sliced
1 clove garlic, crushed
salt and freshly ground
   black pepper

This colorful salad is extraordinarily moist and refreshing. It was created by the chefs at Ottolenghi in Belgravia and is a big hit there. The trick—boiling a whole orange and blitzing it down to a paste—is very effective for many sauces, salsas, and cakes. If you don't like fennel, replace it with a combination of green onion and arugula.

Preheat the oven to 400°F / 200°C. Trim and discard ⅜ inch / 1 cm off the top and tail of the orange and cut it into 12 wedges, keeping the skin on. Remove any seeds.

Place the wedges in a small saucepan with the honey, saffron, vinegar, and just enough water to cover the orange wedges. Bring to a boil and simmer gently for about an hour. At the end you should be left with soft orange and about 3 tablespoons of thick syrup; add water during the cooking if the liquid gets very low. Use a food processor to blitz the orange and syrup into a smooth, runny paste; again, add a little water if needed.

Mix the chicken breast with half the olive oil and plenty of salt and pepper and place on a very hot ridged griddle pan. Sear for about 2 minutes on each side to get clear char marks all over. Transfer to a roasting pan and place in the oven for 15 to 20 minutes, until just cooked.

Once the chicken is cool enough to handle but still warm, tear it with your hands into rough, quite large pieces. Place in a large mixing bowl, pour over half the orange paste, and stir well. (The other half you can keep in the fridge for a few days. It would make a good addition to an herb salsa to serve with oily fish such as mackerel or salmon.) Add the remaining ingredients to the salad, including the rest of the olive oil, and toss gently. Taste, add salt and pepper, and, if needed, more olive oil and lemon juice.

Chicken sofrito

Many of Jerusalem's most iconic dishes—and the most interesting, we dare say—are the result of necessity and straitened circumstances. The Palestinian population of the city and surrounding areas includes many comfortable city folk, but is mostly comprised of village people with very limited means. Of the Jews, the majority of the twentieth-century newcomers were poor in their countries of origin or, if not, became relatively poor in the first years after settling in the city. What all these people cooked, and still do to some extent, reflects the scarcity and costliness of many ingredients.

The Sephardic dish *sofrito*—actually more a cooking method than a dish—is a perfect example of how frugality yields some superb delicacies, and it became tremendously popular in Jerusalem. Originating from the Spanish verb *sofreír* (to fry lightly), it involves slowly cooking meat in a pot on the stove top for a long time, with only oil and very little liquid. The slow braising and steaming of the meat, in its own juices, results in a very tender texture with a distinguishably comforting flavor. This slow cooking method—practiced by Sephardim for centuries—meant that the dish could be made on a Friday for Shabbat and fitted perfectly with the lifestyle in Jerusalem, when, up until not too long ago, only cheap cuts of meat were realistically available and other ingredients were expensive.

---

1 tbsp sunflower oil
1 small free-range chicken, about 3¼ lb / 1.5 kg, butterflied or quartered
1 tsp sweet paprika
¼ tsp ground turmeric
¼ tsp sugar
2½ tbsp freshly squeezed lemon juice
1 large onion, peeled and quartered
sunflower oil, for frying
1⅔ lb / 750 g Yukon Gold potatoes, peeled, washed, and cut into ¾-inch / 2cm dice
25 cloves garlic, unpeeled
salt and freshly ground black pepper

We add potatoes to our sofrito, *which isn't necessary, but trust us, you will never regret doing so because they take on the most gorgeous flavors from the bottom of the pan. If you have a wide enough pan to hold the whole chicken flat, butterfly it by cutting through the center of the breast with a large knife, in between the two sides, until the bird opens up; you could also ask a butcher to do this for you. In the pan, press the bird down firmly so that it lies completely flat.*

Pour the oil into a large, shallow pan or Dutch oven and put over medium heat. Place the chicken flat in the pan, skin side down, and sear for 4 to 5 minutes, until golden brown. Season all over with the paprika, turmeric, sugar, scant ¼ teaspoon salt, a good grind of black pepper, and 1½ tablespoons of the lemon juice. Turn the chicken over so that the skin faces up, add the onion to the pan, and cover with a lid. Decrease the heat to low and cook for a total of about 1½ hours; this includes the time the chicken is cooked with the potatoes. Lift the lid every now and then to check the amount of liquid in the bottom of the pan. The idea is for the chicken to cook and steam in its own juices, but you may need to add a little bit of boiling water, just so that there is always ¼ inch / 5 mm of liquid at the bottom of the pan.

After the chicken has been cooking for about 30 minutes, pour sunflower oil into a medium saucepan to a depth of 1¼ inches / 3 cm and place over medium-high heat. Fry the potatoes and garlic together in a few batches for about 6 minutes per batch, until they take on some color and crisp up. Use a slotted spoon to lift each batch away from the oil and onto paper towels, then sprinkle with salt.

After the chicken has been cooking for 1 hour, lift it from the pan and spoon in the fried potatoes and garlic, stirring them with the cooking juices. Return the chicken to the pan, placing it on top of the potatoes for the remainder of the cooking time, that is, 30 minutes. The chicken should be falling off the bone and the potatoes should be soaked in the cooking liquid and completely soft. Drizzle with the remaining lemon juice when serving.

Meatballs

Together with cheesy pastries, pickled cucumbers, and a plate of hummus, meatballs are one of the ubiquitous Jerusalem dishes, celebrated by absolutely everyone—traditional Jews, fervent Christians, Palestinian eateries, and funky fusion chefs. But, like *polpette al sugo* (meatballs in tomato sauce) in Italy, they are essentially a "mama" food: something simple, basic, and familiar, yet loaded with memories and associations, and every Jerusalemite will have his or her own version.

There are hundreds of varieties of meatballs—*kofta* (in Arabic) and *ktsitsot* (in Hebrew)—each with its own unique heritage and specific preparation technique. It is, really, as a result of necessity more than anything that meatballs became such an essential part of the local food fabric. In a place where serving whole cuts of meat was, for most of its history, considered a mad extravagance, meatballs, kebabs, and stuffed vegetables (SEE PAGE 152) were a sensible alternative.

Meatballs can be made round, cigar shaped, or as small patties. They can have chopped up vegetables added to them (potato, zucchini, onion, turnip), cracked wheat, rice, bread, or couscous. They are sometimes cooked in sauces—tomato, lemon, tamarind, or stock based—or left plain and served with a wedge of lemon or a light salsa.

In Palestinian culture, the difference between *kofta* and kebab can cause some confusion to an outsider. Both are meatballs made from ground lamb, beef, veal, or a mixture of them. Often the meat is skilfully chopped by hand, using two large knives, along with the onion, garlic, and parsley, and then seasoned. In the Old City markets, kebab is sold on the street and in kebab shops, often served alongside pita, chopped salad, grilled onions, and tahini sauce. Kebab is always cooked on long steel skewers placed over coal. It is usually shaped into thick fingers.

Kofta, on the other hand, are normally cooked at home and can be made in any shape: flat patties, thin fingers, or torpedoes. They can be wrapped in vine or other leaves. They can be cooked on the stove top in sauce, grilled, or baked in the oven on a sheet pan (a *siniyah* in Arabic), often with other elements: tahini, tomato, or potato. Palestinian housewives sometimes get the butcher to grind the meat for their *kofta* together with parsley, garlic, and onion, saving them work and also ensuring that the flavors and textures are well blended.

PALESTINIAN HOUSEWIVES SOMETIMES GET THE BUTCHER TO GRIND THE MEAT FOR THEIR KOFTA TOGETHER WITH PARSLEY, GARLIC, AND ONION, SAVING THEM WORK AND ALSO ENSURING THAT THE FLAVORS AND TEXTURES ARE WELL BLENDED.

Kofta b'siniyah

⅔ cup / 150 g light tahini
   paste
3 tbsp freshly squeezed
   lemon juice
½ cup / 120 ml water
1 medium clove garlic,
   crushed
2 tbsp sunflower oil
2 tbsp / 30 g unsalted
   butter or ghee (optional)
toasted pine nuts, to
   garnish
finely chopped flat-leaf
   parsley, to garnish
sweet paprika, to garnish
salt

KOFTA

14 oz / 400 g ground lamb
14 oz / 400 g ground veal
   or beef
1 small onion (about 5 oz /
   150 g), finely chopped
2 large cloves garlic,
   crushed
7 tbsp / 50 g toasted pine
   nuts, coarsely chopped
½ cup / 30 g finely chopped
   flat-leaf parsley
1 large medium-hot red
   chile, seeded and finely
   chopped
1½ tsp ground cinnamon
1½ tsp ground allspice
¾ tsp grated nutmeg
1½ tsp freshly ground
   black pepper
1½ tsp salt

For these kofta, *buy your meat freshly ground by your butcher, if you can. The lamb should be shoulder and the beef a good nonstewing cut. If you get the meat from a supermarket or another grocer, cook it through, just to be on the safe side. Finish the dish with butter only if you are serving it straightaway and consuming it all at once. Otherwise, leave it out, as it sets quickly, which isn't very nice. Serve with pita and cucumber and tomato salad* (SPICED CHICKPEAS AND FRESH VEGETABLE SALAD, PAGE 56, MINUS THE CHICKPEAS).

Put all the kofta ingredients in a bowl and use your hands to mix everything together well. Now shape into long, torpedo-like fingers, roughly 3¼ inches / 8 cm long (about 2 oz / 60 g each). Press the mix to compress it and ensure each kofta is tight and keeps its shape. Arrange on a plate and chill until you are ready to cook them, for up to 1 day.

Preheat the oven to 425°F / 220°C. In a medium bowl, whisk together the tahini paste, lemon juice, water, garlic, and ¼ teaspoon salt. The sauce should be a bit runnier than honey; add 1 to 2 tablespoons water if needed.

Heat the sunflower oil in a large frying pan over high heat and sear the kofta. Do this in batches so they are not cramped together. Sear them on all sides until golden brown, about 6 minutes per batch. At this point, they should be medium-rare. Lift out of the pan and arrange on a baking sheet. If you want to cook them medium or well done, put the baking sheet in the oven now for 2 to 4 minutes.

Spoon the tahini sauce around the kofta so it covers the base of the pan. If you like, also drizzle some over the kofta, but leave some of the meat exposed. Place in the oven for a minute or two, just to warm up the sauce a little.

Meanwhile, if you are using the butter, melt it in a small saucepan and allow it to brown a little, taking care that it doesn't burn. Spoon the butter over the kofta as soon as they come out of the oven. Scatter with the pine nuts and parsley and then sprinkle with the paprika. Serve at once.

Beef meatballs with fava beans & lemon

4½ tbsp olive oil

2⅓ cups / 350 g fava beans, fresh or frozen

4 whole thyme sprigs

6 cloves garlic, sliced

8 green onions, cut at an angle into ¾-inch / 2cm segments

2½ tbsp freshly squeezed lemon juice

2 cups / 500 ml chicken stock

salt and freshly ground black pepper

1½ tsp each chopped flat-leaf parsley, mint, dill, and cilantro, to finish

MEATBALLS

10 oz / 300 g ground beef

5 oz / 150 g ground lamb

1 medium onion, finely chopped

scant 1 cup / 120 g bread crumbs

2 tbsp each chopped flat-leaf parsley, mint, dill, and cilantro

2 large cloves garlic, crushed

4 tsp baharat spice mix (store-bought or see recipe, page 299)

4 tsp ground cumin

2 tsp capers, chopped

1 egg, beaten

Fresh, sharp, and very, very tasty, these meatballs are our idea of the perfect spring supper dish. Serve them with Basmati rice and orzo (PAGE 103) and there isn't need for much else. Whole blanched almonds would be a good addition, for texture. Add them to the pan along with the unshelled fava beans.

Place all of the meatball ingredients in a large mixing bowl. Add ¾ teaspoon salt and plenty of black pepper and mix well with your hands. Form into balls about the same size as Ping-Pong balls. Heat 1 tablespoon of the olive oil over medium heat in an extra-large frying pan for which you have a lid. Sear half the meatballs, turning them until they are brown all over, about 5 minutes. Remove, add another 1½ teaspoons of the olive oil to the pan, and cook the other batch of meatballs. Remove from the pan and wipe it clean.

While the meatballs are cooking, throw the fava beans into a pot with plenty of salted boiling water and blanch for 2 minutes. Drain and refresh under cold water. Remove the skins from half the fava beans and discard the skins.

Heat the remaining 3 tablespoons olive oil over medium heat in the same pan in which you seared the meatballs. Add the thyme, garlic, and green onion and sauté for 3 minutes. Add the unpeeled fava beans, 1½ tablespoons of the lemon juice, ⅓ cup / 80 ml of the stock, ¼ teaspoon salt, and plenty of black pepper. The beans should be almost covered with liquid. Cover the pan and cook over low heat for 10 minutes.

Return the meatballs to the frying pan holding the fava beans. Add the remaining stock, cover the pan, and simmer gently for 25 minutes. Taste the sauce and adjust the seasoning. If it is very runny, remove the lid and reduce a little. Once the meatballs stop cooking, they will soak up a lot of the juices, so make sure there is still plenty of sauce at this point. You can leave the meatballs now, off the heat, until ready to serve.

Just before serving, reheat the meatballs and add a little water, if needed, to get enough sauce. Add the remaining herbs, the remaining 1 tablespoon lemon juice, and the peeled fava beans and stir very gently. Serve immediately.

Lamb meatballs with barberries, yogurt & herbs

1²⁄₃ lb / 750 g ground lamb

2 medium onions, finely chopped

²⁄₃ oz / 20 g flat-leaf parsley, finely chopped

3 cloves garlic, crushed

¾ tsp ground allspice

¾ tsp ground cinnamon

6 tbsp / 60 g barberries

1 large free-range egg

6½ tbsp / 100 ml sunflower oil

1½ lb / 700 g banana or other large shallots, peeled

¾ cup plus 2 tbsp / 200 ml white wine

2 cups / 500 ml chicken stock

2 bay leaves

2 thyme sprigs

2 tsp sugar

5 oz / 150 g dried figs

scant 1 cup / 200 g Greek yogurt

3 tbsp mixed mint, cilantro, dill, and tarragon, coarsely torn

salt and freshly ground black pepper

The sweet-and-sour flavors of these meatballs are prominent yet tempered by the yogurt, making this a very soothing main course, best served with couscous or rice. Barberries—small dried sour berries—are available online or from Middle Eastern groceries. They can be substituted with cranberries. The figs get quite soggy during the long cooking but are essential for the flavor they add. You can remove and discard them at the end if you wish.

Place the lamb, onions, parsley, garlic, allspice, cinnamon, barberries, egg, 1 teaspoon salt, and ½ teaspoon black pepper in a large bowl. Mix with your hands, then roll into balls about the size of golf balls.

Heat one-third of the oil over medium heat in a large, heavy-bottomed pot for which you have a tight-fitting lid. Put in a few meatballs and cook and turn them around for a few minutes until they color all over. Remove from the pot and set aside. Cook the remaining meatballs the same way.

Wipe the pot clean and add the remaining oil. Add the shallots and cook them over medium heat for 10 minutes, stirring frequently, until golden brown. Add the wine, leave to bubble for a minute or two, then add the chicken stock, bay leaves, thyme, sugar, and some salt and pepper. Arrange the figs and meatballs among and on top of the shallots; the meatballs need to be almost covered in liquid. Bring to a boil, cover with the lid, decrease the heat to very low, and leave to simmer for 30 minutes. Remove the lid and simmer for about another hour, until the sauce has reduced and intensified in flavor. Taste and add salt and pepper if needed.

Transfer to a large, deep serving dish. Whisk the yogurt, pour on top, and scatter with the herbs.

Turkey & zucchini burgers with green onion & cumin

1 lb / 500 g ground turkey
1 large zucchini, coarsely grated (scant 2 cups / 200 g in total)
3 green onions, thinly sliced
1 large free-range egg
2 tbsp chopped mint
2 tbsp chopped cilantro
2 cloves garlic, crushed
1 tsp ground cumin
1 tsp salt
½ tsp freshly ground black pepper
½ tsp cayenne pepper
about 6½ tbsp / 100 ml of sunflower oil, for searing

SOUR CREAM & SUMAC SAUCE

scant ½ cup / 100 g sour cream
scant ⅔ cup / 150 g Greek yogurt
1 tsp grated lemon zest
1 tbsp freshly squeezed lemon juice
1 small clove garlic, crushed
1½ tbsp olive oil
1 tbsp sumac
½ tsp salt
¼ tsp freshly ground black pepper

The creamy sumac sauce served with these burgers is fantastically sharp and will go well with most nonred meats (CHICKEN SOFRITO, PAGE 190, FOR EXAMPLE) and also with grilled vegetables and fritters. You can make it in advance, or double the quantity, and keep it refrigerated. After a day the flavors will mellow, so you may want to reinvigorate it by adding extra sumac and lemon juice. The burgers are very portable. You can have them as a snack from the fridge, and they are also ideal for taking to a friend's house or in a lunch box to work.

First make the sour cream sauce by placing all the ingredients in a small bowl. Stir well and set aside or chill until needed.

Preheat the oven to 425°F / 220°C. In a large bowl, combine all the ingredients for the meatballs except the sunflower oil. Mix with your hands and then shape into about 18 burgers, each weighing about 1½ oz / 45 g.

Pour enough sunflower oil into a large frying pan to form a layer about 1/16 inch / 2 mm thick on the pan bottom. Heat over medum heat until hot, then sear the meatballs in batches on all sides. Cook each batch for about 4 minutes, adding oil as needed, until golden brown.

Carefully transfer the seared meatballs to a baking sheet lined with waxed paper and place in the oven for 5 to 7 minutes, or until just cooked through. Serve warm or at room temperature, with the sauce spooned over or on the side.

Polpettone

On the Pesach (Passover) seder table of Yotam's Nonna Luciana, you could always count on finding a sliced meat loaf, beautifully presented, studded with pistachios and gherkins. It was served alongside other Italian Jewish delicacies, such as fried zucchini in vinegar and artichokes fried in olive oil, a creation of the Jews of Rome.

Polpettone is a very old dish of Italian Jews. Claudia Roden gives a much more complicated version than Luciana's in *The Book of Jewish Food*, originating from Piedmont. Hers is also cooked for Passover and it involves wrapping ground veal and turkey mixed with pistachios, egg, nutmeg, and garlic in turkey skin, and poaching this in turkey stock made out of the carcass. Talk about thrift!

In Jerusalem, Jews from Aleppo cook *koisat*, a meat loaf simpler than Luciana's *polpettone* but also stuffed with pistachios (Aleppo is known for the best pistachios and the nut is often referred to as an Aleppine pistachio). Ashkenazic Jews cook *klops*, which is a baked meat loaf, typically a simple—some would even say bland—dish, yet somehow it is highly popular.

---

3 large free-range eggs
1 tbsp chopped flat-leaf
   parsley
2 tsp olive oil
1 lb / 500 g ground beef
scant 1 cup / 100 g bread
   crumbs
½ cup / 60 g unsalted
   pistachios
½ cup / 80 g gherkins (3 or
   4), cut into ⅜-inch / 1cm
   pieces
7 oz / 200 g cooked beef
   tongue (or ham), thinly
   sliced
1 large carrot, cut into
   chunks
2 celery stalks, cut into
   chunks
1 thyme sprig
2 bay leaves
½ onion, sliced
1 tsp chicken stock base
boiling water, to cook
salt and freshly ground
   black pepper

Okay, this is not your average Ottolenghi dish. It is slightly challenging technically, but it is highly impressive and loved by everybody. Make it in advance, when you have a bit of time, and serve as a starter. The salsina, *diminutive for salsa (a grammatical form Yotam's dad enjoys using all the time), is a sharp, yet luscious sauce that can also come in handy with plainly prepared chicken or lamb.*

Start by making a flat omelet. Whisk together 2 of the eggs, the chopped parsley, and a pinch of salt. Heat the olive oil in a large frying pan (about 11 inches / 28 cm in diameter) over medium heat and pour in the eggs. Cook for 2 to 3 minutes, without stirring, until the eggs set into a thin omelet. Set aside to cool down.

In a large bowl, mix together the beef, bread crumbs, pistachios, gherkins, the remaining egg, 1 teaspoon salt, and ½ teaspoon pepper. Lay a large clean tea towel (you may want to use an old one you don't mind getting rid of; cleaning it will be a slight menace) over your work surface. Now take the meat mix and spread it on the towel, shaping it with your hands into a rectangular disk, ⅜ inch / 1 cm thick and roughly 12 by 10 inches / 30 by 25 cm. Keep the edges of the cloth clear.

Cover the meat with the tongue slices, leaving ¾ inch / 2 cm around the edge. Cut the omelet into 4 wide strips and spread them evenly over the tongue.

SALSINA VERDE

scant 2 oz / 50 g flat-leaf
  parsley sprigs
1 clove garlic, crushed
1 tbsp capers
1 tbsp freshly squeezed
  lemon juice
1 tbsp white wine vinegar
1 large free-range egg,
  hard boiled and peeled
⅔ cup / 150 ml olive oil
3 tbsp bread crumbs,
  preferably fresh
salt and freshly ground
  black pepper

Lift the cloth to help you start rolling the meat inward from one of its wide sides. Continue rolling the meat into a large sausage shape, using the towel to assist you. In the end you want a tight, jelly-roll-like loaf, with the ground beef on the outside and the omelet in the center. Cover the loaf with the towel, wrapping it up well so it is sealed inside. Tie the ends with string and tuck any excess cloth underneath the log so you end up with a tightly bound bundle.

Place the bundle inside a large pan or Dutch oven. Throw the carrot, celery, thyme, bay, onion, and stock base around the loaf and pour over boiling water to almost cover it. Cover the pot with a lid and leave to simmer for 2 hours.

Remove the loaf from the pan and set it aside to allow some of the liquid to drain (the poaching stock would make a great soup base). After about 30 minutes, place something heavy on top to remove more of the juices. Once it reaches room temperature, put the meat loaf in the fridge, still covered in cloth, to chill thoroughly, 3 to 4 hours.

For the sauce, put all the ingredients in a food processor and pulse to a coarse consistency (or, for a rustic look, chop the parsley, capers, and egg by hand and stir together with the rest of the ingredients). Taste and adjust the seasoning.

To serve, remove the loaf from the towel, cut into slices ⅜ inch / 1 cm thick, and layer on a serving plate. Serve the sauce on the side.

Braised eggs with lamb, tahini & sumac

This concoction is Jerusalem fusion food at its very best. It incorporates traditional elements that are purely Palestinian with ingredients characteristic of various Jewish cuisines, and puts them all together in a completely nontraditional way. It was inspired by a very young classic, *hamshukah*, signature dish at Machneyuda, the market restaurant that currently serves the most innovative food in town.

This dish can be served at the center of an informal supper. The flavors are intense and the contrasting colors and textures are also pretty dramatic, so you should really serve it on its own, with minimal distractions and just a piece of bread. The list of ingredients isn't set in stone. Other typical Jerusalem ingredients—roasted eggplant, red pepper strips, Swiss chard, cooked chickpeas, chopped almonds, za'atar—can be added or used as substitutes. The various components can be prepared in advance and cooked together at the very last minute.

1 tbsp olive oil
1 large onion, finely chopped (1¼ cups / 200 g in total)
6 cloves garlic, sliced thinly
10 oz / 300 g ground lamb
2 tsp sumac, plus extra to finish
1 tsp ground cumin
scant ½ cup / 50 g toasted unsalted pistachios, crushed
7 tbsp / 50 g toasted pine nuts
2 tsp harissa paste (store-bought or see recipe, page 301)
1 tbsp finely chopped preserved lemon peel (store-bought or see recipe, page 303)
1⅓ cups / 200 g cherry tomatoes
½ cup / 120 ml chicken stock
4 large free-range eggs
¼ cup / 5 g picked cilantro leaves, or 1 tbsp Zhoug (page 301)
salt and freshly ground black pepper

YOGURT SAUCE

scant ½ cup / 100 g Greek yogurt
1½ tbsp / 25 g tahini paste
2 tbsp freshly squeezed lemon juice
1 tbsp water

Heat the olive oil over medium-high heat in a medium, heavy-bottomed frying pan for which you have a tight-fitting lid. Add the onion and garlic and sauté for 6 minutes to soften and color a bit. Raise the heat to high, add the lamb, and brown well, 5 to 6 minutes. Season with the sumac, cumin, ¾ teaspoon salt, and some black pepper and cook for another minute. Turn off the heat, stir in the nuts, harissa, and preserved lemon and set aside.

While the onion is cooking, heat a separate small cast-iron or other heavy pan over high heat. Once piping hot, add the cherry tomatoes and char for 4 to 6 minutes, tossing them in the pan occasionally, until slightly blackened on the outside. Set aside.

Prepare the yogurt sauce by whisking together all the ingredients with a pinch of salt. It needs to be thick and rich, but you may need to add a splash of water if it is stiff.

You can leave the meat, tomatoes, and sauce at this stage for up to an hour. When you are ready to serve, reheat the meat, add the chicken stock, and bring to a boil. Make 4 small wells in the mix and break an egg into each well. Cover the pan and cook the eggs over low heat for 3 minutes. Place the tomatoes on top, avoiding the yolks, cover again, and cook for 5 minutes, until the egg whites are cooked but the yolks are still runny.

Remove from the heat and dot with dollops of the yogurt sauce, sprinkle with sumac, and finish with the cilantro. Serve at once.

Slow-cooked veal with prunes & leek

A unique piece of Jerusalem food is the cuisine of some Sephardic Jews, also referred to as Spanioli, a proud community that has lived in the city for many generations, long before the advent of Zionism. Because many of them arrived from Spain after the Jewish expulsion of 1492, either directly or via other countries, their dishes are a real fusion of old Spanish food, elements picked up along the route, plus local Arab traditions and influences of the Ashkenazic Jews of the city. The result is the most fascinating mishmash, including, among others, *albóndigas* (Spanish meatballs), stuffed savory pastries from Turkey and the Balkans, many of the iconic Palestinian mezes, and *kugel* (noodles and caramel slowly cooked in a pot overnight), an Ashkenazic staple to which the Sephardim added tons of black pepper (we are more than happy to skip this one if offered it).

The combination of meat and dried fruit, as in this dish, is a clear mark of most Sephardic traditions. This clearly differentiates Sephardic cuisine from Palestinian cooking, which never mixes sweet and savory, despite many other similarities.

scant ½ cup / 110 ml sunflower oil
4 large osso buco steaks, on the bone (about 2¼ lb / 1 kg in total)
2 large onions, finely chopped (about 3 cups / 500 g in total)
3 cloves garlic, crushed
6½ tbsp / 100 ml dry white wine
1 cup / 250 ml chicken or beef stock
one 14-oz / 400g can chopped tomatoes
5 thyme sprigs, leaves finely chopped
2 bay leaves
zest of ½ orange, in strips
2 small cinnamon sticks
½ tsp ground allspice
2 star anise
6 large leeks, white part only (1¾ lb / 800 g in total), cut into ⅔-inch / 1.5cm slices
7 oz / 200 g soft prunes, pitted
salt and freshly ground black pepper

TO SERVE
½ cup / 120 g Greek yogurt
2 tbsp finely chopped flat-leaf parsley
2 tbsp grated lemon zest
2 cloves garlic, crushed

This dish takes about four hours to cook and is fairly complex, but the result is quite spectacular. Instead of osso buco steaks, which aren't always easy to get and are expensive, 3¼ lb / 1.5 kg of oxtail can be used here. You'd need to work just a little bit harder getting the meat off the bones, but the flavor is as good. Serve with Mejadra (PAGE 120) *or plain rice.*

Preheat the oven to 350°F / 180°C.

Heat 2 tablespoons of the oil in a large, heavy-bottomed pan over high heat. Fry the veal pieces for 2 minutes on each side, browning the meat well. Transfer to a colander to drain while you prepare the tomato sauce.

Remove most of the fat from the pan, add 2 more tablespoons of the oil, and add the onions and garlic. Return to medium-high heat and sauté, stirring occasionally and scraping the bottom of the pan with a wooden spoon, for about 10 minutes, until the onions are soft and golden. Add the wine, bring to a boil, and simmer vigorously for 3 minutes, until most of it has evaporated. Add half the stock, the tomatoes, thyme, bay, orange zest, cinnamon, allspice, star anise, 1 teaspoon salt, and some black pepper. Stir well and bring to a boil. Add the veal pieces to the sauce and stir to coat.

Transfer the veal and sauce to a deep baking pan about 13 by 9½ inches / 33 by 24 cm, and spread it around evenly. Cover with aluminum foil and place in the oven for 2½ hours. Check a couple of times during the cooking to make sure the sauce is not becoming too thick and burning around the sides; you'll probably need to add a little water to prevent this. The meat is ready when it comes away easily from the bone. Lift the veal from the sauce and place it in a large bowl. When it is cool enough to handle, pick all the meat from the bones and use a small knife to scrape out all the marrow. Discard the bones.

Heat the remaining oil in a separate frying pan and brown the leeks well over high heat for about 3 minutes, stirring occasionally. Spoon them over the tomato sauce. Next, in the pan in which you made the tomato sauce, mix together the prunes, the remaining stock, and the pulled meat and bone marrow and spoon this over the leeks. Re-cover with the foil and continue to cook for another hour. Once out of the oven, taste and season with salt and more black pepper if needed.

Serve hot, with cold yogurt spooned on top and sprinkled with a mixture of the parsley, lemon zest, and garlic.

Lamb

Before chicken, lamb and mutton were the key meats in the Palestinian diet. Shepherds were prevalent all around the hills of Jerusalem when we were children, and still are now, although to a lesser extent. Lamb is slaughtered on special occasions and is a sign of celebration—births, weddings, return of a family member— and religious holidays, such as Easter and Eid al-Adha (Festival of Sacrifice or "Greater Eid"). Lamb and mutton are in many ways the essence of Palestinian cooking. The best-quality lamb is sold by Palestinian butchers, a fact recognized by many chefs in Tel Aviv, who regularly get their supply from them.

_____

THE BEST-QUALITY LAMB IS SOLD BY PALESTINIAN BUTCHERS, A FACT RECOGNIZED BY MANY CHEFS IN TEL AVIV, WHO REGULARLY GET THEIR SUPPLY FROM THEM.

——

In their book, *The Flavor of Jerusalem*, Joan Nathan and Judy Stacey Goldman mention a lamb recipe they found in the 1970s in the Anglican Church's school in Jerusalem. It consists of lamb, potatoes, peas, and mint, a very English-sounding recipe but made quite local by the fact that the peas and mint are added shortly before serving, keeping them bright and fresh.

The Anglican Christ Church in Jerusalem, built in the 1840s, is the oldest Anglican church in the Middle East. The bishop of the church in Jerusalem at the time was a converted Jew, Michael Solomon Alexander. One of his missions was to convert local Jews to Anglicanism. He built a house that supplied free food to the city's poor. Not many came. Only when he started serving kosher soups and bread did his mission start to pick up speed.

Lamb shawarma

Jerusalem proudly boasts its own indigenous Hebrew vocabulary, made up of random words that substitute the common names for words like licorice, piggyback, lollipop, and others. The flatbread referred to in the city as *esh tanur* (burning furnace) is the carb of choice for encasing *shawarma*, slices of spiced meat and fat arranged on a large spit that rotates continuously near a hot grill and is regularly "shaved" with a large knife for passing customers. In addition to the meat, the flatbread includes chopped salad, tahini, fries, pickles, and *amba*, a mango and fenugreek sauce originally from India that has been adopted into the Jewish version of *shawarma* via Iraqi immigrants.

Sami remembers that when he was growing up going for *shawarma* was a bit of a luxury, as it was quite expensive. In Arab shops it was sold in a pita with a condiment of onion marinated with salt and sumac. The fries had to be good!

This is hardly a proper shawarma *recipe. But then again, we wouldn't expect most readers to have a vertical rotating spit at home. Still, the marinated lamb leg ends up tasting close enough to the real thing, which is as common and popular in Jerusalem as it is everywhere else in the Middle East.*

The first eleven ingredients, also known as Lebanese spice mix (SIMILAR TO THE YEMENITE HAWAYEJ ON PAGE 226), *make a versatile mixture that can be used to marinate fish, meat, or root vegetables before roasting or grilling. You can double their quantity and keep half in a sealed jar for up to three weeks. If you don't have a spice grinder, you can use a mortar and pestle to make this mix, but you would need to substitute ground cinnamon for cinnamon sticks, cardamom powder for pods, and leave out the star anise.*

Always serve the shawarma *with fresh cucumber and tomato salad, dressed with lemon juice, olive oil, garlic, and chopped parsley or cilantro. It really needs the freshness and moisture. On top of that, you can serve rice or bulgur and/or Tahini sauce* (PAGE 298). *If you wish, you can add some peeled waxy potatoes to the roasting pan about 1½ hours before the lamb is ready, and toss them in the cooking liquids every now and then as they roast.*

---

2 tsp black peppercorns
5 whole cloves
½ tsp cardamom pods
¼ tsp fenugreek seeds
1 tsp fennel seeds
1 tbsp cumin seeds
1 star anise
½ cinnamon stick
½ whole nutmeg, grated
¼ tsp ground ginger
1 tbsp sweet paprika
1 tbsp sumac
2½ tsp Maldon sea salt
scant 1 oz / 25 g fresh
  ginger, grated
3 cloves garlic, crushed
⅔ cup / 40 g chopped
  cilantro, stems and
  leaves
¼ cup / 60 ml freshly
  squeezed lemon juice
½ cup / 120 ml peanut oil
1 bone-in leg of lamb, about
  5½ to 6½ lb / 2.5 to 3 kg
1 cup / 240 ml boiling
  water

Put the first 8 ingredients in a cast-iron pan and dry-roast over medium-high heat for a minute or two, until the spices begin to pop and release their aromas. Take care not to burn them. Add the nutmeg, ginger, and paprika, toss for a few more seconds, just to heat them, then transfer to a spice grinder. Process the spices to a uniform powder. Transfer to a medium bowl and stir in all the remaining ingredients, except the lamb.

Use a small, sharp knife to score the leg of lamb in a few places, making slits ⅔ inch / 1.5 cm deep through the fat and meat to allow the marinade to seep in. Place in a large roasting pan and rub the marinade all over the lamb; use your hands to massage the meat well. Cover the pan with aluminum foil and leave aside for at least a couple of hours or, preferably, chill overnight.

Preheat the oven to 325°F / 170°C.

Put the lamb in the oven with its fatty side facing up and roast for a total of about 4½ hours, until the meat is completely tender. After 30 minutes of roasting, add the boiling water to the pan and use this liquid to baste the meat every hour or so. Add more water, as needed, making sure there is always about ¼ inch / 0.5 cm in the bottom of the pan. For the last 3 hours, cover the lamb with foil to prevent the spices from burning. Once done, remove the lamb from the oven and leave to rest for 10 minutes before carving and serving.

> The best way to serve this, to our mind, is inspired by Israel's most renowned *shakshuka* eatery (SEE RECIPE, PAGE 66), Dr Shakshuka, in Jaffa, owned by Bino Gabso. Take six individual pita pockets and brush them liberally inside with a spread made by mixing together ⅔ cup / 120 g chopped canned tomatoes, 2 teaspoons / 20 g harissa paste, 4 teaspoons / 20 g tomato paste, 1 tablespoon olive oil, and some salt and pepper. When the lamb is ready, warm the pitas in a hot ridged griddle pan until they get nice char marks on both sides. Slice the warm lamb and cut the slices into ⅔-inch / 1.5cm strips. Pile them high over each warm pita, spoon over some of the roasting liquids from the pan, reduced, and finish with chopped onion, chopped parsley, and a sprinkle of sumac. And don't forget the fresh cucumber and tomato. It's a heavenly dish.

See picture on the following page

FISH

Fish in Jerusalem

Jerusalem is not a city of fish. Situated on the verge of the Judean Desert, and with no substantial water source nearby, fish dishes were never a culinary focal point. As a kid, Sami can only remember one fish shop in the whole of the Old City, as opposed to dozens of butchers.

Still, twentieth-century immigration and technology brought fish onto the tables of many Jerusalemites, particularly Jewish immigrants who brought with them old traditions and cooking methods. In Machne Yehuda market and in some supermarkets, fish tanks full of live carp were a highlight. The person in charge would lift one out with a small net, hit it on the head, clean it, and wrap it in newspaper. For a city child, it was a mesmerizing experience, as close as one gets to an African safari.

INGENIOUS RELATIVES GOT BUSY INVENTING ALL SORTS OF CREATIVE WAYS TO DISTRACT THE SOLDIERS AND SNEAK SOME BEAUTIFUL FRESH FISH ACROSS THE BARBED WIRE.

In their book, *The Flavor of Jerusalem*, Joan Nathan and Judy Stacey Goldman tell this story about fish, or the lack of them: As a result of Jerusalem's division in 1948, between 1948 and 1967 a barbed wire barrier ran through the middle of Beit Tsafafa, dividing this Arab village in southwest Jerusalem between Jordan and Israel. Families were separated and neighbors and relatives divided. Residents of the Jordanian side of Beit Tsafafa were also cut off from the Mediterranean and its fish. To deal with the situation, their ingenious relatives got busy inventing all sorts of creative ways to distract the soldiers and sneak some beautiful fresh fish across the barbed wire.

Panfried sea bass with harissa & rose

3 tbsp harissa paste
  (store-bought or see
  recipe, page 301)
1 tsp ground cumin
4 sea bass fillets, about
  1 lb / 450 g in total,
  skinned and with pin
  bones removed
all-purpose flour, for
  dusting
2 tbsp olive oil
2 medium onions, finely
  chopped
6½ tbsp / 100 ml red
  wine vinegar
1 tsp ground cinnamon
scant 1 cup / 200 ml water
1½ tbsp honey
1 tbsp rose water
scant ½ cup / 60 g currants
  (optional)
2 tbsp coarsely chopped
  cilantro (optional)
2 tsp small dried edible
  rose petals
salt and freshly ground
  black pepper

This dish originates from Bizerte, the northernmost city in Africa. It is sweet and spicy and beautifully aromatic. It is adapted from a recipe kindly given to us by Rafram Hadad (SEE MORE ON HADAD ON PAGE 244). Serve it as a main course with some plain rice or couscous and something green, like sautéed spinach or Swiss chard. Dried rose petals are available in Middle Eastern stores and also online.

First marinate the fish. Mix together half the harissa paste, the ground cumin, and ½ teaspoon salt in a small bowl. Rub the paste all over the fish fillets and leave them to marinate for 2 hours in the fridge.

Dust the fillets with a little flour and shake off the excess. Heat the olive oil in a wide frying pan over medium-high heat and fry the fillets for 2 minutes on each side. You may need to do this in two batches. Set the fish aside, leave the oil in the pan, and add the onions. Stir as you cook for about 8 minutes, until the onions are golden.

Add the remaining harissa, the vinegar, the cinnamon, ½ teaspoon salt, and plenty of black pepper. Pour in the water, lower the heat, and let the sauce simmer gently for 10 to 15 minutes, until quite thick.

Add the honey and rose water to the pan along with the currants, if using, and simmer gently for a couple more minutes. Taste and adjust the seasoning and then return the fish fillets to the pan; you can slightly overlap them if they don't quite fit. Spoon the sauce over the fish and leave them to warm up in the simmering sauce for 3 minutes; you may need to add a few tablespoons of water if the sauce is very thick. Serve warm or at room temperature, sprinkled with the cilantro, if using, and the rose petals.

Fish & caper kebabs with burnt eggplant & lemon pickle

Capers are not widely used in any of the local cuisines but the plants are abundant in the city. They are extremely hardy and grow out of cracks in stone walls. In fact, the Wailing Wall is covered with small caper bushes. The buds must be picked and pickled before the bush flowers, quite beautifully, around April and May.

---

2 medium eggplants (about 1⅔ lb / 750 g in total)
2 tbsp Greek yogurt
1 clove garlic, crushed
2 tbsp chopped flat-leaf parsley
about 2 tbsp sunflower oil, for frying
2 tsp Quick Pickled Lemons (page 303)
salt and freshly ground black pepper

FISH KEBABS

14 oz / 400 g haddock or any other white fish fillets, skinned and pin bones removed
½ cup / 30 g fresh bread crumbs
½ large free-range egg, beaten
2½ tbsp / 20 g capers, chopped
⅔ oz / 20 g dill, chopped
2 green onions, finely chopped
grated zest of 1 lemon
1 tbsp freshly squeezed lemon juice
¾ tsp ground cumin
½ tsp ground turmeric
½ tsp salt
¼ tsp ground white pepper

The combination of the kebabs with the eggplant and pickled lemon makes a wonderfully rich main course; serve it with plain rice or bulgur. The lemon and eggplant condiments, however, are not necessary. You can easily serve the kebabs as a starter with just a squeeze of lemon and a small green salad.

Start with the eggplants. Burn, peel, and drain the eggplant flesh following the instructions in the Burnt eggplant with garlic, lemon, and pomegranate seeds recipe (PAGE 79). Once well drained, coarsely chop the flesh and place in a mixing bowl. Add the yogurt, garlic, parsley, 1 teaspoon salt, and plenty of black pepper. Set aside.

Cut the fish into very thin slices, only about 1/16 inch / 2 mm thick. Cut the slices into tiny dice and put in a medium mixing bowl. Add the remaining ingredients and stir well. Dampen your hands and shape the mixture into 12 patties or fingers, about 1½ oz / 45 g each. Arrange on a plate, cover with plastic wrap, and leave in the fridge for at least 30 minutes.

Pour enough oil into a frying pan to form a thin film on the bottom and place over medium-high heat. Cook the kebabs in batches for 4 to 6 minutes for each batch, turning until colored on all sides and cooked through.

Serve the kebabs while still hot, 3 per portion, alongside the burnt eggplant and a small amount of pickled lemon (careful, the lemons tend to dominate).

Panfried mackerel with golden beet & orange salsa

Although oranges aren't grown in Jerusalem, the famous Jaffa oranges, cultivated along the coast, have made their mark on the city's skyline, sort of.

In 1860, during the Ottoman rule, a complex of buildings was erected in Jerusalem by the Russian czar to serve the increasing number of Russian Christian pilgrims arriving in the city during Christmas and Easter. This included hostels, a hospital, a bathhouse, and a church that were later used as the British headquarters during their mandate. The whole area became known as Migrash Harussim, or the Russian Compound.

In 1964, Israel signed a rental agreement with the Soviet Union for the right to use this property. The deal became known as "the oranges deal," as nearly half the sum was paid out in exported Jaffa oranges.

The salsa for the fish is inspired by a Moroccan orange and olive salad. You can add some bitter leaves and make it into a salad. Red beets can be used instead of golden.

---

1 tbsp harissa paste (store-bought or see recipe, page 301)
1 tsp ground cumin
4 mackerel fillets (about 9 oz / 260 g in total), with skin
1 medium golden beet (3½ oz / 100 g in total)
1 medium orange
1 small lemon, halved widthwise
¼ cup / 30 g pitted Kalamata olives, quartered lengthwise
½ small red onion, finely chopped (¼ cup / 40 g in total)
¼ cup / 15 g chopped flat-leaf parsley
½ tsp coriander seeds, toasted and crushed
¾ tsp cumin seeds, toasted and crushed
½ tsp sweet paprika
½ tsp chile flakes
1 tbsp hazelnut or walnut oil
½ tsp olive oil
salt

Mix together the harissa paste, ground cumin, and a pinch of salt and rub the mixture into the mackerel fillets. Set aside in the fridge until ready to cook.

Boil the beet in plenty of water for about 20 minutes (it may take much longer, depending on the variety), until a skewer slides in smoothly. Allow to cool down, then peel, cut into ¼-inch / 0.5cm dice, and place in a mixing bowl.

Peel the orange and 1 lemon half, getting rid of all the outer pith, and cut them into quarters. Remove the middle pith and any seeds and cut the flesh into ¼-inch / 0.5cm dice. Add to the beet along with the olives, red onion, and parsley.

In a separate bowl, mix together the spices, the juice of the remaining lemon half, and the nut oil. Pour this onto the beet and orange mix, stir, and season to taste with salt. It's best to allow the salsa to stand at room temperature for at least 10 minutes to allow all the flavors to mingle.

Just before serving, heat the olive oil in a large nonstick frying pan over medium heat. Place the mackerel fillets skin side down in the pan, and cook, turning once, for about 3 minutes, until cooked through. Transfer to serving plates and spoon the salsa on top.

Cod cakes in tomato sauce

3 slices white bread,
  crusts removed (about
  2 oz / 60 g in total)
1⅓ lb / 600 g cod
  (sustainably sourced),
  halibut, hake, or pollock
  fillet, skinned and pin
  bones removed
1 medium onion, finely
  chopped (about 1 cup /
  150 g in total)
4 cloves garlic, crushed
1 oz / 30 g flat-leaf parsley,
  finely chopped
1 oz / 30 g cilantro, finely
  chopped
1 tbsp ground cumin
1½ tsp salt
2 extra-large free-range
  eggs, beaten
4 tbsp olive oil

TOMATO SAUCE

2½ tbsp olive oil
1½ tsp ground cumin
½ tsp sweet paprika
1 tsp ground coriander
1 medium onion, chopped
½ cup / 125 ml dry white
  wine
one 14-oz / 400g can
  chopped tomatoes
1 red chile, seeded and
  finely chopped
1 clove garlic, crushed
2 tsp superfine sugar
2 tbsp mint leaves,
  coarsely chopped
salt and freshly ground
  black pepper

With their sweet and slightly sharp sauce, these fish cakes, typical of Syrian Jews, manage to capture much of the spirit of Sephardic food. They are delicate, almost brittle, and thus very comforting and very popular, perfect for a large family gathering where there are many, often fussy diners to please. The cakes are almost better the day after they are cooked; just remember to bring them back to room temperature or warm them up before serving. Serve with bulgur, rice, couscous, or bread, alongside sautéed spinach or Swiss chard.

First, make the tomato sauce. Heat the olive oil over medium heat in a very large frying pan for which you have a lid. Add the spices and onion and cook for 8 to 10 minutes, until the onion is completely soft. Add the wine and simmer for 3 minutes. Add the tomatoes, chile, garlic, sugar, ½ teaspoon salt, and some black pepper. Simmer for about 15 minutes, until quite thick. Taste to adjust the seasoning and set aside.

While the sauce is cooking, make the fish cakes. Place the bread in a food processor and blitz to form bread crumbs. Chop the fish very finely and place in a bowl along with the bread and everything else, except the olive oil. Mix together well and then, using your hands, shape the mixture into compact cakes about ¾ inch / 2 cm thick and 3¼ inches / 8 cm in diameter. You should have 8 cakes. If they are very soft, refrigerate for 30 minutes to firm up. (You can also add some dried bread crumbs to the mix, though do this sparingly; the cakes need to be quite wet.)

Heat half the olive oil in a frying pan over medium-high heat, add half of the cakes, and sear for 3 minutes on each side, until well colored. Repeat with the remaining cakes and oil.

Gently place the seared cakes side by side in the tomato sauce; you can squeeze them a bit so they all fit. Add just enough water to cover the cakes partially (about a scant 1 cup / 200 ml). Cover the pan with the lid and simmer over very low heat for 15 to 20 minutes. Turn off the heat and leave the cakes to settle, uncovered, for at least 10 minutes before serving warm or at room temperature, sprinkled with the mint.

Grilled fish skewers with hawayej & parsley

2¼ lb / 1 kg firm white fish
fillets, such as monkfish
or halibut, skinned, pin
bones removed, and cut
into 1-inch / 2.5cm cubes
scant 1 cup / 50 g finely
chopped flat-leaf parsley
2 large cloves garlic,
crushed
½ tsp chile flakes
1 tbsp freshly squeezed
lemon juice
2 tbsp olive oil
salt
lemon wedges, to serve

15 to 18 long bamboo
skewers, soaked in water
for 1 hour

HAWAYEJ SPICE MIX

1 tsp black peppercorns
1 tsp coriander seeds
1½ tsp cumin seeds
4 whole cloves
½ tsp ground cardamom
1½ tsp ground turmeric

Hawayej is a high-potency Yemeni spice mix used to flavor hearty soups and stews. Here we apply it to fish, which it lifts and spices up tremendously well. Cook this on a grill or a barbecue and serve alongside Balilah (PAGE 102), Fattoush (PAGE 29), Yogurt with cucumber (PAGE 299), or a simple diced tomato and red onion salad with vinegar and olive oil.

Start with the hawayej mix. Place the peppercorns, coriander, cumin, and cloves in a spice grinder or mortar and work until finely ground. Add the ground cardamom and turmeric, stir well, and transfer to a large mixing bowl.

Place the fish, parsley, garlic, chile flakes, lemon juice, and 1 teaspoon salt in the bowl with the hawayej spices. Mix well with your hands, massaging the fish in the spice mixture until all pieces are well coated. Cover the bowl and, ideally, leave to marinate in the fridge for 6 to 12 hours. If you can't spare that time, don't worry; an hour should also be fine.

Place a ridged griddle pan over high heat and leave for about 4 minutes until hot. Meanwhile, thread the fish chunks onto the skewers, 5 to 6 pieces on each, making sure to leave gaps between the pieces. Gently brush the fish with a little olive oil and place the skewers on the hot griddle in 3 to 4 batches so they aren't too close together. Grill for about 1½ minutes on each side, until the fish is just cooked through. Alternatively, cook them on a grill or under a broiler, where they will take about 2 minutes on each side to cook.

Serve immediately with the lemon wedges.

Fricassee salad

This salad is a deconstruction of Tunisian fricassee: a fried bun stuffed with tuna, harissa, olives, anchovies, a spicy pumpkin relish, pickled lemon, cooked potato, and hard-boiled egg. We are not quite sure how it got to signify something so different from the common French term *fricassée*, which is a type of meat stew, but the resemblance to another French classic, Niçoise salad, is no coincidence and is evidence of the interaction between French and Tunisian cuisines during the years of French occupation. The fried buns arrived in Jerusalem in the mid-twentieth century with Tunisian immigrants and joined a long list of favorite fast foods.

Here we confit fresh tuna, a method of preservation that gives the fish both a rich flavor and a wonderful texture. Use olive oil of the best quality and reuse it later for preparing other fish and seafood dishes. You can, however, skip the long process of preservation by getting a good canned tuna. We like Ortiz brand the best, though it is expensive. Turn this into a sandwich by halving the amount of potato and sticking everything inside a hearty baguette.

4 rosemary sprigs
4 bay leaves
3 tbsp black peppercorns
about 1⅔ cups / 400 ml extra virgin olive oil
10½ oz / 300 g tuna steak, in one piece or two
1⅓ lb / 600 g Yukon Gold potatoes, peeled and cut into ¾-inch / 2cm pieces
½ tsp ground turmeric
5 anchovy fillets, coarsely chopped
3 tbsp harissa paste (store-bought or see recipe, page 301)
4 tbsp capers
2 tsp finely chopped preserved lemon peel, (store-bought or see recipe, page 303)
½ cup / 60 g black olives, pitted and halved
2 tbsp freshly squeezed lemon juice
5 oz / 140 g preserved piquillo peppers (about 5 peppers), torn into rough strips
4 large eggs, hard boiled, peeled, and quartered
2 baby gem lettuces (about 5 oz / 140 g in total), leaves separated and torn
⅔ oz / 20 g flat-leaf parsley, leaves picked and torn
salt

To prepare the tuna, put the rosemary, bay leaves, and peppercorns in a small saucepan and add the olive oil. Heat the oil to just below the boiling point, when tiny bubbles begin to surface. Carefully add the tuna (the tuna must be completely covered; if it isn't, heat more oil and add to the pan). Remove from the heat and leave aside for a couple hours, uncovered, then cover the pan and refrigerate for at least 24 hours.

Cook the potatoes with the turmeric in plenty of salted boiling water for 10 to 12 minutes, until cooked. Drain carefully, making sure none of the turmeric water spills (the stains are a pain to remove!), and place in a large mixing bowl. While the potatoes are still hot, add the anchovies, harissa, capers, preserved lemon, olives, 6 tbsp / 90 ml of the tuna preserving oil, and some of the peppercorns from the oil. Mix gently and leave to cool.

Lift the tuna from the remaining oil, break it into bite-size chunks, and add to the salad. Add the lemon juice, peppers, eggs, lettuce, and parsley. Toss gently, taste, add salt if it needs it and possibly more oil, then serve.

See the following pages for pictures of raw and confit tuna

Keeping kosher

Kosher rules and the deviation from them were a source of illicit excitement for Yotam in his teens. Although the Ottolenghi household was always blatantly nonkosher, the vast majority of Jews in Jerusalem felt, and still feel, inclined to observe at least some of the Jewish dietary laws—very uncool in a teenager's eyes. Yotam felt particularly proud that his mother would buy pork "under the counter" from a local butcher and prepare ham sandwiches for his lunch box, a fact that he was sworn to keep "discreet." It all felt terribly special and brave.

———

THE OBSERVANCE OF KASHRUT RULES IS A DIVISIVE ISSUE IN THE CITY AS IT IS IN THE REST OF ISRAEL. YOUR IDENTITY IS TO SOME DEGREE DETERMINED BY HOW STRICT YOU ARE.

———

Youths' vanity aside, the observance of kashrut rules is a divisive issue in the city as it is in the rest of Israel. Your identity is to some degree determined by how strict you are: whether or not you fast on Yom Kippur, how far you try to keep meat and dairy separate, whether you eat in a nonkosher friend's home, whether you'd consume bread over Passover, and a dozen other questions, big and small. The way you answer those questions is taken as an indication as to how traditional you are, how cosmopolitan, how nationalistic.

What made eating nonkosher food especially thrilling in the 1970s and 1980s was that it was hardly ever consumed in public places. This is probably one of the reasons why Yotam was almost obsessive about Sea Dolphin, a restaurant in east Jerusalem serving prawns, squid, lobster, and other forbidden creatures. His idea of the perfect birthday present was their famous plate of prawns with butter and garlic (and we are talking about a ten-year-old!).

The story of Sea Dolphin reflects much of the city's spirit and its taboos. It was set up in 1967 by Shraga Rosenzweig, son of a German Jewish family who settled in Jerusalem in the 1930s, just like Yotam's mother's family. The Rosenzweigs opened a small fish shop in Machne Yehuda market and have run it successfully for years, despite the difficulties in transporting fresh fish from the ports on the Mediterranean during periods of war and the city's division. After the 1967 war, Shraga decided to start a restaurant and teamed up with a Palestinian partner to open Sea Dolphin in east Jerusalem. The place was a huge hit with Jews, Arabs, and international guests and became a small Mecca for all seafood lovers. Naturally, it also drew a fair amount of hostility. At one point, it was blown up and had to be closed down and revamped.

In the late 1980s the first intifada broke out, east Jerusalem became dangerous, and the Jewish customers all but disappeared. Shraga relocated the restaurant to Tel Aviv, marking an end to the Palestinian partnership. During the 1990s, the restaurant moved back to Jerusalem, to its current location in the west part of the city, still serving fish and seafood and basking in over forty years of culinary glory.

Prawns, scallops & clams
with tomato & feta

1 cup / 250 ml white wine
2¼ lb / 1 kg clams,
  scrubbed
3 cloves garlic, thinly sliced
3 tbsp olive oil, plus extra
  to finish
3½ cups / 600 g peeled
  and chopped Italian
  plum tomatoes (fresh or
  canned)
1 tsp superfine sugar
2 tbsp chopped oregano
1 lemon
7 oz / 200 g tiger prawns,
  peeled and deveined
7 oz / 200 g large scallops
  (if very large, cut in half
  horizontally)
4 oz / 120 g feta cheese,
  broken into ¾-inch /
  2cm chunks
3 green onions, thinly
  sliced
salt and freshly ground
  black pepper

This unusual combination of seafood and cheese deserves a place of honor on Ottolenghi's catering menu, making regular appearances for over ten years and always hailed by our customers as "unexpectedly delicious." It works especially well in dinner-party situations, where you can cook everything in advance up to the stage when the prawns and scallops are added, chill the cooked clams, and then reheat and put everything together at the very last minute. To save time and work, or if clams are not available, this dish can be done without them; just add the white wine after cooking the garlic, reduce, and then continue as directed without the clams. Add some chile flakes to the sauce if you want a little heat. Serve with rice, couscous, or bread.

Place the wine in a medium saucepan and boil until reduced by three-quarters. Add the clams, cover immediately with a lid, and cook over high heat for about 2 minutes, shaking the pan occasionally, until the clams open. Transfer to a fine sieve to drain, capturing the cooking juices in a bowl. Discard any clams that don't open, then remove the remainder from their shells, leaving a few with their shells to finish the dish, if you like.

Preheat the oven to 475°F / 240°C.

In a large frying pan, cook the garlic in the olive oil over medium-high heat for about 1 minute, until golden. Carefully add the tomatoes, clam liquid, sugar, oregano, and some salt and pepper. Shave off 3 zest strips from the lemon, add them and simmer gently for 20 to 25 minutes, until the sauce thickens. Taste and add salt and pepper as needed. Discard the lemon zest.

Add the prawns and scallops, stir gently, and cook for just a minute or two. Fold in the shelled clams and transfer everything to a small ovenproof dish. Sink the feta pieces into the sauce and sprinkle with the green onion. Top with some clams in their shells, if you like, and place in the oven for 3 to 5 minutes, until the top colors a little and the prawns and scallops are just cooked. Remove the dish from the oven, squeeze a little lemon juice on top, and finish with a drizzle of olive oil.

Salmon steaks in chraimeh sauce

In Jerusalem, just as famous as gefilte fish is *chraimeh*, the "queen" of all dishes for Tripolitan (Libyan) Jews. It is a must-feature for many Sephardim, just like its Ashkenazic counterpart, on Rosh Hashanah, Passover, and often on Shabbat meal tables. Despite the obvious differences—gefilte is beige and sweet, *chraimeh* is red, hot, and spicy—they are similar in one essential element. In both dishes the flavor of the fish is really irrelevant; it is merely a vehicle for the flavors of the sauce or condiment, be it sweet, sharp, or hot. Families pride themselves on their particular *chraimeh* recipe. It showcases the true skills of the Tripolitan cook—and, with variations on this theme, of other North African cooks—evident in the texture of the sauce, its color, piquancy, and heat.

Claudia Roden tells of the Jews of Livorno, Italy, and a similar traditional dish of a whole fish cooked in a sweet tomato sauce. The Marranos, Jews from Portugal and Spain who arrived in Italy in the seventeenth century, were among the first to introduce tomatoes to Italy and, as many of the Livornese Jewish merchants maintained a presence throughout the Mediterranean, Tripoli included, it is likely that these culinary traditions traveled with them.

Chraimeh is commonly made using greater amberjack steaks, but any type of white fish can be used. We use salmon here because salmon steaks are the most widely available. If you find a large sea bass, that would be the best. White fish fillets are another acceptable compromise.

Chraimeh is served as a starter, warm or at room temperature, with challah (you can use any good white bread) for dipping, a slice of lemon, and a jug of water to calm the heat. This dish is easily reheated and the sauce is so tasty that you may want to double the amount so you have more for dipping the bread. Serve with couscous or rice.

---

scant ½ cup / 110 ml
   sunflower oil
3 tbsp all-purpose flour
4 salmon steaks, about
   1 lb / 950 g
6 cloves garlic, coarsely
   chopped
2 tsp sweet paprika
1 tbsp caraway seeds,
   dry toasted and freshly
   ground
1½ tsp ground cumin
rounded ¼ tsp cayenne
   pepper
rounded ¼ tsp ground
   cinnamon
1 green chile, coarsely
   chopped
⅔ cup / 150 ml water
3 tbsp tomato paste
2 tsp superfine sugar
1 lemon, cut into 4 wedges,
   plus 2 tbsp freshly
   squeezed lemon juice
2 tbsp coarsely chopped
   cilantro
salt and freshly ground
   black pepper

Heat 2 tablespoons of the sunflower oil over high heat in a large frying pan for which you have a lid. Place the flour in a shallow bowl, season generously with salt and pepper, and toss the fish in it. Shake off the excess flour and sear the fish for a minute or two on each side, until golden. Remove the fish and wipe the pan clean.

Place the garlic, spices, chile, and 2 tablespoons of the sunflower oil in a food processor and blitz to form a thick paste. You might need to add a little bit more oil to bring everything together.

Pour the remaining oil into the frying pan, heat well, and add the spice paste. Stir and fry for just 30 seconds, so that the spices don't burn. Quickly but carefully (it may spit!) add the water and tomato

paste to stop the spices from cooking. Bring to a simmer and add the sugar, lemon juice, ¾ teaspoon salt, and some pepper. Taste for seasoning.

Put the fish in the sauce, bring to a gentle simmer, cover the pan and cook for 7 to 11 minutes, depending on the size of the fish, until it is just done. Remove the pan from the heat, take off the lid, and leave to cool down. Serve the fish just warm or at room temperature. Garnish each serving with the cilantro and a lemon wedge.

Cold fish

"Gefilte fish" is the answer you normally get when you ask someone what Jewish food is. Well, not in Jerusalem, at least not for everyone. Sami, needless to say, didn't have it until the age of eighteen. But he isn't Jewish. Yotam's first memory of this dish is from the age of ten, when the school initiated an evening of culinary exchange and asked every child to bring food representing his community—something typical of the country his parents or grandparents came from. Luckily for Yotam he could bring a pizza made by his dad and so quadrupled his popularity swiftly and effortlessly. Others were less fortunate. They brought gefilte fish.

In our childhoods, gefilte fish, a poached mix of ground fish shaped into flat cakes, was plainly abhorred by almost everyone. Sweet, gray, and smeared with gelatinous gunk, it was perceived as a typical remnant of the old Ashkenazic world that was best left behind in eastern Europe. Compared with the sexy falafel or Yotam's mouthwatering pizza, it did indeed pale.

> SWEET, GRAY, AND SMEARED WITH GELATINOUS GUNK, GEFILTE FISH WAS PERCEIVED AS A TYPICAL REMNANT OF THE OLD ASHKENAZIC WORLD THAT WAS BEST LEFT BEHIND IN EASTERN EUROPE.

Still, despite everything, Yotam did develop a taste for gefilte fish, especially when liberally doused with *chrein*, the obligatory horseradish and beet sauce that makes all the difference.

Cold fish, sweetened or pickled, can actually be a real delicacy and is common in both Ashkenazic and Sephardic cooking. As Jews often didn't have access to fresh fish and needed to cook them in advance for Shabbat, all sorts of preserving methods were developed in order to serve them cold, at the same time satisfying the Jewish love for all things sweet.

Apart from salting and pickling—as with the famous herring—many dishes involve coating fish in egg or batter, frying it, and leaving it to cool down, often dipping it in a sugar-and-vinegar-based marinade. The Sephardic version is normally called *escabèche* and is popular with North African Jews. The Roman Jews used pine nuts and raisins. These were mixed with olive oil, vinegar, and sugar and spooned over red mullet; it was baked, not fried.

Marinated sweet & sour fish

3 tbsp olive oil
2 medium onions, cut into
⅜-inch / 1cm slices
(3 cups / 350 g in total)
1 tbsp coriander seeds
2 peppers (1 red and
1 yellow), halved
lengthwise, seeded, and
cut into strips ⅜ inch /
1 cm wide (3 cups /
300 g total)
2 cloves garlic, crushed
3 bay leaves
1½ tbsp curry powder
3 tomatoes, chopped
(2 cups / 320 g in total)
2½ tbsp sugar
5 tbsp cider vinegar
1 lb / 500 g pollock, cod
(sustainably sourced),
halibut, haddock, or
other white fish fillets,
divided into 4 equal
pieces
seasoned all-purpose flour,
for dusting
2 extra-large eggs, beaten
⅓ cup / 20 g chopped
cilantro
salt and freshly ground
black pepper

This dish is best served at room temperature, preferably after resting for a day or two in the fridge, with a chunk of bread. It makes a substantial starter or can be served at the center of a light meal. Small whole fish are also good here: red mullet, sardines, or small mackerel, scaled and gutted. We would like to thank Danielle Postma for this recipe.

Preheat the oven to 375°F / 190°C.

Heat 2 tablespoons of the olive oil in a large ovenproof frying pan or Dutch oven over medium heat. Add the onions and coriander seeds and cook for 5 minutes, stirring often. Add the peppers and cook for a further 10 minutes. Add the garlic, bay leaves, curry powder, and tomatoes, and cook for another 8 minutes, stirring occasionally. Add the sugar, vinegar, 1½ teaspoons salt, and some black pepper and continue to cook for another 5 minutes.

Meanwhile, heat the remaining 1 tablespoon oil in a separate frying pan over medium-high heat. Sprinkle the fish with some salt, dip in the flour, then in the eggs, and fry for about 3 minutes, turning once. Transfer the fish to paper towels to absorb the excess oil, then add to the pan with the peppers and onions, pushing the vegetables aside so the fish sits on the bottom of the pan. Add enough water just to immerse the fish (about 1 cup / 250 ml) in the liquid.

Place the pan in the oven for 10 to 12 minutes, until the fish is cooked. Remove from the oven and leave to cool to room temperature. The fish can now be served, but it is actually better after a day or two in the fridge. Before serving, taste and add salt and pepper, if needed, and garnish with the cilantro.

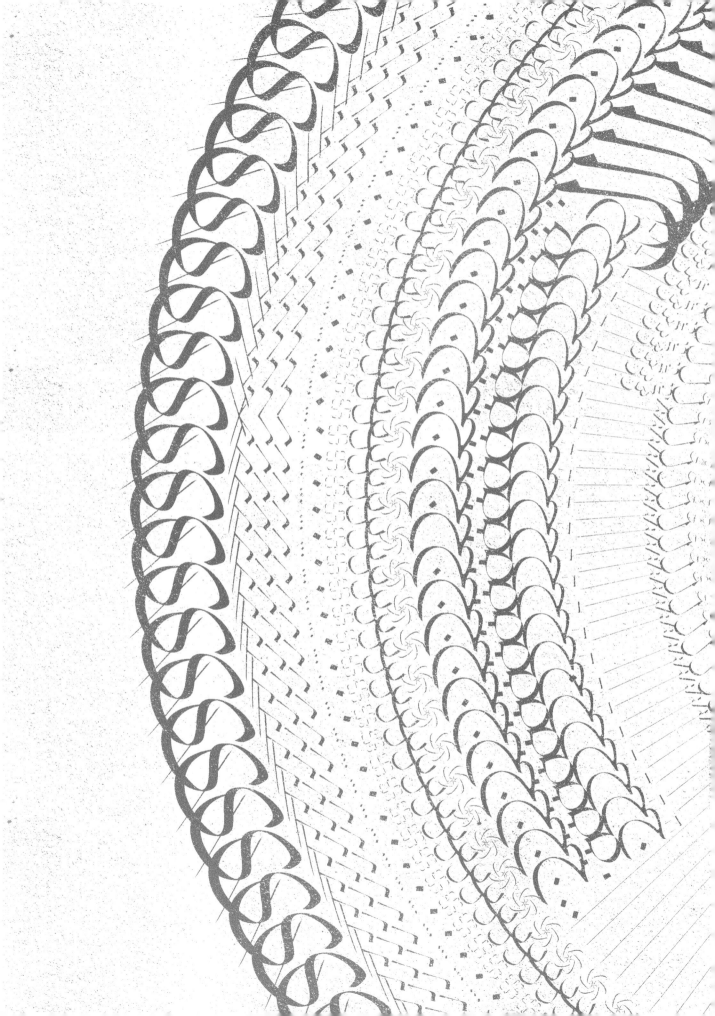

SAVORY
PASTRIES

Red pepper & baked egg galettes

Sit in any Arab restaurant in Jerusalem and before you know it the table fills up with tons of little salady mezes of every consistency and color (we always wonder how anyone manages to stomach anything after this, but once the famous grilled meat skewers arrive, it is plainly obvious, in a very practical way). Roasted red peppers are respectable members of the meze clan. They are sweet (everybody loves sweet in Jerusalem), juicy, and wonderfully colorful.

---

4 medium red peppers, halved, seeded, and cut into strips ⅜ inch / 1 cm wide

3 small onions, halved and cut into wedges ¾ inch / 2 cm wide

4 thyme sprigs, leaves picked and chopped

1½ tsp ground coriander

1½ tsp ground cumin

6 tbsp olive oil, plus extra to finish

1½ tbsp flat-leaf parsley leaves, coarsely chopped

1½ tbsp cilantro leaves, coarsely chopped

9 oz / 250 g best-quality, all-butter puff pastry

2 tbsp / 30 g sour cream

4 large free-range eggs (or 5½ oz / 160 g feta cheese, crumbled), plus 1 egg, lightly beaten

salt and freshly ground black pepper

The contrast of the red peppers and the egg yolk make these pastries stunning to look at. They are quite easy to make and taste brilliant; kids in particular love them. The egg can be substituted with feta or any other young and salty white cheese (check if there's a Turkish grocer in your neighborhood), which is ideal if you are not eating the galettes straightaway.

Preheat the oven to 400°F / 210°C. In a large bowl, mix together the peppers, onions, thyme leaves, ground spices, olive oil, and a good pinch of salt. Spread out in a roasting pan and roast for 35 minutes, stirring a couple of times during the cooking. The vegetables should be soft and sweet but not too crisp or brown, as they will cook further. Remove from the oven and stir in half of the fresh herbs. Taste for seasoning and set aside. Turn the oven up to 425°F / 220°C.

On a lightly floured surface, roll out the puff pastry into a 12-inch / 30cm square about ⅛ inch / 3 mm thick and cut into four 6-inch / 15cm squares. Prick the squares all over with a fork and place them, well spaced, on a baking sheet lined with parchment paper. Leave to rest in the fridge for at least 30 minutes.

Remove the pastry from the fridge and brush the top and sides with beaten egg. Using an offset spatula or the back of a spoon, spread 1½ teaspoons of the sour cream over each square, leaving a ¼-inch / 0.5cm border around the edges. Arrange 3 tablespoons of the pepper mixture on top of the sour cream–topped squares, leaving the borders clear to rise. It should be spread fairly evenly, but leave a shallow well in the middle to hold an egg later on.

Bake the galettes for 14 minutes. Take the baking sheet out of the oven and carefully crack a whole egg into the well in the center of each pastry. Return to the oven and cook for another 7 minutes, until the eggs are just set. Sprinkle with black pepper and the remaining herbs and drizzle with oil. Serve at once.

Brick

We were given this recipe by Rafram Hadad, a very colorful character. Hadad was born in Djerba, a Tunisian island with a Jewish minority that settled there over twenty-five hundred years ago, and arrived in Israel with his family in the 1970s. The main Tunisian community in Jerusalem, which arrived earlier—in the 1950s and 1960s—was very small, so it was "annexed" to the much larger Moroccan community and lost some of its unique heritage. Hadad, however, is extremely proud of his unique Tunisian food heritage. He still has some family in Tunisia and he returns on a regular basis guiding culinary trips. He is also the Slow Food movement coordinator in Israel, an artist, a political activist, and a food writer. He is one of those people who surfs life's waves, taking it all in as part of an adventure. In 2010, he got mixed up in an ordeal that resulted in him being kept in solitary confinement in a Libyan prison for five months. He was arrested after having been seen wandering in Tripoli taking photographs of the city and was released following a major diplomatic effort involving, among others, Tony Blair, Vladimir Putin, and Silvio Berlusconi.

---

about 1 cup / 250 ml
   sunflower oil
2 circles feuilles de brick
   pastry, 10 to 12 inches /
   25 to 30 cm in diameter
3 tbsp chopped flat-leaf
   parsley
1½ tbsp chopped green
   onion, both green and
   white parts
2 large free-range eggs
salt and freshly ground
   black pepper

Brick is the commercial name given to a paper-thin pastry, similar to filo, only sturdier and crunchier (spring-roll wrappers make a good substitute). It gets its name from a popular Tunisian street snack, also called brick. *Other Tunisian staples can be added, such as crushed cooked potato seasoned with cinnamon, fried onion, ground meat, black olives, harissa paste, or canned tuna.*

You will need to have the ingredients for the brick *filling ready so that once your oil is at the right temperature, you can assemble the parcels quickly and fry them as soon as they're made. The parcels won't hold together well if you don't fry them immediately.*

Pour the sunflower oil into a medium saucepan; it should come about ¾ inch / 2 cm up the sides of the pan. Place over medium heat and leave until the oil is hot. You don't want it too hot or the pastry will burn before the egg is cooked; tiny bubbles will start to surface when it reaches the right temperature.

Place one of the pastry circles inside a shallow bowl. (You can use a larger piece if you don't want to waste much pastry and fill it up more.) You will need to work quickly so that the pastry does not dry out and become stiff. Put half the parsley in the center of the circle and sprinkle with half the green onion. Create a little nest in which to rest an egg, then carefully crack an egg into the nest. Sprinkle generously with salt and pepper and fold in the sides of the pastry to create a parcel. The four folds will overlap so that the egg is fully enclosed. You can't seal the pastry, but a neat fold should keep the egg inside.

Carefully turn the parcel over and gently place it in the oil, seal side down. Cook for 60 to 90 seconds on each side, until the pastry is golden brown. The egg white should be set and the yolk still runny. Lift the cooked parcel from the oil and place between paper towels to soak up the excess oil. Keep warm while you cook the second pastry. Serve both parcels at once.

Sfiha or Lahm Bi'ajeen

Only a few decades ago, when many Palestinian families didn't have ovens at home, housewives used to bring a risen dough and lamb topping to their nearby bakery. The baker would deftly shape the dough for them, scatter over the ground lamb, and bake the pastries in his wood-fired oven. His payment came in the form of a little gastronomic return: a couple of *sfiha* pastries.

Sfiha or *lahm bi'ajeen*, a Levantine lamb-topped dough, is a bit like a pizza and is as popular as its Italian cousin. Sami's mother used to make special small individual versions for her kids that she would bake and then top with heaps of fresh ingredients: parsley, radish, mint, green onion, and lemon juice. The little ones folded them into portable sandwiches that they gobbled in seconds.

These little savory pastries can easily be taken to work, where they can be heated up or served as they are, with a squeeze of lemon. The dough is quite wet and sloppy when you first mix it. Once you start kneading it, however, it should be fine, so don't be tempted to add much more flour.

TOPPING

9 oz / 250 g ground lamb
1 large onion, finely chopped (1 heaping cup / 180 g in total)
2 medium tomatoes, finely chopped (1½ cups / 250 g)
3 tbsp light tahini paste
1¼ tsp salt
1 tsp ground cinnamon
1 tsp ground allspice
⅛ tsp cayenne pepper
scant 1 oz / 25 g flat-leaf parsley, chopped
1 tbsp freshly squeezed lemon juice
1 tbsp pomegranate molasses
1 tbsp sumac
3 tbsp / 25 g pine nuts
2 lemons, cut into wedges

DOUGH

1⅔ cups / 230 g bread flour
1½ tbsp powdered milk
½ tbsp salt
1½ tsp fast-rising active dry yeast
½ tsp baking powder
1 tbsp sugar
½ cup / 125 ml sunflower oil
1 large free-range egg
scant ½ cup / 110 ml lukewarm water
olive oil, for brushing

Start with the dough. Put the flour, powdered milk, salt, yeast, baking powder, and sugar in a large mixing bowl. Stir well to mix, then make a well in the center. Put the sunflower oil and egg in the well, then stir as you add the water. When the dough comes together, transfer it to a work surface and knead for 3 minutes, until elastic and uniform. Put in a bowl, brush with some olive oil, cover with a towel in a warm spot, and leave for 1 hour, at which point the dough should have risen a little.

In a separate bowl, use your hands to mix together all of the topping ingredients except the pine nuts and lemon wedges. Set aside.

Preheat the oven to 450°F / 230°C. Line a large baking sheet with parchment paper.

Divide the risen dough into scant 2-oz / 50g balls; you should have about 14. Roll out each ball into a circle about 5 inches / 12 cm in diameter and 1/16 inch / 2 mm thick. Brush each circle lightly on both sides with olive oil and place on the baking sheet. Cover and leave to rise for 15 minutes.

Use a spoon to divide the filling among the pastries, and spread it evenly so it covers the dough fully. Sprinkle with the pine nuts. Set aside to rise for another 15 minutes, then put in the oven for about 15 minutes, until just cooked. You want to make sure the pastry is just baked, not overbaked; the topping should be slightly pink inside and the pastry golden on the underside. Remove from the oven and serve warm or at room temperature with the lemon wedges.

Abadi cookies

Sold in iconic red printed bags carrying the founding father's portrait, Abadi's savory cookies, *ka'ach bilmalch*, are dangerously addictive and immediately recognizable by generations of Jerusalemites. It was the pleasant crunch, hard crumble, and roasted sesame seed topping that made the ring-shaped cookies so popular when they first burst onto the scene in 1838.

It all began in Aleppo, when one of the family's ancestors set up a small neighborhood bakery. In 1926, the family moved to Palestine carried on donkeys' backs and settled in Jerusalem, where they ran a tiny bakery from their house near Machne Yehuda market. Yosef, the son, who was born in Jerusalem, joined the bakery at the age of thirteen, and worked there for years perfecting his trade.

In 1949, Yosef and his wife, Simcha, extended the bakery and, based on Simcha's idea, the famous ring-shaped cookies were now made much smaller. The new size proved tremendously popular, so the business expanded and the manual cart used for deliveries made way for a bike, then motorcycles, and finally, in the 1960s, delivery trucks. Eventually, word got out and the cookies outgrew the city. Nowadays, they are sold nationally in supermarkets, but the artisanal, small-scale image has stuck, and they are still wonderful.

Variations on Abadi's hard and short savory biscuits appear all over the Arab and Sephardic worlds, normally shaped as rings and sprinkled with sesame seeds. Moroccans and Tripolitans make a similar cookie and serve it with black coffee. The ancient Sephardic community of Jerusalem call them *biskochos salados* and often shape them as sticks. However, it is the Aleppine Jews' version that has the richest flavor, often containing lots of aromatic "surprises" like aniseeds, *mahleb* (the ground stones of St. Lucie cherries), coriander seeds, and cumin seeds.

Recipe on next page

Ka'ach bilmalch

4 cups / 500 g all-purpose
flour, sifted
6½ tbsp / 100 ml sunflower
oil
6½ tbsp / 100 g unsalted
butter, diced and left to
soften
1 tsp fast-rising active
dry yeast
1 tsp baking powder
1 tsp sugar
1½ tsp salt
½ tsp ground cumin
1½ tbsp fennel seeds,
toasted and very lightly
crushed
about 6½ tbsp / 100 ml
water
1 large free-range egg,
beaten
2 tsp white and black
sesame seeds

DIPPING SAUCE

1¼ oz / 35 g flat-leaf
parsley (stems and
leaves)
1 clove garlic, crushed
scant 2 tbsp / 25 g light
tahini paste
½ cup / 125 g Greek yogurt
5 tsp / 25 ml freshly
squeezed lemon juice
pinch of salt

These simple savory cookies are normally kept at home in a jar, ready to be snacked on at any moment (Yotam's dad tends to sneak into the kitchen in the middle of the night and devour a couple—without anyone noticing, of course). They aren't very rich, so they will go well with a cheese dip or on their own with a glass of cold beer, arak on ice, or black coffee. The dipping sauce given here is optional; make it if you want to upgrade them to a predinner party appetizer.

Preheat the oven to 400°F / 200°C. Place the sifted flour in a large bowl and make a well in the center. Pour the oil into the well, add the butter, yeast, baking powder, sugar, salt, and spices, and stir together well until a dough forms. Add the water gradually while stirring until the dough is smooth. Knead for a couple minutes.

Line a baking sheet with parchment paper. Pinch pieces of the dough into small balls, about a scant 1 oz / 25 g each. On a clean surface, roll the balls into long snakes about ⅜ inch / 1 cm thick and 5 to 5½ inches / 12 to 13 cm long. Form each snake into a closed ring and arrange on the baking sheet, spacing them about ¾ inch / 2 cm apart. Brush each ring with the egg and sprinkle lightly with the sesame seeds. Leave to proof for 30 minutes.

Bake the biscuits for 22 minutes, until golden brown. Allow to cool down before storing them in a clean jar or an airtight container. They keep for up to 10 days.

To make the dipping sauce, just blitz all the ingredients together to get a uniformly green sauce. Add a tablespoon or so of water if the sauce is very thick; you want a nice coating consistency.

Herb pie

The extravagant use of herbs in our cooking is definitely to be blamed on Jerusalem. Herbs are sold there, quite literally, by the bucketload. Fallahat, Palestinian peasant women, come into the city with baskets and sacks brimming with fresh produce from the surrounding countryside to sell on the curbside. They used to carry the sacks of produce on their heads with amazing acts of graceful balance. Herbs are always there—particularly mint, parsley, *za'atar*, cilantro, sage, and dill—but also plenty of other vegetables and fruits in season. Housewives buy liberal quantities ready to go into salads, aromatic pastes, vegetable stuffings, and most other dishes as well. It seems almost ironic that it is Israeli and Palestinian herbs that fill the miserly bags of fresh herbs sold in most UK supermarkets today, given that no sane cook there would consider buying anything less than five times the amount.

This pie, inspired by all kinds of Sephardic pastries from Turkey and the Balkans, can happily sit at the center of a light vegetarian meal. Serve it after the Burnt eggplant and mograbieh soup (PAGE 141).

---

2 tbsp olive oil, plus extra for brushing the pastry
1 large onion, diced
1 lb / 500 g Swiss chard, stems and leaves finely shredded but kept separate
5 oz / 150 g celery, thinly sliced
1¾ oz / 50 g green onion, chopped
1¾ oz / 50 g arugula
1 oz / 30 g flat-leaf parsley, chopped
1 oz / 30 g mint, chopped
⅔ oz / 20 g dill, chopped
4 oz / 120 g anari or ricotta cheese, crumbled
3½ oz / 100 g aged Cheddar cheese, grated
2 oz / 60 g feta cheese, crumbled
grated zest of 1 lemon
2 large free-range eggs
⅓ tsp salt
½ tsp freshly ground black pepper
½ tsp superfine sugar
9 oz / 250 g filo pastry

Preheat the oven to 400°F / 200°C. Pour the olive oil into a large, deep frying pan over medium heat. Add the onion and sauté for 8 minutes without browning. Add the chard stems and the celery and continue cooking for 4 minutes, stirring occasionally. Add the chard leaves, increase the heat to medium-high, and stir as you cook for 4 minutes, until the leaves wilt. Add the green onion, arugula, and herbs and cook for 2 minutes more. Remove from the heat and transfer to a colander to cool.

Once the mixture is cool, squeeze out as much water as you can and transfer to a mixing bowl. Add the three cheeses, lemon zest, eggs, salt, pepper, and sugar and mix well.

Lay out a sheet of filo pastry and brush it with some olive oil. Cover with another sheet and continue in the same manner until you have 5 layers of filo brushed with oil, all covering an area large enough to line the sides and bottom of a 8½-inch / 22cm pie dish, plus extra to hang over the rim. Line the pie dish with the pastry, fill with the herb mix, and fold the excess pastry over the edge of the filling, trimming the pastry as necessary to create a ¾-inch / 2cm border.

Make another set of 5 filo layers brushed with oil and place them over the pie. Scrunch up the pastry a little to create a wavy, uneven top and trim the edges so it just covers the pie. Brush generously with olive oil and bake for 40 minutes, until the filo turns a nice golden brown. Remove from the oven and serve warm or at room temperature.

Sweet filo cigars

There was a time when you couldn't go to a bar mitzvah or Jewish wedding in Jerusalem without getting at least one type of "cigar" pastry— filo stuffed and rolled, usually with a spiced meat filling, sometimes cheese. They were the heritage of various Sephardic communities, particularly Moroccan, one of the largest in the city. Luckily, those days are mostly over. Not so much because it is a bad idea, but mostly due to the poor quality of the execution and due to overexposure, a bit like the British prawn cocktail, a relic of the same era.

In actual fact, cigars can be completely wonderful. Iraqi Jews have a version with chopped chicken, onion, and parsley. The famous Moroccan ones are stuffed with ground beef, sautéed onion, sweet spices, lemon juice, and parsley. We particularly like the sweet varieties that are found throughout the region, in various configurations, the difference being whether they are baked or deep-fried and whether they are soaked in sweet syrup or just sprinkled with confectioners' sugar.

scant 1 cup / 80 g sliced
 almonds
½ cup / 60 g unsalted
 pistachios, plus extra,
 crushed, to garnish
5 tbsp water
scant ½ cup / 80 g vanilla
 sugar
1 large free-range egg,
 separated, white beaten
1 tbsp grated lemon zest
filo pastry, cut into twelve
 7½-inch / 18cm squares
peanut oil, for frying
scant ½ cup / 180 g good-
 quality honey

These cigars, stuffed with almonds and pistachios, are a traditional Tunisian Jewish sweet served at Purim. They are wonderful served with black coffee as a snack or after a meal. Stored in an airtight container, they keep for up to three days. The recipe was kindly given to us by Rafram Hadad.

In a food processor, bring the almond and pistachio together into a fine paste. Place the ground nuts in a frying pan and add 4 tablespoons of the water and the sugar. Cook over very low heat until the sugar has dissolved, about 4 minutes. Remove the pan from the heat and add the egg yolk and lemon zest, stirring them into the mixture.

Put 1 sheet of pastry on a clean surface. Spread about 1 tablespoon of the nut mixture in a thin strip along the edge closest to you, leaving ¾ inch / 2 cm clear on the left and right sides. Fold the two sides over the paste to hold it in at both ends and roll away from you to create a compact cigar. Tuck the top edge in and seal it with a little bit of the beaten egg white. Repeat with the pastry and filling.

Pour enough oil into a frying pan to come ¾ inch / 2 cm up the sides. Heat the oil over medium-high heat and fry the cigars for 10 seconds on each side, until golden.

Place the cigars on a plate lined with paper towels and allow to cool. Place the honey and the remaining 1 tablespoon water in a small saucepan and bring to a boil. When the honey and water are hot, lightly dip the cooled cigars in the syrup for a minute and stir gently until well coated. Remove and arrange on a serving plate. Sprinkle with the crushed pistachios and leave to cool.

Ghraybeh

One of Yotam's oldest memories of the Old City—it stands out clearly from all others—is a confectionery shop near David Street selling yellowish shortbread cookies with the most delectable melting texture. The flavor is one of those childhood sensations that cannot be replicated. They were sweet, almost sandy in texture, disappearing as soon as they hit the mouth, with the most wonderful aroma of rose water. These were, most probably, *ghraybeh* cookies.

Ghraybeh, meaning "swoon" in Arabic, are found in Palestine, Syria, Lebanon, and other countries in the region. They can be made in various shapes, either as a thin bracelet with a nut "cementing" the two ends together, as a diamond with a nut in the middle, or as a round cake as we make them here.

¾ cup plus 2 tbsp / 200 g ghee or clarified butter, from the fridge so it is solid

scant ⅔ cup / 70 g confectioners' sugar

3 cups / 370 g all-purpose flour, sifted

½ tsp salt

scant 4 tsp orange blossom water

2½ tsp rose water

about 5 tbsp / 30 g unsalted pistachios

Tripolitan Jews sometimes add semolina to their ghraybeh. *Some Sephardic Jews use margarine or oil, which makes them both kosher and shorter. Jews from Aden (Yemen) make similar cookies called* nayem; *they are flavored with ground cardamom and each cookie is studded with a clove. All these are possible variations.*

The flavors of orange blossom and rose water are quite intense here. Reduce them if you like. Serve the ghraybeh *with black coffee or tea.*

In a stand mixer fitted with the whip attachment, cream together the ghee and confectioners' sugar for 5 minutes, until fluffy, creamy, and pale. Replace the whip with the beater attachment, add the flour, salt, and orange blossom and rose waters, and mix for a good 3 to 4 minutes, until a uniform, smooth dough forms. Wrap the dough in plastic wrap and chill for 1 hour.

Preheat the oven to 350°F / 180°C. Pinch a piece of dough, weighing about ½ oz / 15 g, and roll it into a ball between your palms. Flatten it slightly and place on a baking sheet lined with parchment paper. Repeat with the rest of the dough, arranging the cookies on lined sheets and spacing them well apart. Press 1 pistachio into the center of each cookie.

Bake for 17 minutes, making sure the cookies don't take on any color but just cook through. Remove from the oven and leave to cool down completely. Store the cookies in an airtight container for up to 5 days.

Sweet cheese

Underneath the Ethiopian church inside the ancient walls of the Old City, in a rundown gloomy room, behind an unmarked iron door at the bottom of a stairway, is Zalatimo, a pastry shop like no other. People come here from all parts of town to indulge in one rare delicacy: a crisp-edged baked pastry known as *mutabbaq*, prepared by the Zalatimo family shops in Jerusalem and Amman. The opening hours are unpredictable, and inside the ancient arched ceiling, Roman pillars and medieval flooring contrast sharply with exposed fluorescent tubes and simple Formica furniture.

Zalatimo begins by preparing the filo dough, flipping it in the air and then rolling and stretching it by hand on a marble work surface. The paper-thin dough is brushed with *smen*— smoked and aged clarified butter—then folded into a misshaped rectangle. The pastry is sprinkled with either walnuts and cinnamon or crumbled unsalted sheep's milk cheese and then baked. Still warm from the oven, the crispy-edged *mutabbaq* is drizzled with sugar syrup and the faintest hint of rose water. Around the Old City, everybody knows this version simply as a Zalatimo.

Mutabbaq, also known as *kellaj*, is a favorite sweet of Palestinians. But it isn't quite as famous as *knafeh*, which is also made with sheep's milk cheese. *Knafeh* uses semolina or vermicelli-like dough (*kadaifi*), food coloring, pistachios, and a copious amount of sugar syrup. We prefer *mutabbaq*.

PEOPLE COME HERE FROM ALL PARTS OF TOWN TO INDULGE IN ONE RARE DELICACY— A CRISP-EDGED BAKED PASTRY KNOWN AS MUTABBAQ.

The use of sweetened young white cheese in desserts is widespread in the city. Ashkenazim use it for krantz cakes (PAGE 284), for a range of baked cheesecakes, and for blintzes, stuffed crepes. Palestinians, however, are the only ones using sweet fresh sheep's milk cheese in sweets. Traditionally, the cheese is made in spring, when the pastures are lush and the milk is plentiful. Some of the milk is cooked and the cheese is preserved in jars or cans in salted water. It is later hydrated and used for a variety of savory recipes.

Mutabbaq

2⁄3 cup / 130 g unsalted
   butter, melted
14 sheets filo pastry,
   12 by 15½ inches /
   31 by 39 cm
2 cups / 500 g ricotta
   cheese
9 oz / 250 g soft goat's
   milk cheese
crushed unsalted
   pistachios, to garnish
   (optional)

SYRUP

6 tbsp / 90 ml water
rounded 1⅓ cups / 280 g
   superfine sugar
3 tbsp freshly squeezed
   lemon juice

Mutabbaq (SEE PAGE 261) *is a good dessert when you have guests. It is unusual yet utterly delicious, it looks impressive and it can be made in advance, kept in the fridge and then baked to serve. Add a couple of drops of orange blossom water to the syrup if you like. An alternative, yet common filling you can use consists of crushed walnuts (2 cups / 200 g), superfine sugar (¼ cup / 50 g), cinnamon (1 tsp), and melted unsalted butter (3 tbsp)—all mixed together.*

Heat the oven to 450°F / 230°C. Brush a shallow-rimmed baking sheet about 11 by 14½ inches / 28 by 37 cm with some of the melted butter. Spread a filo sheet on top, tucking it into the corners and allowing the edges to hang over. Brush all over with butter, top with another sheet, and brush with butter again. Repeat the process until you have 7 sheets evenly stacked, each brushed with butter.

Place the ricotta and goat's milk cheese in a bowl and mash together with a fork, mixing well. Spread over the top filo sheet, leaving ¾ inch / 2 cm clear around the edge. Brush the surface of the cheese with butter and top with the remaining 7 sheets of filo, brushing each in turn with butter.

Use scissors to trim about ¾ inch / 2 cm off the edge but without reaching the cheese, so it stays well sealed within the pastry. Use your fingers to tuck the filo edges gently underneath the pastry to achieve a neat edge. Brush with more butter all over. Use a sharp knife to cut the surface into roughly 2¾-inch / 7cm squares, allowing the knife almost to reach the bottom but not quite. Bake for 25 to 27 minutes, until golden and crisp.

While the pastry is baking, prepare the syrup. Put the water and sugar in a small saucepan and mix well with a wooden spoon. Place over medium heat, bring to a boil, add the lemon juice, and simmer gently for 2 minutes. Remove from the heat.

Slowly pour the syrup over the pastry the minute you take it out of the oven, making sure it soaks in evenly. Leave to cool for 10 minutes. Sprinkle with the crushed pistachios, if using, and cut into portions. Serve warm.

Semolina, coconut & marmalade cake

Semolina cakes soaked in syrup are so numerous all over the Middle East and vary in so many ways it is hard to find a single definition or an accurate enough name to fit. Some cakes have coconut in them; some have yogurt; some bakers prefer flavoring them with citrus syrups, others with flower blossoms; some use sugar and others honey. In any case, the moist yet light texture and the aromatic flavors are what it's all about.

¾ cup / 180 ml sunflower oil

1 cup / 240 ml freshly squeezed orange juice

½ cup / 160 g orange marmalade (fine-cut or without peel)

4 large free-range eggs

grated zest of 1 orange

⅓ cup / 70 g superfine sugar

¾ cup / 70 g shredded dried coconut

¾ cup / 90 g all-purpose flour

1 cup plus 1½ tbsp / 180 g semolina

2 tbsp ground almonds

2 tsp baking powder

thick Greek yogurt, flavored with 1 or 2 drops orange blossom water, to serve

SOAKING SYRUP

1 cup / 200 g superfine sugar

½ cup plus 1½ tbsp / 140 ml water

1 tbsp orange blossom water

These cakes will keep well for at least five days if wrapped carefully in parchment paper or aluminum foil; as a matter of fact, they improve with time. You can serve them with the yogurt as a simple dessert, or without it if you are just having them with a cup of tea. Instead of two 1-lb / 500g loaves, you can make a single large loaf, which will take at least 20 to 30 minutes longer to bake.

Preheat the oven to 350°F / 180°C. Whisk together the oil, orange juice, marmalade, eggs, and orange zest until the marmalade dissolves. In a separate bowl, mix together all the dry ingredients and add to the wet ingredients. Mix until well combined. The mixture should be runny.

Grease and line two 1-lb / 500g loaf pans (8½ by 4½ inches / 21 by 11 cm) with waxed paper. Divide the filling evenly between them. Bake for 45 to 60 minutes, until a skewer inserted in a cake comes out clean and the tops turn an orangey brown.

Near the end of the baking time, place the syrup ingredients in a small saucepan and bring to a boil, then remove from the heat. As soon as the cakes come out of the oven, start brushing them with the hot syrup using a pastry brush; you'll need to do this in a few goes, allowing the syrup to soak in for a minute or two before you carry on brushing with more syrup. Make sure you use up all the syrup and it is all absorbed into the cakes.

Once the cakes have cooled down a little, remove them from the pan and leave to cool completely. Serve with the Greek yogurt, flavored with a drop of orange blossom water.

Poached pears in white wine *&* cardamom

Cardamom is one of our favorite spices. Like allspice and cinnamon, it has its own sweetness—not in a sugary sense, but more in an aromatic way—but it gets an extra dimension when it appears in sweet contexts. This is why it makes total sense that walking the streets of east Jerusalem you are most likely to smell cardamom near coffee sellers. Arab coffee, fiercely bitter and strong, is traditionally served with very generous amounts of sugar and often flavored with cardamom. When grinding the coffee, the expert grinder holds in his palm just the right proportion of coffee to cardamom pods and feeds it into the machine. A scent of cardamom always surrounds young waiters walking with brass trays around the Old City delivering freshly made coffee in little jugs.

2 cups / 500 ml dry white wine

1½ tbsp freshly squeezed lemon juice

¾ cup / 150 g superfine sugar

15 cardamom pods, lightly crushed

½ tsp saffron threads

pinch of salt

4 firm pears, peeled

crème fraîche, to serve

We regularly teach this dessert in our classes at Leiths School in London. Students are always impressed by how simple it is to prepare and how impressive the final result is. We think it is all to do with our magic ingredient, cardamom. Cardamom pods are best crushed lightly with the side of the knife so they release their flavor. They vary in potency. Often, even pods bought freshly from supermarkets are not very aromatic, hence the large number specified in this recipe. However, if you get yours fresh from a Middle Eastern or Indian grocer, you will find you may not need as many.

Pour the wine and lemon juice into a medium saucepan and add the sugar, cardamom, saffron, and salt. Bring to a light simmer and place the pears in the pan. Make sure they are immersed in the liquid; add water if needed. Cover the surface with a disk of waxed paper and simmer the pears, turning them occasionally, for 15 to 25 minutes, until they are cooked through but not mushy. To check if the pears are ready, insert a knife into the flesh; it should slide in smoothly.

Remove the pears from the liquid and transfer to four serving bowls. Increase the heat and reduce the liquid by about two-thirds, or until thick and syrupy. Pour over the pears and leave to cool down. Serve cold or at room temperature, with crème fraîche on the side or spooned on top.

Yogurt pudding with poached peaches

We are not big on spirits in Jerusalem. Come to think of it, we are not big drinkers at all. Arak, however, is the local spirit of choice for those who do drink. It is always associated with the famous meze spread, where a sip of arak makes an effective palate cleanser between bites. The diner is often served a tray with a bottle of arak, a pitcher of water, and some ice, which they mix together, instantly turning the clear spirit into a beautiful milky liquid. Arak is great for cooking, mainly with fish and desserts, imparting its anisey flavor gently yet clearly.

Peaches have a delicate flavor, so they work well with this light and creamy pudding. You can also use pears here, apricots, and even strawberries. Each fruit, though, would need a different cooking time. All the components of this dish are prepared in advance and assembled at the last minute.

4 sheets (leaves) gelatin (0.2 oz / 7 g in total)
¾ cup plus 2 tbsp / 200 ml heavy cream
¾ cup plus 2 tbsp / 200 ml whole milk
scant 1 cup / 190 g superfine sugar
½ vanilla bean, seeds scraped
grated zest of ½ orange
scant 1 cup / 200 g Greek yogurt
1 cup / 250 ml water
½ cup / 125 ml arak, ouzo, or Pernod, plus 1 tsp to drizzle at the end
4 flat white peaches, or regular yellow peaches if unavailable (14 oz / 400 g in total)
4 tbsp lemon juice
3 tbsp / 20 g slivered Iranian (or crushed regular) pistachios

Place the gelatin sheets in a bowl with plenty of cold water and leave to soften for a few minutes.

Pour the cream and milk into a small saucepan and add a scant ½ cup / 90 g of the sugar, the vanilla pod and half its seeds, and the orange zest. Place over medium heat, bring to a simmer, and remove immediately from the heat. Remove the vanilla pod and rinse it well.

Put the yogurt in a medium mixing bowl and whisk constantly as you pour in the hot milk and cream in a slow stream. Squeeze the water out of the gelatin sheets, add them to the bowl, and stir until they dissolve completely.

Pour the mixture into four ⅔-cup / 150ml individual molds (darioles or ramekins) and leave to set in the fridge for at least 5 hours. You can also leave them in the fridge overnight, covered with plastic wrap.

To prepare the poached peaches, put the water, arak, rinsed vanilla pod, and the remaining vanilla seeds and sugar in a medium saucepan. Bring to a boil and add the peaches (they need to be submerged in the liquid so if they are large and plump, cut them in half and remove the pits). Simmer gently for 8 to 12 minutes, depending on the ripeness of the peaches; they need to be completely soft. Remove from the heat and leave to cool down in the pan.

Once cool, stir in the lemon juice and refrigerate for up to 2 days if you are not serving at this point. Before you use them, halve each peach, remove the pit, and cut each half into 2 or 3 wedges.

When ready to serve, dip the molds in a bowl of hot water for a minute or two to assist in tipping out the puddings. Turn them over onto individual serving plates. You may need to shake the molds gently; don't worry, the puddings will come out eventually. Once out, arrange the peaches and some of the syrup around the puddings, spoon more syrup over them, and add a drizzle of arak. Sprinkle with the pistachios and serve.

Cardamom rice pudding with pistachios & rose water

Rachela Shrefler, now in her seventies, came to Jerusalem from Iran as a child and later met her husband, Ezra Shrefler, a Turkish Kurdish Jew. They are both cooks and own Azura (SEE PAGE 166), a restaurant in Machne Yehuda market. Rachela, though, is the one cooking at home. Among the many pots she has on the stove on a Friday for the Saturday "raid"—when dozens of hungry family members will descend on their house—is a pot with rice pudding. The rice sits on the hot platter until Saturday morning, when the family members sit together and eat it. It is simple and delicious, containing only rice, milk, and sugar, with a dusting of ground cinnamon.

Rice pudding was the most common everyday dessert throughout the old Sephardic world, with variations according to community, and was eaten hot or cold, at various times of the day. Possible additions would be honey, saffron, mastic, cinnamon, and other sweet spices.

Rice pudding is also common in Arab homes. Sami's mother used to prepare it for the family on occasion, causing the kids to go into serious clashes over the caramelized bits that formed at the bottom of the pot. They would have it with sugar syrup flavored with flower blossom.

For this recipe, we must thank John Meechan, a Glaswegian (!), who developed it for the menu of our London restaurant, NOPI. It is highly aromatic and rich, not muted down for the European palate.

1⅔ cups / 400 ml whole milk

½ cup / 120 ml heavy cream

1 vanilla bean, seeds scraped

8 cardamom pods, lightly crushed

scant ⅔ cup / 120 g short-grain rice

2 tbsp / 30 g unsalted butter, diced

2 tbsp condensed milk

1 tbsp acacia or other mild-flavored honey

salt

3 tbsp roasted and slivered or lightly crushed unsalted pistachios, to garnish

1 tbsp dried edible rose petals, to garnish

SYRUP

1 tbsp honey or other mild-flavored honey

1½ tsp rose water

1 tsp water

Put the whole milk, cream, vanilla (bean and seeds), and cardamom in a medium saucepan and place over high heat. As soon as the mix is about to boil, remove from the heat, allow to cool down, and leave in the fridge to infuse overnight, or at least a couple hours.

To prepare the syrup, stir together the honey, rose water, and water until the honey dissolves. Set aside.

Add the rice to the pan with the infused milk and cream, bring to a boil, and simmer over medium heat, stirring all the time, for 20 minutes. The rice should be cooked through but still retain a bite and the pudding should be thick. You will need to add a little bit of water, up to 3½ tablespoons / 50 ml, toward the end of the cooking if the pudding becomes too thick before the rice is done.

Remove the pan from the heat and carefully pick out the cardamom pods and vanilla pod. Stir in the butter, condensed milk, honey, and a pinch of salt. You can chill the mix now (and reheat in a microwave oven later) or serve immediately in little flat bowls, sprinkled with pistachios and rose petals and drizzled with the syrup.

Muhallabieh

Muhallabieh, malabi, ksab, sutlaj, sahleb—these are all names for puddings or thick sweet drinks that are dear to Jerusalemites, almost as much as the sacred stones of the Old City. Well, not quite, but it is fair to say that Arabs and Jews share a real fascination with these milky desserts.

In Jerusalem, before the days of Coke and lattes, tamarind drink and *soos* (made from a licorice twig) were the typical refreshing summer beverages (wandering vendors would carry them in ornamental glass, clay, or metal vats, attached to their backs with leather straps); their winter counterpart was *sahleb.*

When we were kids, *sahleb* was sold by vendors outside Damascus Gate in the Old City. In winter, we would go there in groups, hang around, and eat the warm and soothing thick beverage, topped with ground ginger, cinnamon, walnuts, and shredded dried coconut. The name *sahleb* means "orchid" in Hebrew and Arabic, as the pudding was thickened with ground orchid root. But this is now rare and expensive, so today cornstarch or rice flour, with no fragrance but very cheap, is used instead.

Muhallabieh *or* malabi (SEE PICTURE OPPOSITE AND ON PAGES 272–73) *are the dessert forms of* sahleb. *On the face of it, we must admit, a milk pudding doesn't sound promising at all. Imagination doesn't work here; you just need to try it. Once more, we bring in Claudine and Alison, our devoted recipe testers, who thought the description sounded horrible but actually loved it. What makes it so special is the lightness and simplicity of the base pudding (which is like a lean version of panna cotta), combined with the flavor and character coming from the condiments that are spooned on top. In Israel, both fancy restaurants and simple street stalls sell* malabi *and it is the topping that varies.*

We chose not to use the ubiquitous rose water for this version of the famous pudding, but a more subtle bay leaf syrup; you can easily add a couple drops of rose water at the end if you wish. A few pomegranate seeds would also make for a beautiful addition on top. You will have bay syrup left over; it will keep for a few weeks in a sterilized sealed jar (SEE PAGE 303) *stored in a cool place. Consider spooning it over a fruit salad.*

To use this recipe to make sahleb, *follow the instructions but decrease the cornstarch to 5 tablespoons / 40 g. When hot and thick, pour into small glasses and top with ground ginger, ground cinnamon, chopped walnuts, shredded dried coconut, and a tiny drizzle of orange blossom water. Serve at once.*

PUDDING

6 tbsp / 50 g cornstarch
2 cups / 500 ml whole milk
¾ cup plus 2 tbsp / 200 ml
  water
6½ tbsp / 80 g superfine
  sugar
6 tbsp / 25 g shredded
  dried coconut, to garnish
3½ tbsp / 25 g chopped
  unsalted pistachios, to
  garnish

SYRUP

5 tbsp / 60 g superfine
  sugar
¼ cup / 60 ml water
1 bay leaf, fresh or dried
¼ vanilla bean, seeds
  scraped

Start with the pudding. Whisk the cornstarch with 6½ tablespoons / 100 ml of the milk to make a smooth paste. Pour the remaining milk, along with the water and sugar, into a medium saucepan and heat gently to dissolve the sugar. When the milk mixture begins to release steam, whisk in the cornstarch paste. Continue whisking until the mixture boils and thickens so that it resembles thick custard. Remove from the heat and pour into six individual bowls or wineglasses. Cover the top of each pudding with plastic wrap to prevent a skin from forming (the plastic wrap should touch the surface) and place in the fridge for at least 3 hours, until set.

For the syrup, place the sugar, water, bay leaf, and vanilla bean and seeds in a small saucepan and heat gently just until the sugar dissolves. Remove from the heat and leave to cool.

To serve, top each serving with the coconut, pistachios, and about 1 tablespoon of the syrup.

Walnut & fruit crumble cream

FIG COMPOTE

1 lb / 500 g ripe figs, quartered
2 tbsp freshly squeezed lemon juice
1 tbsp superfine sugar

GUAVA & PLUM COMPOTE

4 guavas, seeded and cut into 1¼-inch / 3cm pieces (about 2 cups / 300 g in total)
6 plums, pitted and cut into quarters (about 2 cups / 300 g in total)
2 tbsp superfine sugar
1 tbsp freshly squeezed lemon juice
1 tbsp water

CRUMBLE

⅓ cup / 40 g whole-wheat flour
⅓ cup / 40 g all-purpose flour
3½ tbsp / 50 g unsalted butter, chilled and cut into ¾-inch / 2cm cubes
3½ tbsp / 50 g light brown sugar
pinch of salt
1 cup / 100 g walnuts, coarsely broken

CREAM

⅔ cup / 150 ml heavy cream
6½ tbsp / 100 g Greek yogurt
6½ tbsp / 100 g mascarpone cheese
1 tbsp superfine sugar
½ tsp vanilla extract
½ tsp ground cardamom
½ star anise, ground

It's an old and much-loved trick—layering cream with seasonal fresh or cooked fruit—and it works every time; but it is much more clever to spike the cream and fruit with additional layers of flavor that rhyme with one another and "play games" with the taste buds. Here we chose fruits that grow in or around Jerusalem and some typical spices. You can opt for one of our combinations or go for something that is local and seasonal to you and enhance it with your favorite sweet spices (allspice, cinnamon, mace, clove), herbs (thyme, rosemary, marjoram, basil), various citrus zests, and scented syrups. Just remember to adjust the cooking time and the amount of sugar and lemon juice to your particular fruit.

We have only recently discovered that plum and guava are a spectacular match. If you increase the quantity of sugar in the compote to 1½ cups / 300 g and cook the fruit longer, you will end up with the most fragrant jam.

Preheat the oven to 375°F / 190°C. Start with the fruit, whichever option you choose. Mix all the ingredients together in a medium saucepan. Cook over medium-low heat for 15 to 20 minutes, until the fruits are completely soft, stirring occasionally. Remove from the heat and set aside to cool down.

To make the crumble, place both types of flour in a large mixing bowl with the butter, sugar, and salt. Use your fingers to rub the mixture into a bread crumb texture and then stir in the walnuts. Spread on a baking sheet lined with parchment paper and place in the oven for 15 to 20 minutes, until dry and cooked through. Remove and leave to cool.

For the cream, place all the ingredients in a large mixing bowl and whisk to soft peaks, taking care not to overwhip (it is quite thick to start with, so it shouldn't take more than 30 seconds).

To assemble, just spoon a nice dollop of cream into a bowl, top with some compote, and sprinkle with some crumble. For a fancier look, spoon one-third of the crumble into the bottom of four medium glasses or glass bowls. Cover this with two-thirds of the fruit, then two-thirds of the cream. Another one-third of the crumble goes on top of this, followed by the remaining fruit and then cream. Serve at once, or chill for a few hours before serving. Scatter the remaining crumble on top just before serving.

Spice cookies

During the late nineteenth century, as part of their Protestant beliefs, the Templars arrived in Jerusalem from Europe and established the German colony, a picturesque little neighborhood southwest of the Old City that to this day feels unusually central European. This is the "civilized" part of town, where you go for a coffee and a slice of Sacher torte if you wish to escape the harsh Levantine reality.

Germanic influences on the city's food are evident in Christian contexts—the famous Austrian hospice at the heart of the Old City serves superb strudels and proper schnitzels—but Czech, Austrian, Hungarian, and German Jews arriving in the city from the 1930s have also managed to stamp their mark, opening cafés and bakeries serving many Austro-Hungarian classics (SEE PAGE 284). *Duvshanyot*, round iced cookies, made with honey and spices, typically for Rosh Hashanah, are possibly a result of this heritage; they are similar to *Pfeffernüsse*.

¾ cup plus 2 tbsp / 125 g
   currants
2 tbsp brandy
scant 2 cups / 240 g all-
   purpose flour
1½ tsp best-quality cocoa
   powder
½ tsp baking powder
¼ tsp baking soda
½ tsp each ground
   cinnamon, allspice,
   ginger, and nutmeg
¼ tsp salt
5 oz / 150 g good-quality dark
   chocolate, coarsely grated
½ cup / 125 g unsalted
   butter, at room
   temperature
⅔ cup / 125 g superfine
   sugar
1 tsp vanilla extract
½ tsp grated lemon zest
½ tsp grated orange zest
½ large free-range egg
1 tbsp diced candied
   citrus peel

GLAZE

3 tbsp freshly squeezed
   lemon juice
1⅓ cups / 160 g
   confectioners' sugar

These are very loosely inspired by duvshanyot, *or* Pfeffernüsse. *They are actually more closely related to an Italian spice cookie and are hugely popular on the sweet counter at Ottolenghi over Easter and Christmas. The recipe was adapted from the excellent* The International Cookie Cookbook *by Nancy Baggett.*

Soak the currants in the brandy for 10 minutes. Mix together the flour, cocoa powder, baking powder, baking soda, spices, salt, and dark chocolate. Mix well with a whisk.

Put the butter, sugar, vanilla, and lemon and orange zest in a stand mixer fitted with the beater attachment and beat to combine but not aerate much, about 1 minute. With the mixer running, slowly add the egg and mix for about 1 minute. Add the dry ingredients, followed by the currants and brandy. Mix until everything comes together.

Gently knead the dough in the bowl with your hands until it comes together and is uniform. Divide the dough into 1¾-oz / 50g chunks and shape each chunk into a perfectly round ball. Place the balls on 1 or 2 baking sheets lined with parchment paper, spacing them about ¾ inch / 2 cm apart, and let rest in the fridge for at least 1 hour.

Preheat the oven to 375°F / 190°C. Bake the cookies for 15 to 20 minutes, until the top firms up but the center is still slightly soft. Remove from the oven. Once the cookies are out of the oven, allow to cool for only 5 minutes, and then transfer to a wire rack. While the cookies are still warm, whisk together the glaze ingredients until a thin and smooth icing forms. Pour 1 tablespoon of the glaze over each biscuit, leaving it to drip and coat the biscuit with a very thin, almost transparent film. Finish each with 3 pieces of candied peel placed at the center. Leave to set and serve, or store in an airtight container for a day or two.

Yeasted cakes

Yeasted doughs, enriched with eggs, sugar, and oil, butter or margarine, are at the heart of Ashkenazic cuisine. On Fridays, particularly in Me'ah She'arim and other Orthodox neighborhoods, you will find people queuing in bakeries for their challah (see picture on page 281)—wonderful, sweet braided Shabbat bread loved by all—just as they have done for generations in eastern and central Europe. Challah was adopted by Jews in southern Germany in the Middle Ages and spread all over the Ashkenazic world, where it was given various shapes, all having different religious significances.

(see picture on page 281)

ON FRIDAYS, YOU WILL FIND PEOPLE QUEUING IN BAKERIES FOR THEIR CHALLAH—WONDERFUL, SWEET BRAIDED SHABBAT BREAD LOVED BY ALL—JUST AS THEY HAVE DONE FOR GENERATIONS IN EASTERN AND CENTRAL EUROPE.

Another enriched yeasted dough product is the most popular cake in the west side of Jerusalem, and probably in the whole of the country. It is the *krantz* cake or *babbka*. This archetypal cake is also known as yeast cake (*ugat shmarim*), and as unattractive as the name may sound, the cake is scrumptiously soft and sweet, like a cross between a rum baba and a Danish pastry. People go crazy for it. There are industrial varieties sold in airtight packs in supermarkets and artisanal varieties baked fresh in specialized bakeries. They can be filled with a sweet, soft cheese (like ricotta), poppy seeds, chocolate, or nuts, to name but a few possibilities.

Like many other foods, this very Ashkenazic cake has completely crossed the lines from the world it started off in and has conquered the hearts and stomachs of the general Israeli public. Kadosh, a popular café set up in 1967 in the center of the city, is run by Itzik and Keren Kadosh, he a Sephardi and she from a Moroccan family. Yotam has seen them in action. It is unbelievable! Keren and Itzik bake hundreds of *krantzes* every Friday, the cheese one being the most popular, and droves of Jerusalemites of every possible background come to buy them for Shabbat.

Chocolate krantz cakes

4¼ cups / 530 g all-purpose flour, plus extra for dusting

½ cup / 100 g superfine sugar

2 tsp fast-rising active dry yeast

grated zest of 1 small lemon

3 extra-large free-range eggs

½ cup / 120 ml water

rounded ¼ tsp salt

⅔ cup / 150 g unsalted butter, at room temperature, cut into ¾-inch / 2cm cubes

sunflower oil, for greasing

CHOCOLATE FILLING

scant ½ cup / 50 g confectioners' sugar

⅓ cup / 30 g best-quality cocoa powder

4½ oz / 130 g good-quality dark chocolate, melted

½ cup / 120 g unsalted butter, melted

1 cup / 100 g pecans, coarsely chopped

2 tbsp superfine sugar

SYRUP (ENOUGH TO COVER BOTH CAKES)

⅔ cup / 160 ml water

1¼ cups / 260 g superfine sugar

Making a krantz isn't easy or quick (SEE PICTURES ON PAGES 283 AND 286–87). *You need to let the dough rise overnight and then fill and shape it, which is quite an elaborate process. But, and it is a big but, we were guaranteed by two of our recipe testers, Claudine and Alison, that it is well worth it! (Their exclamation mark.)*

Although this recipe makes two fairly large cakes, there isn't really any risk of anything going to waste. They are just the sort of thing everyone hurls themselves at as soon as they come out of the oven. They will also keep for up to two days at room temperature, wrapped in foil, and up to a couple of weeks when frozen.

For a fabulous alternative to the chocolate filling, brush each dough half with 6 tbsp / 80 g melted unsalted butter and then sprinkle with ½ cup / 120 g light muscovado sugar, 1½ tbsp ground cinnamon, and scant ½ cup / 50 g coarsely chopped walnuts; then roll as described in the chocolate version.

For the dough, place the flour, sugar, yeast, and lemon zest in a stand mixer fitted with the dough hook and mix on low speed for 1 minute. Add the eggs and water and mix on low speed for a few seconds, then increase the speed to medium and mix for 3 minutes, until the dough comes together. Add the salt and then start adding the butter, a few cubes at a time, mixing until it is incorporated into the dough. Continue mixing for about 10 minutes on medium speed, until the dough is completely smooth, elastic, and shiny. During the mixing, you will need to scrape down the sides of the bowl a few times and throw a small amount of flour onto the sides so that all of the dough leaves them.

Place the dough in a large bowl brushed with sunflower oil, cover with plastic wrap, and leave in the fridge for at least half a day, preferably overnight.

Grease two 2¼-lb / 1kg loaf pans (9 by 4 inches / 23 by 10 cm) with some sunflower oil and line the bottom of each pan with a piece of waxed paper. Divide the dough in half and keep one-half covered in the fridge.

Make the filling by mixing together the confectioners' sugar, cocoa powder, chocolate, and butter. You will get a spreadable paste. Roll out the dough on a lightly floured surface into a rectangle measuring 15 by 11 inches (38 by 28 cm). Trim the sides to make them even, then position the dough so that a long side is closest to you. Use an offset spatula to spread half the chocolate mixture over the rectangle, leaving a ¾-inch / 2cm border all around. Sprinkle half the pecans on top of the chocolate, then sprinkle over half the superfine sugar.

Brush a little bit of water along the long end farthest away from you. Use both hands to roll up the rectangle like a roulade, starting from the long side that is closest to you and ending at the other long end. Press to seal the dampened end onto the roulade and then use both hands to even out the roll into a perfect thick cigar. Rest the cigar on its seam.

Trim about ¾ inch / 2 cm off both ends of the roulade with a serrated knife. Now use the knife to gently cut the roll into half lengthwise, starting at the top and finishing at the seam. You are essentially dividing the log into two long even halves, with the layers of dough and filling visible along the length of both halves. With the cut sides facing up, gently press together one end of each half, and then lift the right half over the left half. Repeat this process, but this time lift the left half over the right, to create a simple, two-pronged plait. Gently squeeze together the other ends so that you are left with the two halves, intertwined, showing the filling on top. Carefully lift the cake into a loaf pan. Cover the pan with a wet tea towel and leave to rise in a warm place for 1 to 1½ hours. The cake will rise by 10 to 20 percent. Repeat the whole process to make the second cake.

Preheat the oven to 375°F / 190°C, making sure you allow plenty of time for it to heat fully before the cakes have finished rising. Remove the tea towels, place the cakes on the middle rack of the oven, and bake for about 30 minutes, until a skewer inserted in the center comes out clean.

While the cakes are in the oven, make the syrup. Combine the water and sugar in a saucepan, place over medium heat, and bring to a boil. As soon as the sugar dissolves, remove from the heat and leave to cool down. As soon as the cakes come out of the oven, brush all of the syrup over them. It is important to use up all the syrup. Leave the cakes until they are just warm, then remove them from the pans and let cool completely before serving.

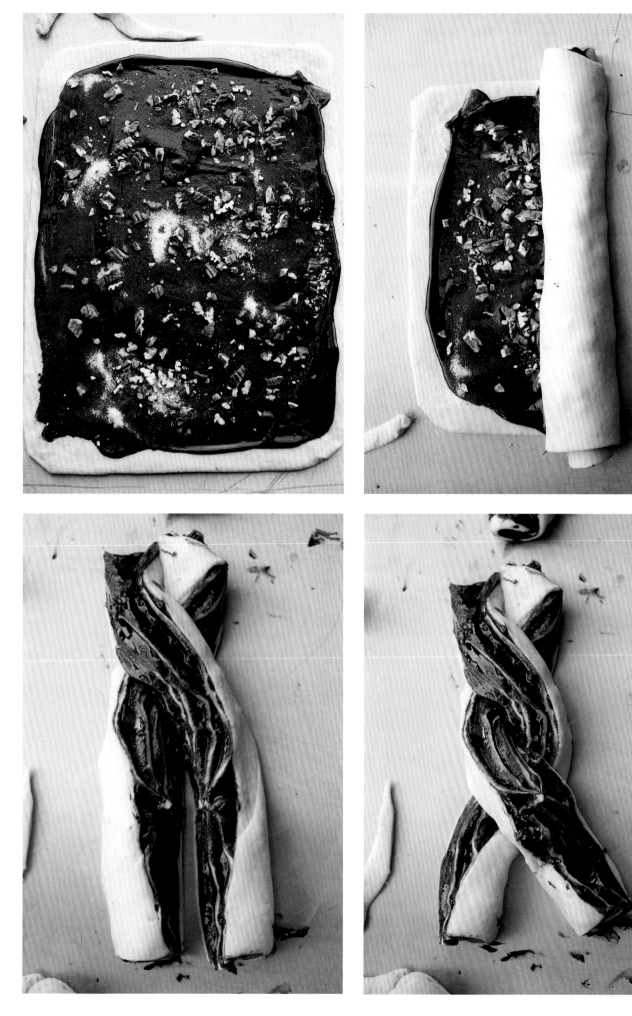

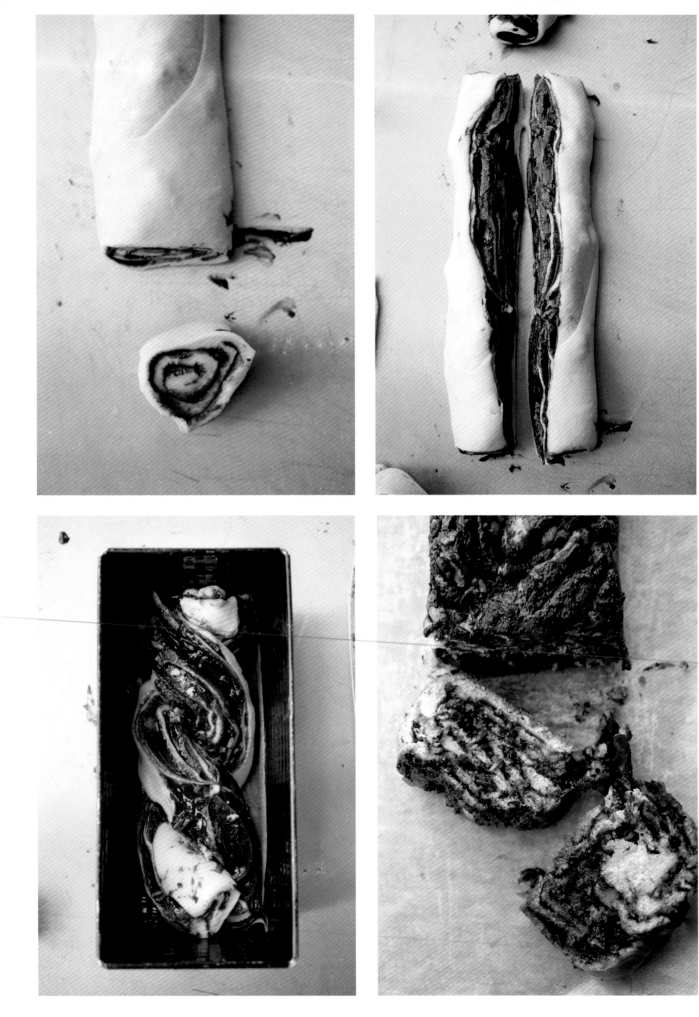

Ma'amul

During the month of Ramadan, many shops and restaurants are closed, but special pastries and confections make a seasonal appearance on the streets and in the bakeries of east Jerusalem. One particular favorite is *mushabak*, a type of batter that is poured into hot oil and fried, then drenched in syrup and sold in bulk for the breaking-of-the-fast feast after sunset. They are displayed piled up over a light that shines though the colorful see-through pastries.

An end-of-Ramadan specialty is *ma'amul*, probably the most popular of Arab cookies. *Ma'amul* are short biscuits made with semolina and/or flour, stuffed with nuts or dates, and daintily decorated with a special wooden mold or jagged tweezers. The date variety is round and flat, the nut one high and domed.

Sami clearly remembers a woman, whom the kids used to call "auntie," who went around all the houses in the neighborhood toward the end of Ramadan helping housewives make the cookies. The women of the extended family used to work together in a large, chatty group gathered around "auntie." They had to make a lot of cookies, enough for the many guests that come and go during this time, and some for the poor or those who couldn't afford to make them. Anyone coming to the house would encounter piles of cookies everywhere, white with fresh confectioners' sugar, like little snowballs.

Our ma'amul *cookies lack the distinctive dainty finish of the traditional version but have the typical short and dry casing with moist and nutty center and floral aroma. We mix together nuts and dates. You can substitute the walnuts with pistachios as is common in Nablus and the Galilee. The cookies keep well (up to five days if stored in an airtight container), so consider doubling the quantities. This recipe is adapted from one by Anissa Helou, a friend and a huge expert on Middle Eastern, particularly Lebanese, cuisine.*

---

2 cups plus 1½ tbsp / 350 g semolina

⅓ cup / 40 g all-purpose flour

3½ tbsp / 40 g superfine sugar

pinch of salt

¾ cup / 180 g unsalted butter, cut into 1¼-inch / 3cm cubes

2 tbsp orange blossom water

1 tbsp rose water

1½ tsp water

confectioners' sugar, to finish

WALNUT FILLING

2¼ cups / 225 g walnuts

⅓ cup / 45 g Medjool dates, coarsely chopped

3½ tbsp / 45 g superfine sugar

1 tsp ground cinnamon

1½ tsp rose water

1 tbsp orange blossom water

Put the semolina, flour, sugar, and salt in a large mixing bowl and stir together. Add the butter and work with your fingers until the texture is like bread crumbs. Add the orange blossom and rose waters and the water and use your hands to bring the mixture together into a ball. Remove to a clean surface and knead the dough for about 5 minutes, until completely smooth. Cover with a damp tea towel and leave to rest for 30 minutes.

To make the filling, place the walnuts, dates, sugar, and cinnamon in a food processor and process until the nuts are chopped quite finely but not completely ground. Add the rose and orange blossom waters and pulse briefly until you get a uniform coarse paste.

Preheat the oven to 400°F / 210°C. To mold the cookies, have a bowl of water handy to keep your hands damp while you work; this will help form the dough and prevent it from cracking. Remove walnut-size pieces of pastry, weighing a scant 1 oz / 25 g, and roll into a ball. Flatten each ball in the cup of your hand, turning it around as you do so and using your thumb to press it flat. Lift the edges to shape a little pot. The sides need to be ⅛ inch / 3 mm thick and 1 inch / 2.5 cm high.

Fill the pastry with a heaping tablespoon of the filling. Pinch the dough over the filling so that the pot is sealed, then roll it into a ball again. Flatten the ball between the palms of your hands—the sides should now be 1¼ inches / 3 cm high—and then place on a baking sheet lined with parchment paper. Repeat until all the dough and filling is used. Using the back of a fork, press down gently on top of each cookie to make a pattern of lines with the tines.

Bake for 12 to 14 minutes. The cookies need to be cooked through but must not take on any color. Remove from the oven and transfer to a wire rack to cool down. Before serving, sprinkle liberally with confectioners' sugar. The cookies will keep for up to 5 days in an airtight container.

Helbeh (fenugreek cake)

3 cups / 500 g fine
   semolina
⅔ cup / 75 g all-purpose
   flour
½ cup / 70 g pine nuts,
   blitzed into large crumbs
⅓ cup / 80 ml olive oil
⅓ cup / 80 ml sunflower oil
2½ tbsp /40 g unsalted
   butter, melted, plus extra
   to grease the pan
1½ tsp fenugreek seeds
2½ cups / 600 ml water
1½ tsp fast-rising active
   yeast
½ tsp baking powder
½ tsp salt
3 tbsp / 25 g whole
   almonds, blanched
   and peeled

SYRUP

1½ cups / 300 g superfine
   sugar
6½ tbsp / 100 ml water
2 tbsp freshly squeezed
   lemon juice
1½ tbsp rose water
1½ tbsp orange blossom
   water

This cake is one of Sami's childhood favorites. It is essentially a semolina cake soaked in syrup, similar to many other Levantine cakes (SEE SEMOLINA, COCONUT, AND MARMALADE CAKE, PAGE 264), but the fenugreek gives it a very unusual edge. We haven't come across it anywhere else.

Sami's grandmother used to say that breastfeeding mothers must eat *helbeh* because fenugreek will encourage milk production. Despite their firm protests, bitter fenugreek tea was always given to kids to cure minor illnesses. It was believed to have a great medicinal effect but, unfortunately, had a flavor to match.

Helbeh cake comes with a disclaimer. Not everyone likes it. In a quick survey we did among the chefs in our restaurant NOPI, only five out of seven approved. But those five absolutely loved it! Fenugreek, the ultimate curry ingredient, has a strong savory association in many people's minds and some can't shake it off. However, a bit like cardamom, it works in a sweet context very well and adds magical "exoticism" that really appeals to others. If you like cardamom, rose water, and intense sweetness, you are likely to enjoy helbeh. It is fantastic with a small cup of strong black coffee.

Always make helbeh *at least a day ahead of serving and don't be tempted to tuck into it sooner; the flavors need the time to come together properly.*

Mix the semolina, flour, and pine nuts in a large bowl. Add the oils and melted butter and mix well. Set aside.

Put the fenugreek seeds and water in a medium saucepan and bring to a boil over high heat. Decrease the heat to low and simmer for about 25 minutes, until the seeds are plump and tender. Drain the seeds, reserving the cooking water, and add them to the semolina mix. Add the yeast, baking powder, and salt, then gradually stir in ¾ cup / 180 ml of the hot fenugreek water; if you don't have enough liquid, make it up with water. Knead the dough on a work surface until it is completely smooth.

Grease a 9½-inch / 24cm round cake pan with butter and line it with parchment paper so that the paper comes three-quarters of the way up the sides of the pan. Pour in the semolina mixture and press it down with your hand so it is level and smooth.

Use a small, sharp knife to score the surface of the cake with parallel lines 2 inches / 5 cm apart, followed by another set of lines at a 45-degree angle, creating a diamond pattern. Place 1 almond in the

center of each diamond. Cover the cake pan with a clean tea towel and set it aside somewhere warm for about 1 hour. Toward the end of the resting time, preheat the oven to 425°F / 220°C, making sure you allow plenty of time for your oven to heat fully.

Put the cake on the lower oven rack and bake for 20 minutes. Lower the heat to 400°F / 200°C and bake for 20 minutes longer, until it is golden brown and a skewer inserted in the center comes out clean.

Prepare the syrup while the cake is in the oven. Place the sugar and water in a small saucepan and mix well with a wooden spoon. Bring to a boil, add the lemon juice, and simmer gently for 4 minutes. Take the syrup off the heat, allow it to cool down just a little, and then add the orange blossom and rose waters.

When the cake is ready, remove it from the oven and immediately drizzle the syrup all over it, making sure you use all of the syrup. Leave the cake to cool completely, then cover well with aluminum foil or parchment paper. Serve the next day.

Tahini cookies

When it comes to food, Israelis can be very fickle. One day, without any notice, everybody discovers a brand-new favorite delight and treats it as the absolute best thing since sliced bread. This normally doesn't last long, before something new and equally exciting makes a surprise appearance. This was the case when tahini, or halva, cookies were at the height of their popularity a few years ago. There was no escaping them. You could find them in all the cafés, in every bakery, and in the cookie jar of any avid home baker, echoing the taste and texture of local halva, the crumbly dense Arab confection made with sesame paste and honey or sugar.

Tahini is very much the local version of peanut butter (SEE PAGE 298) and this is by no means the only time it crosses sides from savory to sweet. Raw tahini paste mixed with honey makes the most delicious breakfast spread. A staple Palestinian breakfast snack is chunks of bread dipped in tahini mixed with grape molasses. Iraqi Jews serve dates drenched in tahini to end the meal on a sweet note.

The cookie buzz has now died down, but the passion for halva lives on. These days it is served as ice cream at Machneyuda, the most creative of the city's new restaurants (SEE PAGE 205). It has also found its way into Kadosh Café's chocolate-halva *krantz* cake (PAGE 284).

⅔ cup / 130 g superfine
   sugar
⅔ cup / 150 g unsalted
   butter, at room
   temperature
scant ½ cup / 110 g light
   tahini paste
½ tsp vanilla extract
5 tsp / 25 ml heavy cream
2 cups plus 1½ tbsp / 270 g
   all-purpose flour
1 tsp ground cinnamon

These cookies are like a hybrid between a short biscuit and halva, with the typical melting texture of the former and the nutty, unctuous flavor of the latter. For us, who used to spread halva over white bread and gulp it down for breakfast, they are a real throwback to childhood.

Preheat the oven to 400°F / 200°C. Place the sugar and butter in a stand mixer fitted with the beater attachment and beat on medium speed for 1 minute, until just combined but not aerated much. With the machine running, add the tahini, vanilla, and cream, then add the flour and beat for about 1 minute, until the dough comes together. Transfer to a work surface and knead until smooth.

Pinch off ⅔ oz / 20 g of the dough and roll into a ball between your palms. Use the back of a fork to push down lightly on top of the ball so that it flattens just slightly and takes on the marks from the tines. Place on a baking sheet lined with parchment paper (you may need 2 sheets, depending on size). Continue with the rest of the dough, spacing the cookies 1¼ inches / 3 cm apart. Sprinkle a little cinnamon on each cookie and then bake for 15 to 17 minutes, until golden brown. Transfer to a wire rack to cool before serving. They will keep in a sealed container for up to 10 days.

Almond memories

Almonds originated in the Middle East and for centuries were a rare and expensive commodity reserved for special occasions. In Sephardic culture, *mazapán*, or "marzipan," is the pinnacle of all culinary achievements. Daniela Lerrer, owner of the Sephardic bar, Barood, refers to the sweet almond paste as "the holiest of holy." Marzipan was, and still is, prepared only for very special occasions such as births and weddings in her family. She recalls that after giving birth, her mother, in addition to passing her down the frying pan she had been using for decades, also prepared marzipan.

The Bulgarian Jews' marzipan is considered the finest. Celebrated Jerusalem-born author Meir Shalev gives a highly detailed account of marzipan making in his book, *Esau*, based on his wife's Bulgarian aunt's recipe. That same aunt showed up on his wedding day, elegant and beautiful, carrying a large tray of traditional marzipan she had made especially for the occasion. Upon noticing the groom's side of the family—a bunch of salt-of-the-earth but scruffy farmers—she held the tray close to her, tightly, and whispered to the bride, "This, is for Bulgarians only."

> EVERYBODY WATCHED CLOSELY AS ONE OF THE KIDS WARILY POPPED AN ALMOND INTO HIS MOUTH AND THEN ALL BURST INTO NASTY, VICIOUS LAUGHTER AT THE SIGHT OF ONE VERY CONTORTED FACE.

There were two very similar almond trees in the communal playgrounds just outside Yotam's house. School ended early in those days—around 12 or 1 p.m.—so Yotam and his friends used to spend long afternoons trying to keep themselves entertained with anything even remotely exciting, from playing with all sorts of creepy crawlies and stray cats to taunting younger kids. When they ran out of options, the almond trees supplied the all-too-necessary distraction for the gang. It was their version of Russian roulette.

As one of the trees produced only bitter almonds and the other beautifully sweet ones, and the dried nuts could only be picked off the ground, it was completely impossible to know what went into one's mouth until it was too late. Everybody watched closely as one of the kids warily popped an almond into his mouth and then all burst into nasty, vicious laughter at the sight of one very contorted face.

Green almonds, a young nut encased in a velvety green shell that later falls off, make a fleeting appearance in markets during the spring. They are sold over ice sprinkled with salt and eaten raw; they are extremely sour. When making stuffed vegetables, Sami's mother used to line the bottom of the pan with them, where they would impart a sharp aroma.

Clementine & almond syrup cake

¾ cup plus 2 tbsp / 200 g
  unsalted butter
scant 2 cups / 380 g
  superfine sugar
grated zest and juice of
  4 clementines
grated zest and juice of
  1 lemon
2½ cups / 280 g ground
  almonds
5 large free-range eggs,
  beaten
¾ cup plus 1 tbsp / 100 g
  all-purpose flour, sifted
pinch of salt
long strips of orange zest
  to garnish

CHOCOLATE ICING
(OPTIONAL)

6 tbsp / 90 g unsalted
  butter, diced
5 oz / 150 g good-quality
  dark chocolate,
  broken up
2½ tsp honey
1½ tsp Cognac

This fragrant cake has a wonderful light texture and will keep, covered, for at least a week. Oranges will make an adequate substitute for the clementines. A citrus zester, inexpensive and widely available, is the ideal tool for getting long, even strips of orange zest to garnish the cake.

Preheat the oven to 350°F / 180°C. Lightly grease a 9½-inch / 24cm springform pan with butter and line the sides and bottom with parchment paper.

Place the butter, 1½ cups / 300 g of the sugar, and both zests in a stand mixer fitted with the beater attachment and beat on low speed to combine everything well. Do not work the mixture too much or incorporate too much air. Add half the ground almonds and continue mixing until combined.

With the machine running, gradually add the eggs, stopping to scrape the bottom and sides of the bowl a couple of times as you go. Add the remaining ground almonds, the flour, and the salt and beat until completely smooth.

Pour the cake batter into the pan and level it with an offset spatula.

Bake the cake for 50 to 60 minutes. Check to see if it is ready by inserting a skewer into the center. It should come out a little bit moist.

When the cake is almost done, place the remaining ⅓ cup / 80 g sugar and the citrus juices in a small saucepan and bring to a boil (the juices should total about ½ cup / 120 ml; remove some juice if needed). When the syrup boils, remove it from the heat.

As soon as the cake comes out of the oven, brush it with the boiling syrup, making sure all the syrup soaks in. Leave the cake to cool down completely in the pan before you remove it. You can then serve it as it is, garnished with orange zest strips, or store it for up to 3 days in an airtight container.

If you wish to ice the cake, we recommend doing it on the day you want to serve it so the icing is fresh and shiny. Put the butter, chocolate, and honey in a heatproof bowl and place over a saucepan of simmering water (make sure the bowl does not touch the water). Stir until everything is melted, then immediately remove from the heat and fold in the Cognac. Pour the icing over the cooled cake, allowing it to dribble naturally down the sides without covering the cake completely. Let the icing set and then garnish the center of the cake with the orange zest strips.

CONDIMENTS

Dukkah

½ cup / 70 g hazelnuts,
    with skins
2 tbsp sunflower seeds
1 tsp fennel seeds
1 tbsp cumin seeds
1 tbsp dried green
    peppercorns (or white,
    as an alternative)
3 tbsp coriander seeds
1½ tbsp sesame seeds
½ tsp nigella seeds
½ tsp Maldon sea salt
1 tsp sweet paprika

This is an Egyptian aromatic seed-and-nut mix that can be sprinkled over leafy salads, roasted vegetables, bean pastes such as hummus, and simply cooked rice or lentils. It adds an exotic charm. You can prepare it in advance and store it in an airtight container for a month or so. When making, be sure not to burn the seeds, removing them from the heat as soon as they begin to pop, and also not to process them much with the mortar and pestle so that they keep their texture.

Preheat the oven to 325°F / 160°C.

Spread the hazelnuts on a baking sheet and place in the oven for 20 minutes. Add the sunflower seeds after 10 minutes, keeping them apart from the nuts. Remove from the oven and leave to cool while you toast the seeds.

Put a cast-iron pan or heavy-bottomed frying pan over medium heat and leave for 5 minutes to heat up. Spread the fennel seeds in the pan and dry-toast them for 30 seconds. Add the cumin seeds and cook for another 30 seconds, until they start to pop, then transfer them both to a little bowl. Keeping the pan over the heat, add the green peppercorns and cook for about 30 seconds, until they start to pop. Transfer to a separate bowl. Dry-toast the coriander seeds for up to a minute, until they start to pop. Keep separate.

Decrease the heat to low and cook the sesame and nigella seeds together, stirring occasionally, until the sesame seeds turn light brown, then remove from the pan.

Rub the hazelnuts between the palms of your hands to remove and discard some of the skins. Use a mortar and pestle to chop them coarsely, then transfer to a medium bowl. Lightly crush the cumin and fennel seeds and add to the hazelnuts. Do the same with the coriander seeds, followed by the green peppercorns and then the sunflower seeds. Add the sesame and nigella seeds, the salt, and the paprika and mix well. Store in an airtight container for up to 1 month.

Harissa

1 red pepper
½ tsp coriander seeds
½ tsp cumin seeds
½ tsp caraway seeds
1½ tbsp olive oil
1 small red onion, coarsely
   chopped (scant ⅔ cup /
   90 g in total)
3 cloves garlic, coarsely
   chopped
3 hot red chiles, seeded
   and coarsely chopped
1½ tsp tomato paste
2 tbsp freshly squeezed
   lemon juice
½ tsp salt

Harissa, the basic flavoring agent in Tunisian cuisine, is extremely versatile. Use it as a condiment for grilled meat or fish, add it to roasted vegetables, or stir into stews and soups. We particularly like it with couscous or rice. Adjust the amount of heat by increasing or reducing the number of chiles. Just remember, it is meant to be hot!

Place the pepper under a very hot broiler, turning occasionally for about 25 minutes, until blackened on the outside and completely soft. Transfer to a bowl, cover with plastic wrap, and allow to cool. Peel the pepper and discard its skin and seeds.

Place a dry frying pan over low heat and lightly toast the coriander, cumin, and caraway seeds for 2 minutes. Remove them to a mortar and use a pestle to grind to a powder.

Heat the olive oil in a frying pan over medium heat, and fry the onion, garlic, and chiles for 10 to 12 minutes, until a dark smoky color and almost caramelized.

Now use a blender or a food processor to blitz together all of the paste ingredients until smooth, adding a little more oil if needed.

Store in a sterilized jar (SEE PAGE 303) in the fridge for up to 2 weeks or even longer.

Zhoug

1¼ oz / 35 g cilantro
   (leaves and stems),
   coarsely chopped
⅓ oz / 10 g flat-leaf parsley
   (leaves and stems),
   coarsely chopped
2 hot green chiles,
   coarsely chopped
½ tsp ground cumin
¼ tsp ground cardamom
¼ tsp ground cloves
⅛ tsp superfine sugar
¼ tsp salt
1 clove garlic, crushed
2 tbsp olive oil
2 tbsp water

Jews arriving from Yemen in the first part of the twentieth century are responsible for zhoug, the Israeli national chile paste. It is an "official" component of the famous pita with falafel and of shawarma.

Zhoug is a wonderful condiment that is believed to have health benefits for the immune system and the stomach. You can spoon it over anything that requires an additional kick. However, it is best served alongside some freshly grated tomatoes. Dunk a slice of white bread in each and you are in heaven. You can also spoon both over a rich piece of meat or a stew, as a Middle Eastern kind of gremolata.

The texture of zhoug is important. It needs to be coarse, as if it were made traditionally with grinding stones. It should also be very hot, so use more chiles if yours aren't.

Place all of the ingredients in a small food processor. Blitz in a few pulses to get a coarse paste; make sure not to overmix. Store in a sterilized jar (SEE PAGE 303) in the fridge for up to 3 weeks.

Pilpelchuma

1 large ancho or pasilla
  chile, or other dried chile
  with a little heat (⅓ oz /
  12 g in total)
4½ tbsp / 25 g cayenne
  pepper
3½ tbsp / 25 g sweet
  paprika
2½ tsp ground cumin
1½ tsp caraway seeds,
  ground
20 cloves garlic, peeled
  (2¾ oz / 75 g in total)
¾ tsp salt
5 tbsp / 75 ml sunflower
  oil, plus a little extra

This is an intense chile-and-garlic paste that is used by Jews from Tripoli as a basic seasoning for many of their dishes, a bit like the Tunisian harissa. *It is concentrated and deep in flavor, so use it carefully. It can be smeared over root vegetables before roasting, or mixed with oil and herbs to marinate meats for the grill. It is also wonderful whisked into the eggs when making scrambled eggs.*

Place the chile in a small bowl, cover with hot water, and allow it to soak for 30 minutes. Drain and seed the chile and cut into large chunks.

Spread the ground spices out in a frying pan. Place over medium-low heat and dry-roast them for about 2 minutes. Put the spices in a small food processor, along with the chile, garlic, and salt. Process a little, then, with the machine still running, pour in the oil and process until you get a sticky paste.

Spoon the mixture into a sterilized jar (SEE PAGE 303) and cover with a film of oil to prevent it drying out. Seal and store in the fridge, where it will last for up to 1 month.

Labneh

scant 2 cups / 450 g
  goat's milk yogurt
scant 2 cups / 450 g
  cow's milk yogurt
½ tsp coarse sea salt

Labneh *is yogurt that has been drained of most of its liquid and is almost as thick as cream cheese. It has a sharp, intense flavor. You can make* labneh *with any yogurt, but we like mixing goat's and cow's milk yogurts for a good balance of flavors. You can keep the* labneh *for at least a week in a sealed tub in the fridge, ready to be spread over bread as a quick snack with some sliced cucumber. As part of a meze selection, spread it out on a small plate, drizzle with olive oil, and sprinkle with chopped oregano or some* za'atar.

Line a deep bowl with cheesecloth. In a separate bowl, stir the yogurts together with the salt, then pour into the cloth. Bring the edges together, form a tight bundle, and tie firmly with a string. Hang the bundle over the bowl and place in the fridge. Leave the yogurt to drain for 24 to 36 hours, emptying the bowl once or twice if needed. After this time, much of the liquid will be gone and the yogurt will have turned thick and quite dry; the center may still be creamy.

Preserved lemons

6 unwaxed lemons
6 tbsp coarse sea salt
2 rosemary sprigs
1 large red chile
juice of 6 lemons
olive oil

We've published this recipe before, in Ottolenghi: The Cookbook, *but as pickled lemons are so central to our cooking and so much better homemade, here it is again. Just remember, the preserving process will take at least four weeks, and you really do need to give the lemons this time. The same method can be used with limes.*

Before starting, get a jar just large enough to accommodate all the lemons snugly. To sterilize it, fill it with boiling water, leave for a minute, and then empty it. Allow it to dry out naturally without wiping it so it remains sterilized.

Wash the lemons and cut a deep cross all the way from the top to within ¾ inch / 2 cm from the base. Stuff each lemon with 1 tablespoon of the salt and place in the jar. Push the lemons in tightly so they are squeezed together tightly. Seal the jar and leave in a cool spot for at least a week.

After this initial period, remove the lid and press the lemons as hard as you can to squeeze out as much of the juice as possible. Add the rosemary, chile, and lemon juice and cover with a thin layer of olive oil. Seal the jar and leave in a cool place for at least 4 weeks. The longer you leave them, the better the flavor.

Quick pickled lemons

½ red chile, chopped
3 tbsp freshly squeezed
  lemon juice
3 small-medium unwaxed
  lemons, halved
  lengthwise and sliced
  widthwise as thinly as
  possible
3 tbsp / 35 g superfine
  sugar
1½ tsp coarse sea salt
1 clove garlic, crushed
1 tsp sweet paprika
¼ tsp ground cumin
½ tsp ground turmeric

*For these, you won't need to wait four weeks like you do for preserved lemons (*SEE ABOVE), *just 24 hours. Their aroma won't be quite as perfumed but still magnificently pungent, so much so that they warrant a word of warning: a bit like chile sauce, once you have started accompanying your food with these slices—meat, fish, lentils, couscous—you will find them hard to give up.*

Use a mortar and pestle to smash together the chile with 1 teaspoon of the lemon juice; you want to get a rough-looking paste. Transfer this to a large bowl along with all the other ingredients. Use your hands to mix everything together well so that all the flavors get massaged into the lemons. Leave in a covered bowl overnight, then transfer to a sterilized sealed jar (SEE ABOVE) the next day. The lemon will keep in the fridge for up to 2 weeks.

Pickled cucumbers with dill

There are some foods that can be found on pretty much any dining table in Jerusalem. Pickles, particularly pickled cucumbers, are a safe bet. Their sharp, often overwhelming intensity is completely compatible with the local character.

Pickles are frequently served at the beginning of meals to encourage the appetite, or alongside substantial, often fatty dishes to balance their richness. Palestinian and Jewish restaurants always serve pickles with hummus. The Ashkenazic cucumber pickles, which gained a mythological status, are a must next to Chopped liver (PAGE 186). Sephardim serve them as appetizers before the meal and then with the meal itself, adding a touch of zest to long-cooked stews and *tagines*.

Both Arabs and Sephardim pickle turnips or cauliflowers in beet water (SEE PICKLED TURNIP AND BEET, PAGE 307). It dyes them a familiar pink tinge that adds brightness to the table when placed next to dull-colored dishes such as chickpeas, lentils, and eggplant.

In general, most cuisines in Jerusalem don't add sugar to their pickling liquor and many use brine only, no vinegar, particularly for cucumbers. However, it is hard to draw many generalizations when it comes to pickles, because it is all about using up seasonal ingredients and those obviously vary. On top of that, each cuisine tends to add its own little touches—lemon skin, a spice, chile, herbs—that are unique and distinctive.

These are easy to make and take three to six days. You need to make sure you use small cucumbers. Look for them in Middle Eastern groceries.

4½ cups / 1 liter water
4½ tbsp coarse sea salt
1 tsp black mustard seeds
1 tsp coriander seeds
10 allspice berries
1 tsp fennel seeds
10 black peppercorns
5 whole cloves
1 tsp celery seeds
1 small dried chile
1 large bunch dill
 (1¾ oz / 50 g in total)
7 cloves garlic, unpeeled,
 lightly crushed
6 bay leaves
10 to 13 mini or Lebanese
 cucumbers (about 1 lb /
 900 g in total)

Bring the water and salt to a boil in a medium saucepan. Once the salt has dissolved, remove from the heat.

Place all the spices, the chile, half the dill, the garlic, and the bay leaves in the bottom of a sterilized 1½-quart / 1.5l jar (SEE PAGE 303). Place the cucumbers vertically in the jar, pressing them in to make sure they are tightly packed; try to get in as many as possible.

Fill the jar with the hot brine, making sure the cucumbers are completely covered. Put the rest of the dill on top and cover the jar loosely with the lid (this allows gas to escape from the jar). Store in a cool, dark place for 3 days.

After 3 days, taste a pickle. It should be mildly pickled. Leave to ferment for up to 3 days longer if you want a sharper taste. In any case, once you are happy with the flavor, seal the jar and refrigerate for up to 2 weeks.

Pickled mixed vegetables with curry

¼ small white cabbage, cut
 into 1¼-inch / 3cm cubes
 (2½ cups / 220 g in total)
3 medium carrots, peeled
 and cut at an angle into
 ⅜-inch / 1cm slices
 (2⅔ cups / 330 g in total)
2 mini cucumbers, cut at
 an angle into ⅜-inch /
 1cm slices (scant 2 cups /
 190 g in total)
2 celery stalks, cut into
 1¼-inch / 3cm segments
¼ small cauliflower,
 divided into small florets
 (scant 1 cup / 120 g
 in total)
1 tbsp curry powder
1 tsp ground allspice
6 cloves garlic, sliced
2 red chiles
3¼ cups / 800 ml
 warm water
6½ tbsp / 100 ml cider
 vinegar
fine sea salt

Pick and choose the vegetables you want to use. You can add rutabaga, radish, turnip, kohlrabi, or even unripe plums.

Mix the vegetables in a bowl and place about half at the bottom of a sterilized 1½-quart / 1.5l jar (SEE PAGE 303). Add the curry, allspice, garlic, and chiles. Top with the remaining vegetables.

To make the brine, stir 2 tablespoons salt into the warm water until dissolved. Pour the brine into the jar, filling it to within ¾ inch / 2 cm of the rim. Add the vinegar; the vegetables should be completely covered. If they are not, make more brine by adding 1½ teaspoons salt to each scant 1 cup / 200 ml warm water. Seal the jar.

Place the jar in a well lit, if possible, sunny, spot. The pickles should be ready in 5 days. They should be crunchy and full of sharp and salty flavors. Once ready, keep in the fridge for up to 2 weeks.

Pickled turnip and beet

10 small or 5 large fresh
 turnips (2¼ lb / 1 kg
 in total)
3 small beets (8½ oz /
 240 g in total)
1 green or red chile, cut
 into ⅜-inch / 1cm slices
3 tender celery stalks, cut
 into ¾-inch / 2cm slices
1¼ cups / 300 ml distilled
 white vinegar
3 cups / 720 ml warm
 water
fine sea salt

This is a cinch to make but must be prepared over two days. It is sharp and not too complex in flavor, perfect for serving with unctuous meats (SEE LAMB SHAWARMA, PAGE 210), a tagine, or hummus (PAGE 114).

Peel the turnips and beets, halve them if they are not small, and cut them into slices ¼-inch / 0.5cm thick. Place in a large mixing bowl and sprinkle with 1 teaspoon salt. Stir well, cover, and set aside to marinate overnight at room temperature.

The following day, transfer the vegetables and their juices to a sterilized 1½- to 2-quart / 1.5 to 2l jar (SEE PAGE 303). Add the chile and celery, followed by 3 tablespoons salt, the vinegar, and the water. If needed, add more water and vinegar to fill the jar (two parts water to one part vinegar) to within ¾ inch / 2 cm of the rim. Seal the jar, shake it gently to dissolve the salt, and place in a well-lit spot. After 3 to 4 days, the pickles should be ready. They will keep somewhere cool and dark for up to 1 month.

Index

A

Abadi cookies 247–9
acharuli khachapuri 252–3
a'ja (bread fritters) 64
almond 293–5
    & Clementine syrup cake
      294–5
    date & baby spinach salad 30–1
    sweet filo cigars 258–9
anari cheese, herb pie 250–1
Ansky, Sherry 125, 174
apricot, currants & tamarind,
    with braised quail 176–7
arak
    & Clementines, with roasted
      chicken 178–9
    yogurt pudding with poached
      peaches 268–9
artichoke
    raw, & herb salad 40–1
    stuffed with peas & dill 170–1
arugula, raw artichoke & herb
    salad 40–1

B

baba ghanoush 76
Baggett, Nancy 278
baharat 299
balilah 102
banana shallot
    lamb meatballs, with
      barberries, yogurt & herbs
      198–9
    roasted chicken with
      Jerusalem artichoke & lemon
      180–1
barberry
    chicken with caramelized
      onion & cardamom rice 184–5
    fava bean kuku 38–9
    pistachio & mixed herbs, with
      saffron rice 104–5
    yogurt & herbs, with lamb
      meatballs 198–9
barley
    & parsley salad 80–1
    risotto, with marinated feta
      108–9
    & yogurt hot soup 134

beans
    beans & grains 94–129
    cannellini, & lamb soup 135
    mixed, salad 42–3
    see also fava bean
beef
    kofta b'siniyah 194–5
    kubbeh hamusta 162–3
    meatballs, with fava beans &
      lemon 196–7
    polpette 203
    spicy freekeh soup with
      meatballs 148–9
    stuffed artichoke with peas &
      dill 170–1
    stuffed potatoes 168–9
beet
    golden, & orange salsa, with
      pan-fried mackerel 222–3
    leek & walnut spicy salad 72–3
    puréed, with yogurt
      & za'atar 52–3
    root vegetable slaw with
      labneh 48–9
    & turnip, pickled 307
bread fritters (a'ja) 64
bread crumbs
    beef meatballs with fava beans
      & lemon 196–7
    polpette 202–3
    stuffed potatoes 168–9
brick 244–5
bulgur wheat
    open kibbeh 160–1
    tabbouleh 85
    yogurt & chermoula
      eggplant 58–9
burekas 254–5
burgers, turkey & zucchini,
    with green onion & cumin
    200–1
butternut squash
    & red onion, roasted, with
      tahini & za'atar 36–7
    & tahini spread 68–9

C

cabbage
    pickled mixed vegetables with
      curry 307
    stuffed 153

cakes
    Clementine & almond syrup
      294–5
    helbeh (fenugreek) 290–1
    semolina, coconut &
      marmalade 264–5
    yeasted 280–7
cannellini bean & lamb soup 135
caper & fish kebabs with burnt
    eggplant & lemon pickle 220–1
caramel, prunes & roasted
    potato 86–7
cardamom
    rice 184–5
    rice pudding, with pistachios &
      rose water 270–1
    & white wine, pears poached
      in 266–7
carrot
    clear chicken soup with
      knaidlach 144–5
    pickled mixed vegetables with
      curry 307
    root vegetable slaw with
      labneh 48–9
    spicy freekeh soup with
      meatballs 148–9
    spicy, salad 65
    watercress & chickpea soup
      with rose water & ras el
      hanout 132–3
cashew, parsley & barley salad
    80–1
cauliflower
    fried, with tahini 60–1
    maqluba 125–8
    pickled mixed vegetables with
      curry 307
    roasted, & hazelnut salad 62–3
celeriac
    cannellini bean & lamb soup 135
    root vegetable slaw with
      labneh 48–9
celery
    clear chicken soup with
      knaidlach 144–5
    herb pie 250–1
    kubbeh hamusta 162–3
    pickled mixed vegetables with
      curry 307

roasted cauliflower & hazelnut
salad 62–3
spicy freekeh soup with
meatballs 148–9
challah 280–2
cheddar
burekas 254–5
herb pie 250–1
cheese
sweet 261
see also specific cheeses
chermoula eggplant with bulgur
& yogurt 58–9
chicken
with caramelized onion &
cardamom rice 184–5
clear soup, with knaidlach
144–5
Jerusalem mixed grill 174–5
maqluba 125–8
poached, with sweet spiced
freekeh 182–3
roasted, with Clementines &
arak 178–9
roasted, with Jerusalem
artichoke & lemon 180–1
saffron, & herb salad 188–9
sofrito 190–1
chicken heart, Jerusalem mixed
grill 174–5
chicken liver
chopped 186
Jerusalem mixed grill 174–5
chickpea
balilah 102
basic hummus 114–15
currants & herbs with basmati
& wild rice 106–7
falafel 98–9
hummus kawarma with lemon
sauce 116–18
spiced, & fresh vegetable salad
56–7
warm, with hummus & toasted
pita 119
& watercress soup with rose
water & ras el hanout 132–3
chile
& garlic paste
(pilpelchuma) 302
yogurt & peas with conchiglie
110–11
chocolate
icing 294–5
krantz cake (babbka) 284–7
spice cookies 278–9

chraimeh sauce, salmon steaks
in 234–5
cigars, sweet filo 258–9
cilantro
& pomegranate, with lamb-
stuffed quince 154–5
zhoug 301
clam
prawn & scallop with tomato &
feta 232–3
seafood & fennel soup 136–7
clementine
& almond syrup cake 294–5
& arak with roasted chicken
178–9
coconut, marmalade & semolina
cake 264–5
cod cakes in tomato sauce 224–5
compote
fig 276–7
guava & plum 276–7
conchiglie with yogurt, peas &
chile 110–11
condiments 296–307
cookies
Abadi 247–9
ghraybeh 260
ma'amul 288–9
spice 278–9
tahini 292
cottage cheese, burekas 254–5
couscous 139–41
burnt eggplant & mograbieh
soup 140–1
with tomato & onion 129
crumble, cream, walnut & fruit
276–7
cucumber
pickled with dill 304
yogurt with 299
see also mini cucumber
cumin & green onion with turkey
& zucchini burgers 200–1
currant
herbs & chickpeas with
basmati & wild rice 106–7
spice cookies 278–9
tamarind & apricots, with
braised quail 176–7
curry, pickled mixed vegetables
with 307

D
date
almond & baby spinach salad
30–1
ma'amul 288–9
desserts & sweets 256–95
dill
cucumbers pickled with 304
& peas, artichoke stuffed with
170–1
dukkah 300
dumplings, knaidlach with clear
chicken soup 144–5

E
egg
acharuli khachapuri 252–3
a'ja (bread fritters) 64
baked, & red pepper galettes
242–3
braised, with lamb, tahini &
sumac 204–5
chopped liver 186
fava bean kuku 38–9
fricassee salad 227
polpette 203
sabih 90–1
salsina verde 203
shakshuka 66–7
eggplant 32
baba ghanoush 76
burnt, & lemon pickle with fish
& caper kebabs 220–1
burnt, with lemon &
pomegranate seeds 76–7
burnt, & mograbieh soup 140–1
chermoula, with bulgur &
yogurt 58–9
maqluba 125–8
roasted, with fried onion &
chopped lemon 33
sabih 90–1
stuffed, with lamb & pine nuts
166–7

F
falafel 98–9
Fattoush, Na'ama's 28–9
fava bean
kuku 38–9
& lemon, with beef meatballs
196–7

fennel
    roasted chicken with
        Clementines & arak 178–9
    saffron chicken & herb salad
        188–9
    & seafood soup 136–7
fenugreek cake (helbeh) 290–1
feta
    acharuli khachapuri 252–3
    a'ja (bread fritters) 64
    burekas 254–5
    conchiglie with yogurt, peas
        & chile 110–11
    herb pie 250–1
    marinated, with barley risotto
        108–9
    parsley & barley salad 80–1
    Swiss chard fritters 54–5
    & tomato, with prawns,
        scallops & clams 232–3
feuilles de brick 244–5
fig compote 276–7
filo
    herb pie 250–1
    mutabbaq 261–3
    sweet cigars 258–9
fish 216–39
    & caper kebabs with burnt
        eggplant & lemon pickle
        220–1
    cold 237
    gefilte 237
    grilled skewers, with hawayej
        & parsley 226
    marinated sweet & sour 238–9
    see also specific types of fish
flatbread, Na'ama's Fattoush 28–9
freekeh
    spicy soup, with meatballs
        148–9
    sweet spiced, with poached
        chicken 182–3
fricassee salad 227
fritters
    bread (a'ja) 64
    Swiss chard 54–5

G
galettes, red pepper & baked
    egg 242–3
Gardiner-Scott, Reverend
    William 166
garlic
    cannellini bean & lamb
        soup 135
    & chile paste
        (pilpelchuma) 302

fried tomato with 50–1
    preserved lemon, tomato, &
        charred okra 74–5
gefilte fish 237
gherkin, polpette 203
Ghosh, Nawal Abu 76
ghraybeh 260
goat's milk cheese
    mutabbaq 261–3
    puréed beets with yogurt
        & za'atar 52–3
    roasted sweet potato & fresh
        fig 26–7
Goldman, Judy Stacey 166, 208, 216
grains & beans 94–129
green bean, mixed bean salad
    42–3
green onion & cumin with turkey
    & zucchini burgers 200–1
green pepper, parsley & barley
    salad 80–1
guava & plum compote 276–7

H
Hadad, Rafram 244
haddock & caper kebabs with burnt
    eggplant & lemon pickle 220–1
halloumi, acharuli khachapuri 252–3
harissa 301
    & rose with panfried sea bass
        218–19
hawayej & parsley with grilled fish
    skewers 226
hazelnut
    dukkah 300
    salad, & roasted cauliflower
        62–3
helbeh (fenugreek cake) 290–1
herb(s)
    barberries & yogurt, with
        lamb meatballs 198–9
    chickpeas & currants with
        basmati & wild rice 106–7
    mixed, barberries & pistachio,
        with saffron rice 104–5
    pie 250–1
    salad 40–1, 188–9
honey, sweet filo cigars 258–9
hummus 16, 112–19
    basic 114–15
    kawarma (lamb), with lemon
        sauce 116–18
    warm chickpeas with, &
        toasted pita 119
hyssop *see* za'atar

I
icing
    chocolate 294–5
    lemon glaze 278–9

J
Jerusalem artichoke, lemon &
    roasted chicken 180–1

K
ka'ach bilmalch 248–9
Kadosh bakery 282
kawarma hummus with lemon
    sauce 116–18
kebabs 192
    fish & caper, with burnt
        eggplant & lemon pickle
        220–1
Kedem, Ezra 76
kibbeh 159–63
    kubbeh hamusta 162–3
    open 160–1
kidreh 182
Kissinger Platter 152
knaidlach with clear chicken
    soup 144–5
koftas 192
    b'siniyah 194–5
kohlrabi salad 46–7
Kosher rules 231
krantz cake (babbka) 282
    chocolate 284–7
ktsitsot 192
kubbeh 153
kuku, fava bean 38–9

L
labneh 302
    with root vegetable slaw 48–9
    shakshuka 66–7
Lahm Bi'ajeen 246
lamb 208–13
    -stuffed quince with
        pomegranate & cilantro
        154–5
    & beef meatballs, with fava
        beans & lemon 196–7
    & cannellini bean soup 135
    hummus kawarma with lemon
        sauce 116–18
    kofta b'siniyah 194–5
    meatballs, with barberries,
        yogurt & herbs 198–9

open kibbeh 160–1

& pine nuts, eggplant stuffed with 166–7

Ruth's stuffed Romano peppers 164–5

Sfiha/Lahm Bi'ajeen 246

shawarma 210–13

spicy freekeh soup with meatballs 148–9

tahini & sumac, with braised egg 204–5

latkes 92–3

leek

burekas 254–5

lemony meatballs 44

prunes & slow-cooked veal 206–7

stuffed artichoke with peas & dill 170–1

walnut & spicy beet salad 72–3

wheat berries & Swiss chard with pomegranate molasses 100–1

lemon

& fava beans, with beef meatballs 196–7

chopped, fried onion & roasted eggplant 33

glaze 278–9

Jerusalem artichoke & roasted chicken 180–1

lemony leek meatballs 44

pickle 220–1

pomegranate seeds & burnt eggplant 76–7

preserved 303

preserved, tomato, garlic & charred okra 74–5

quick pickled 303

sauce 116–18, 119

lentil(s), mejadra 120–1

liver *see* chicken liver

M

ma'amul 288–9

mackerel, pan-fried, with golden beet & orange salsa 222–3

mafrum "cakes" 168

maftoul 139

maqluba 125–8

marmalade, semolina & coconut cake 264–5

marzipan 293

matzo, knaidlach 144–5

meat 172–213

meatballs 192–201

beef, with fava beans & lemon 196–7

kofta b'siniyah 194–5

lamb, with barberries, yogurt & herbs 198–9

lemony leek 44

with spicy freekeh soup 148–9

turkey & zucchini burgers with green onion & cumin 200–1

Meitlis, Tamara 44

mejadra 120–1

milk puddings 274–5

mini cucumber

chopped salad 90–1

Na'ama's Fattoush 28–9

pickled mixed vegetables with curry 307

spiced chickpeas & fresh vegetable salad 56–7

mixed grill, Jerusalem 174–5

mograbieh & burnt eggplant soup 140–1

muhallabieh 274–5

musabaha (warm chickpeas with hummus) & toasted pita 119

mushabak 288

mussel, seafood & fennel soup 136–7

mutabbaq 261–3

N

Nathan, Joan 166, 208, 216

O

okra, charred, tomato, garlic & preserved lemon 74–5

one-pots 125–7

onion

caramelized, cardamom rice & chicken 184–5

fried, chopped lemon & roasted eggplant 33

mejadra 120–1

stuffed 157

tomato & couscous 129

see also red onion

orange & golden beet salsa with panfried mackerel 222–3

orzo & basmati rice 103

ox tongue, polpette 203

P

parsley

balilah 102

& barley salad 80–1

brick 244–5

& hawayej with grilled fish skewers 226

salsina verde 203

tabbouleh 85

zhoug 301

parsnip, latkes 92–3

pasta, conchiglie with yogurt, peas & chile 110–11

pastries, savory 240–55

peach, poached, with yogurt pudding 268–9

pear, poached in white wine & cardamom 266–7

pea(s)

chile & yogurt with conchiglie 110–11

& dill, artichoke stuffed with 170–1

pecan, chocolate krantz cake (babbka) 284–7

pecorino, burekas 254–5

pepper

green, parsley & barley salad 80–1

piquillo, fricassee salad 227

Romano, Ruth's stuffed 164–5

yellow, marinated sweet & sour fish 238–9

see also red pepper

pies, herb 250–1

pilpelchuma 302

pine nut

buttered, tahini & yogurt with Swiss chard 88–9

conchiglie with yogurt, peas & chile 110–11

helbeh (fenugreek cake) 290–1

hummus kawarma with lemon sauce 116–18

kofta b'siniyah 194–5

& lamb, eggplant stuffed with 166–7

maqluba 125–8

open kibbeh 160–1

stuffed onions 157

piquillo pepper, fricassee salad 227

pirogen 168

pistachio

ghraybeh 260

mixed herbs & barberries, with saffron rice 104–5

polpette 203

pistachio, *continued*

    & rose water, with cardamom
        rice pudding 270–1

    soup 138

    sweet filo cigars 258–9

pita

    baby spinach salad with dates
        & almond 30–1

    toasted, with hummus & warm
        chickpeas 119

pkhali 71

plum & guave compote 276–7

pollock, marinated sweet &
    sour 238–9

polpette 202–3

pomegranate

    & cilantro, with lamb-stuffed
        quince 154–5

    molasses, with wheat berries &
        Swiss chard 100–1

    seeds, lemon & burnt eggplant
        76–7

potato

    cannellini bean & lamb
        soup 135

    chicken sofrito 190–1

    fricassee salad 227

    latkes 92–3

    roasted, with caramel & prunes
        86–7

    seafood & fennel soup 136–7

    stuffed 168–9

prawn

    scallops & clams with tomato &
        feta 232–3

    tiger, seafood & fennel soup
        136–7

prune

    caramel & roasted potato 86–7

    leek & slow-cooked veal 206–7

ptitim 8, 139

puff pastry

    burekas 254–5

    red pepper & baked egg
        galettes 242–3

Q

quail, braised, with apricots,
    currants & tamarind 176–7

quince, lamb-stuffed, with
    pomegranate & cilantro 154–5

R

radish

    Na'ama's Fattoush 28–9

    spiced chickpeas & fresh
        vegetable salad 56–7

ras el hanout & rose water with
    watercress & chickpea soup
    132–3

red onion & butternut squash,
    roasted, with tahini & za'atar
    36–7

red pepper

    & baked egg galettes 242–3

    harissa 301

    marinated sweet & sour fish
        238–9

    mixed bean salad 42–3

    shakshuka 66–7

    spiced chickpeas & fresh
        vegetable salad 56–7

rice

    basmati

        cardamom 184–5

        maqluba 125–8

        mejadra 120–1

        & orzo 103

        Ruth's stuffed Romano
            peppers 164–5

        saffron, with barberries,
            pistachio & mixed herbs
            104–5

        turnip & veal "cake" 156

        & wild, with chickpeas,
            currants & herbs 106–7

    pudding, cardamom, with
        pistachios & rose water 270–1

    stuffed onions 157

ricotta

    acharuli khachapuri 252–3

    burekas 254–5

    herb pie 250–1

    mutabbaq 261–3

risotto, barley, with marinated
    feta 108–9

Roden, Claudia 202, 234

Romano peppers, Ruth's
    stuffed 164–5

root vegetable slaw, with
    labneh 48–9

rose, harissa & panfried
    sea bass 218–19

rose water

    ghraybeh 260

    & pistachios, with cardamom
        rice pudding 270–1

    & ras el hanout, with
        watercress & chickpea soup
        132–3

Rosenzweig, Shraga 231

S

sabih 90–1

saffron

    chicken & herb salad 188–9

    rice, with barberries, pistachio
        & mixed herbs 104–5

salad

    baby spinach, with dates &
        almond 30–1

    chopped 90–1

    chunky zucchini & tomato 84

    fresh vegetable & spiced
        chickpeas 56–7

    fricassee 227

    hazelnut, & roasted
        cauliflower 62–3

    herb 40–1, 188–9

    kohlrabi 46–7

    mixed bean 42–3

    Na'ama's Fattoush 28–9

    parsley & barley 80–1

    root vegetable slaw with
        labneh 48–9

    spicy beet, leek & walnut 72–3

    spicy carrot 65

salmon steaks in chraimeh sauce
    234–5

salsa, golden beet & orange 222–3

salsina verde 203

scallop, clam & prawn with tomato
    & feta 232–3

sea bass, panfried, with harissa
    & rose 218–19

sea bass, seafood & fennel soup
    136–7

seafood & fennel soup 136–7

semolina, coconut & marmalade
    cake 264–5

Sfiha 246

Sha'ananim, Mishkenot 152

shakshuka 66–7

Shalev, Meir 293

shallot

    stuffed onions 157

    see also banana shallot

Shavit, Tango 252

shawarma, lamb 210–13

shishbarak 153

Shrefler, Elran 166

slaw, root vegetable, with labneh
    48–9

sofrito, chicken 190–1

soup 130–49
    burnt eggplant & mograbieh
        140–1
    cannellini bean & lamb 135
    clear chicken, with knaidlach
        144–5
    hot yogurt & barley 134
    kubbeh hamusta 162–3
    pistachio 138
    seafood & fennel 136–7
    spicy freekeh, with meatballs
        148–9
    tomato & sourdough 142–3
    watercress & chickpea, with
        rose water & ras el hanout
        132–3
sourdough & tomato soup 142–3
sour cream & sumac sauce
    200–1
spice cookies 278–9
spinach, baby, salad, with dates &
    almond 30–1
stuffed foods 150–71
sumac
    lamb & tahini with braised egg
        204–5
    & sour cream sauce 200–1
sweet potato, roasted, & fresh fig
    26–7
sweet & sour marinated fish 238–9
sweets & desserts 256–95
Swiss chard
    fritters 54–5
    herb pie 250–1
    kubbeh hamusta 162–3
    with tahini, yogurt & buttered
        pine nuts 88–9
    & wheat berries, with
        pomegranate molasses 100–1
syrups 262, 264, 270, 275, 284–5,
    290–1

T
tabbouleh 85
tahini
    basic hummus 114–15
    cookies 292
    with fried cauliflower 60–1
    hummus kawarma (lamb) with
        lemon sauce 116–18
    kofta b'siniyah 194–5
    musabaha (warm chickpeas
        with hummus) & toasted pita
        119
    open kibbeh 160–1
    sauce 119, 298
    spread, & butternut squash
        68–9

sumac & lamb with braised egg
    204–5
yogurt sauce 204–5
& yogurt sauce 88–9
za'atar with roasted butternut
    squash & red onion 36–7
tamarind, apricots & currants,
    with braised quail 176–7
tomato
    barley risotto with marinated
        feta 108–9
    braised eggs with lamb, tahini
        & sumac 204–5
    burnt eggplant & mograbieh
        soup 140–1
    chopped salad 90–1
    & feta, with prawns, scallops &
        clams 232–3
    fried with garlic 50–1
    garlic, preserved lemon &
        charred okra 74–5
    maqluba 125–8
    marinated sweet & sour fish
        238–9
    Na'ama's Fattoush 28–9
    onion & couscous 129
    sauce 169, 224–5
    seafood & fennel soup 136–7
    shakshuka 66–7
    & sourdough soup 142–3
    spiced chickpeas & fresh
        vegetable salad 56–7
    spicy freekeh soup with
        meatballs 148–9
    tabbouleh 85
    turnip & veal "cake" 156
    & zucchini chunky salad 84
tuna, fricassee salad 227
turkey & zucchini burgers with
    green onion & cumin 200–1
turnip
    & beet, pickled 307
    clear chicken soup with
        knaidlach 144–5
    & veal "cake" 156

V
veal
    kofta b'siniyah 194–5
    slow-cooked, with prunes &
        leek 206–7
    & turnip "cake" 156
vegetables 24–93

W
walnut
    chunky zucchini & tomato
        salad 84
    & fruit crumble cream 276–7
    leek & spicy beet salad 72–3
    ma'amul 288–9
watercress
    & chickpea soup with rose
        water & ras el hanout 132–3
    kohlrabi salad 46–7
wheat berries & Swiss chard with
    pomegranate molasses 100–1
white wine & cardamom, pears
    poached in 266–7

Y
yeasted cakes 280–7
yellow bean, mixed bean
    salad 42–3
yellow pepper, marinated sweet &
    sour fish 238–9
yogurt
    & barley hot soup 134
    bulgar & chermoula eggplant
        58–9
    chunky zucchini & tomato
        salad 84
    with cucumber 299
    herbs & barberries, with lamb
        meatballs 198–9
    Na'ama's Fattoush 28–9
    peas & chile with conchiglie
        110–11
    pudding, with poached peaches
        268–9
    sauce 204–5
    & tahini sauce 88–9
    & za'atar, with puréed beets
        52–3
    see also labneh

Z
za'atar (hyssop) 34–5
    tahini, roasted butternut
        squash & red onion 36–7
    & yogurt, with puréed beets
        52–3
zhoug 301
    sabih 90–1
zucchini
    kubbeh hamusta 162–3
    & tomato chunky salad 84
    & turkey burgers, with green
        onion & cumin 200–1

Acknowledgments

The idea for this book was our friend and business partner's, Noam Bar, who was also instrumental in every stage in its making. If it wasn't for Noam, there wouldn't be a *Jerusalem* cookbook, it wouldn't look the way it does, and it definitely wouldn't have such a far-reaching scope.

Nomi Abeliovich spent eighteen months doing much of the legwork for us—interviewing, collecting recipes, meticulously collating materials, and just being a constant source of knowledge and inspiration. We are forever grateful for her priceless contribution.

We would like to thank deeply Cornelia Staeubli, who may have not been actively involved in this book but is heavily caught up in every other aspect of our professional lives, running Ottolenghi almost singlehandedly and giving us support, constant advice, and the peace of mind needed to commit to such a big project.

This is the third book that has come about from working with our editor, Sarah Lavelle, and our agent, Felicity Rubinstein. It is always wonderfully uncomplicated working with both of them, making the creative process a real joy. We are grateful to Imogen Fortes for her hard work in making everything make perfect sense. We would also like to thank Fiona MacIntyre, Carey Smith, Ed Griffiths, and Sarah Bennie from Ebury for their constant efforts.

We are sincerely grateful to Caz Hildebrand, Jonathan Lovekin, and Adam Hinton for their distinct contributions to the beauty of this book. All three, in different ways, are extraordinary collaborators. Our friend Alex Meitlis's creative spirit is a constant inspiration.

Sarah Stephens and Tara Wigley have been assisting us for months in trying out the recipes and critically assessing them. We would like to thank them both enormously for their hard work and wise comments. Sarah deserves an extra massive thank you for cooking up all the dishes for the camera; this was a gigantic task. We would like to thank Claudine Boulstridge—and also Alison Quinn and Toni Birbara—for checking and double-checking all the recipes and for always being both meticulous and sincere.

Yotam's partner, Karl Allen, and Sami's partner, Jeremy Kelly, have been implicit collaborators in this project, enduring our extra workload and often failed creations with much love and great patience. We owe them the world.

Thanks to Lindy Wiffen and Gerry Ure of the fabulous Ceramica Blue for the time and effort in selecting some striking dishes for our photo shoot. And thank you to Sanjana Lovekin for collecting all those skip-worthy pieces of metal and other eccentric objects.

We also want to thank a small bunch of close people—family, colleagues, and friends—that have been involved in our work over the years, or are just a constant presence in our lives, giving us support, encouragement, and love: Michael and Ruth Ottolenghi, Tirza, Danny and the Florentin family, Hassan and Na'ama Tamimi, Adrian Von Ferscht, Gianluca Piermaria and his family, Carmel Gedaliahu-Noy, Tali Levin, Eric Rodari, George and Maureen Kelly, Pete and Greta Allen, Tamara Meitlis, Shachar Argov, Garry Chang, Helen Goh, David Kausman, Ramael Scully, Basia Murphy, Lingchee Ang, Colleen Murphy, Angelita Pereira, Francis Pereira, Sarit Packer, Itamar Srulovich, Peter Lowe, Maria Oskarsson, Chris Mok, Savarna Paterson, Charissa Fraser, Heidi Knudsen, Oshrat Yakutiel, Gal Zohar, Gemma Bell, Osnat and Assi Cirlin, Keren Margalit, Yoram Ever-Hadani, Itzik Lederfeind, Ilana Lederfeind, and Amos, Ariela, and David Oppenheim.

The chefs at Ottolenghi and NOPI deserve a special acknowledgment. Many ideas are down to our daily interactions with this amazing group of hardworking and creative people.

For their cooperation and generous assistance while researching the book and shooting *Jerusalem on a Plate*, we are grateful to James Nutt, Lauren Rowles, Katie Buchanan, Zam Baring, Andrew Palmer, Arlette Lugassy, Rachela, Ezra, Elran and Limor Shrefler, Daniella Lerrer, Sherry Ansky, Ezra Kedem, Yossi El'ad, Michal Barenes, Yakub Barhum, Rama Ben Tzvi, Tomer Niv, Keren and Itzik Kadosh, Shai Zeltzer, Ze'ev Dunya, Itzik Gil, Ruba and Rami Khalil, Halil Mussa, Samir Zalatimo, Hanni Zalatimo, Yasser Muhammad Taha (Abu Shukri), Fadi Yasser Taha, Razi Shahin, Muhammad Shahin, Nabil Ibrahim Hijazi, Muhammad Ikermawi, Eli and Aliza Tarazi, Ge'ula Hassidoff Shmu'eli, Meir Shalev, Rafram Haddad, Nawal Abu Gosh, Anat Teitelbaum, Eitan Alon, Micha Shagrir, Itzik Har'el, and the staff and students at Notre Dame Jerusalem cookery school.

We feel particularly indebted to all the people who have bought our books and cooked our food over the past five years and for the endless stream of heartening reactions and comments.

Published in the United States by Ten Speed Press,
an imprint of the Crown Publishing Group,
a division of Random House, Inc., New York.
www.crownpublishing.com
www.tenspeed.com

Originally published in slightly different form in hardcover in
Great Britain by Ebury Press, an imprint of Ebury Publishing,
a Random House Group Company, London

Ten Speed Press and the Ten Speed Press colophon are
registered trademarks of Random House, Inc.

Map on page 18 reproduced by kind permission of
The National Library of Israel (Jerusalem);
Eran Laor Cartographic Collection

Library of Congress Cataloging-in-Publication Data
Ottolenghi, Yotam.
  Jerusalem : a cookbook / Yotam Ottolenghi, Sami Tamimi.
    p. cm.
Includes index.
  Includes index.
1. Cooking, Middle Eastern. 2. Jerusalem—Description and travel.
I. Tamimi, Sami. II. Title.
  TX725.M628O88 2012
  641.5'676—dc23
2012017560

ISBN 978-1-60774-394-1
eISBN 978-1-60774-395-8

Printed in China

Cover design by **Sarah Pulver**
Interior design by **Here Design**
Additional prop styling by **Sanjana Lovekin**
Additional text provided by **Noam Bar**
Additional text, photography, and research by **Nomi Abeliovich**

14 15 16 17

First United States Edition